The Diaspora Story

Overleaf *Jewish immigrants arriving in New York*

The Diaspora Story

The Epic of the Jewish People among the Nations

Joan Comay

in association with Beth Hatefutsoth –
The Nahum Goldmann Museum
of the Jewish Diaspora, Tel Aviv

Random House  New York

All rights reserved under International and Pan-American Copyright Conventions.
Published in the United States by Random House, Inc., New York.
Originally published in Great Britain by George Weidenfeld and Nicolson Ltd., 91
Clapham High Street, London SW4.

Library of Congress Cataloging in Publication Data
Comay, Joan.
    The Diaspora story.

    Includes index.
    1. Jews – History – 70   2. Jews – Diaspora.
I. Bet ha-tefutsot (Tel Aviv, Israel)   II. Title.
DS123.C65 1981   909'.04924   80–6034
ISBN 0–394–51644–3   AACR2

Manufactured in the United States of America

24689753

First American Edition

Contents

(This book is based on the Museum of the Jewish Diaspora, Tel Aviv, and the illustrations are drawn from it.)

Introduction

The term 'Diaspora' comes from a Greek word meaning dispersion. It is used here to denote the world-wide dispersion of the Jewish people outside its ancestral homeland, the Land of Israel.

The Diaspora has lasted for over twenty-five centuries. For most of that time the political independence of the Jewish people was crushed; the central sanctuary of its faith, the Temple of Jerusalem, lay in ruins; and its homeland was a minor province of one imperial power after another. Diaspora was then called Exile (in Hebrew, *Golah* or *Galut*). The stubborn refusal of this little people to disappear, from repression or assimilation, remains one of the startling enigmas of human history.

The first period of the Galut was the Babylonian captivity, starting just before the Hebrew kingdom of Judah was destroyed in 586 BC.

In the 2nd century BC another Jewish Commonwealth arose, after the Maccabean Revolt. It was wiped out by the Romans in AD 70, after four years of war. Jewish independence would not arise again until the State of Israel was proclaimed in 1948. For nearly nineteen centuries before that, the Jews were a minority everywhere, subject to the whims of rulers and the attitudes of the populace. At times they were the hapless victims of intolerance and greed and suffered segregation, economic restrictions, crippling taxes, pogroms and pillage, forced baptism, blood-libel charges, expulsion or death at the stake. At other times they enjoyed periods of relative calm, and they poured their gifts into the surrounding society.

As with other living species, the Jew survived largely through his ability to adapt to his environment. That environment was neither uniform nor static. It changed in different localities and in different periods. Always, Jews strove to reconcile their two worlds. They clung to their own faith and traditions, while in varying degrees adopting the customs, language, dress and occupations of the countries in which they lived.

Migration was in itself a factor of survival. Persecuted in one country, or pushed out of it, Jews found refuge elsewhere. As Diaspora centres declined, others arose. The Jews expelled from Spain at the end of the 15th century AD settled in North Africa, Italy, or the Ottoman Empire. Jews fleeing the persecution of mediaeval Germany were welcomed into Poland-Lithuania. The misery of Jewish life in the 19th-century Russian Pale of Settlement propelled a mass exodus westward. These people went mainly to the United States. Migration

7

constantly widened the frontiers of the Diaspora.

In the last 2,000 years there have been two major streams of Jewish dispersion, with some intermingling between them. The more southerly route remained within the Near East – the Mediterranean area. It comprised the successive centres of Jewish life in Babylonia, North Africa, Spain, and the Ottoman Empire. That part of the Jewish world lay generally in the lands of Islam. It became known as Sephardi, from the Hebrew word for Spanish. The more northerly route was the European one – the Byzantine empire, Franco-Germany, Eastern Europe and the New World. This was the part of Jewry known as Ashkenazi, from the Hebrew word for German. Its involvement was with Christianity.

With the Nazi rise to power in our time, the Jews that came under Hitler's sway found themselves with nowhere to go. The gates of

A replica from the relief on the Arch of Titus. The holy vessels from the destroyed temple in Jerusalem are carried in triumphal procession.

Western countries had been all but closed, and the gates of the Jewish Homeland forcibly barred. Most of the Jewish people ended up in the gas chamber.

After Israel became an independent state in 1948, the surviving Displaced Persons in European camps and the endangered communities in Arab countries streamed back to the land from which their forefathers had started. For them, the wheel of migration had come full circle.

It is unlikely that the Jews as a people would long have survived the disaster of AD 70, unless the instruments of its survival had been forged beforehand in a unique spiritual and cultural heritage. It was as if the nation had instinctively trained itself for exile.

The most important instrument of survival was the Book that the wandering Jew carried in his knapsack. To call the Old Testament a Book is in a sense misleading. It is a sacred anthology of ancient Hebrew literature compiled and edited over a period of more than a thousand years. The works in it include religious writings, historical narratives, laws, legends and folk tales, prophecies, proverbs and poetry. Its central theme is the Covenant between God and the Hebrew people, and everything that happens to the people, for good or bad, is related to that theme. Embedded in the Old Testament is the unique Hebrew creed of monotheism, the Mosaic legal system, and the promise of a Messianic Return to Zion.

After the fall of Jerusalem in AD 70, it was a wise and logical reaction for the sages gathered at Yavneh on the coast to complete the canon of the Writings (the third part of the Old Testament) and thus give the Hebrew Bible its final and enduring shape.

The Oral Law was the body of commentary, rulings and opinions that the religious leaders had been already evolving for centuries before AD 70. It was meant to interpret and expand the biblical Written Law, and apply it to the detailed needs of daily life. At the beginning of the 3rd century AD the Oral Law was given a systematic codification in the Mishnah, later to be broadened into the Jerusalem Talmud (4th century AD) and the more comprehensive Babylonian Talmud (5th-6th century AD). Judaism had consciously become a portable faith and way of life that could function without a State, a Temple or a fixed abode. Its adjustment to changing conditions would continue throughout Diaspora history.

In addition to the Bible and the Oral Law there were other basic institutions that had already been tested during centuries of Diaspora life before the disaster of AD 70, and would help to preserve the identity and cohesion of Jewry after it. They included the tightly-knit family, the autonomous community, the synagogue, the religious education system and the belief in a Messianic Return. Through the vicissitudes of the next nineteen centuries, all these factors would form the survival kit for a dispersed and battered people.

Part One

The Inner World
of the Diaspora

*A grandmother and granddaughter in Eastern Europe
before the Second World War.*

Contemporary Jewish Faces

These faces are some of a group of nearly 200 camera portraits gathered by Cornell Capa, an internationally-known photographer. The assortment provides a random sample of Jewish faces of both sexes, all ages and many countries. The overwhelming impression they make is that there is no standard Jewish physical type.

Chapter One

Faces

The great diversity of Jewish facial characteristics is confirmed by modern scientific surveys. For the anthropologist a key indicator is the cephalic index, the ratio between the length and breadth of the skull. The range of the measurements for Jews is just about as wide as that for the human race as a whole. There are also great variations in different communities regarding the blood type and the colour of the eyes and hair. For instance, up to twenty per cent of Eastern European Jews have blue eyes, compared to less than two per cent of Iraqi Jews.

The wide physical differences between Jews result from three processes that have operated over thousands of years: intermarriage with neighbouring peoples; conversions of non-Jews to the Jewish faith; and environmental factors. As a result, different physical types have evolved in different localities. A Georgian Jew tends to look like other Georgians; a Yemenite Jew tends to look like other Yemenites; but Georgian and Yemenite Jews do not resemble each other.

Throughout later Diaspora history the rate of intermarriage varied. It increased where conditions were relaxed and Jews mingled freely with the general population. It virtually ceased where Jews were persecuted, restricted and segregated. To this day, the Halachic (Jewish Law) definition of a Jew is one whose mother is Jewish or one who has converted to Judaism. The ethnic origin of the mother is the determining factor, and the father need not be Jewish at all.

The Jews have been so widely dispersed for so long that environmental factors, like climate and diet, have also contributed to the diversity of types. Like their neighbours, Jews from tropical and semi-tropical countries are dark-skinned, while their brethren from colder European countries are pale-skinned. Against the historical background of these various processes, it is not surprising that the Jewish people should have such a remarkable variety of faces.

Jewish Faces in Art
See colour pages 17, 18 and 19

Jews portrayed in ancient synagogue wall-paintings, mediaeval manuscripts, church frescoes, and 17th- to 19th-century oil paintings. There are no common facial characteristics.

The artist is not a cameraman. In depicting people, he is influenced by his own personal style and the artistic conventions of his time. He may also be subject to prevailing prejudices, as embodied in group stereotypes.

Anti-Semitic Caricatures

The Jew became the classic victim in Europe of the group-stereotype portrait. Until about the 11th century, Jews were depicted in much the same style as non-Jews. In the Dark Age of persecution that ensued, Jews were forced to wear special hats or badges to distinguish them from Christians. At the same time they were depicted in art as sinister creatures with crooked figures and facial expressions of cunning and greed. There is a direct line of descent from these mediaeval drawings to the vicious Nazi caricatures of *Der Stuermer* and other modern anti-Semitic literature.

Left *A mediaeval caricature of Joseph (Joselman) of Rosheim (c.1478–1554), the greatest of the Jewish* shtadlanim *in Germany in the Middle Ages.* Right *A cartoon from a Polish brochure of the 1930s, 'In the grip of communism'. The Jew leads Death to his harvest in Poland.*

Below *Uncle Sam becomes the modern Moses, parting the waters of intolerance and oppression to welcome European Jews to America. From* Puck, *30 November 1881.*

Chapter Two

The Traditional Jewish Home

The main channel for transmitting Jewish traditions from generation to generation was the home. Being a Jew was first and foremost a family affair.

In the early biblical period (the Patriarchs and the Judges) the social unit was the extended family or family clan, called the *mishpachah*. The head of the family had complete authority over its members – maybe three or four generations of them – and over all family property. Within the extended family group were small sub-units, each made up of parents and their children, and known as a *bet av* ('father's house'). The members of the extended family were responsible for each other's protection and welfare. If one of them was murdered, his kinsmen were duty-bound to avenge him. Each Israelite tribe was a loose combination of such family clans. The heads of the important families were the elders of the tribe.

In the course of time the authority of the family heads and tribal leaders waned as centralized institutions were established: the monarchy, the Temple priesthood, and regular courts to punish wrongdoers and settle disputes. The emphasis shifted to the small family, the 'bet av', as the basic unit of society.

The conditions and needs of the Diaspora strengthened the role of the restricted family as the bastion of traditional values and customs. Ties of sentiment and loyalty continued to exist with a wide circle of blood relatives or relatives by marriage. But the focus of Jewish family law and custom was based on the tight system of relationships between husband and wife and between parent and child. However, even in modern times the wider family unit, the 'clan', remained strong among the communities in Moslem lands.

The Jewish attitude to marriage was always a very positive one. Ideals of celibacy and monasticism which developed in Christianity remained alien to Judaism. In Jewish thought, marriage was the only road to personal fulfilment, and procreation was a sacred duty. The Talmud states: 'He who has no wife lives without joy, without blessing and without goodness.' Another down-to-earth Talmudic saying points out that, were it not for the sexual urge, no man would build a house, marry a wife or beget children.

The relationship between husband and wife required by Judaism

(continued on page 21)

Mezuzah

Two similar passages in the *Book of Deuteronomy* prescribe ways for keeping God's word constantly in men's minds:

'Hear, O Israel: The Lord our God is one Lord; and you shall love the Lord your God with all your heart, and with all your soul, and with all your might. And these words which I command you this day shall be upon your heart; and you shall teach them diligently to your children, and shall talk of them when you sit in your house, and when you walk by the way, and when you lie down, and when you rise. And you shall bind them as a sign upon your hand, and they shall be as frontlets between your eyes. And you shall write them on the

doorposts of your house and on your gates.' (Deut. 6:4–9)

From ancient times the last-mentioned requirement has been fulfilled by inserting a coiled square of parchment, inscribed with these two biblical passages, into a case that is fixed in slanting position to the upper part of the right-hand doorpost. The affixed object is called a *mezuzah*, a Hebrew word that originally referred to the doorpost itself. The word *Shaddai* is written on the back of the parchment so that it is visible through a small aperture in the case. Shaddai is one of the names for the Almighty; the word is also formed by the initial letters of a Hebrew phrase meaning 'guardian of the doors of Israel'.

On passing through the door a pious Jew will kiss the mezuzah or touch it and then kiss his fingers. This is a mark of respect, not a commandment.

Strictly speaking, the mezuzah is required only on the entrance door to a house and on the doors of rooms that are used for living purposes. It has become customary, however, to affix a mezuzah also at the entrances of synagogues and other Jewish public buildings. After the Six-Day War in 1967, a mezuzah was placed on each of the gates leading into the recaptured Old City of Jerusalem.

The mezuzah became a favourite object of Jewish ceremonial art and occurs in many decorative styles from different periods.

Interior of the Jewish home

Such rooms varied in different places and periods, but certain traditional objects remained as constant features of them. In this picture there can be seen the Sabbath candles and *kiddush* sanctification cup, the *chanukkiah* and the *mizrach*.

The chanukkiah is a candelabrum used in a Jewish home for the celebration of the Feast of Chanukkah (Dedication) that occurs about the time of Christmas.

In 164 BC, the leader of the Maccabean Revolt, Judah the Maccabee,

A table set for the Sabbath meal in 18th-century Poland

recaptured Jerusalem, restored the defiled Temple and re-dedicated it. According to the accepted Jewish legend, only a small jar of undefiled holy oil was found, sufficient to light the great candelabrum for one night; but by a miracle the oil replenished itself and lasted for eight days. Therefore it was laid down that the event would be commemorated each year by the Feast of Chanukkah, sometimes called the Feast of Lights, which would also last for eight days.

In celebrating the festival, one candle on the chanukkiah is lit the first night and an additional one on each succeeding night until all eight have been lit. A ninth candle, popularly known as a *shammash* (beadle) is used to light the others.

The chanukkiah was originally a round or star-shaped oil lamp with the requisite number of wicks. From the late Middle Ages onwards the oil was replaced by candles. The chanukkiah varies greatly in appearance in different times and places, and can be made of silver, metal, pottery or stone.

The Hebrew word *mizrach* means 'east'. It is applied in Western countries to a wall-plaque which is hung on the eastern wall of a living-room or synagogue, so that Jews can face towards Jerusalem when praying. (Naturally, communities living to the east, north or south of the Holy Land would face Jerusalem from those directions.)

The plaque usually has the word 'mizrach' in the centre, surrounded by biblical verses and pictures of holy places, animals, birds, fruit, flowers, or other decorative motifs. The painting may be done on parchment or metal, or it may consist of tinted paper cut-outs between sheets of glass, a popular form of Jewish folk-art in Eastern Europe.

Faces in Art

Previous page '*A Jewess from Morocco*', a detail from a painting by Alfred Dehondencq, 19th century.

Left '*Rabbi Jacob Sasportas*' of Amsterdam, a detail from a painting by I. Luttichuys, 1671.

Right '*A Jewess*', a detail of the oil painting by Maurycy Gottlieb, c.1878.

Moses, from the 3rd-century synagogue murals of Dura Europos.

'*Personification of Autumn*'. *A replica of the mosaic from the 4th-century synagogue of Hammath-Tiberias.*

Jews from France. A replica of part of a 15th-century cavalry, from Carcassonne.

'Süsskind of Trimberg', a detail from the Minnesänger manuscript, Germany, 14th century.

Left *The Ketubbah. An illuminated 'ketubbah' from Rome, 1771.*

Below *The Circumcision Ceremony. A model of a circumcision ceremony in Algeria, 19th century.*

was summarized by the great 12th-century scholar, Maimonides:

Thus the sages lay down that a man shall honour his wife more than his own self and shall love her as he loves himself, and shall constantly seek to benefit her according to his means; that he shall not unduly impose his authority on her and shall speak gently with her; that he shall be neither sad nor irritable. Similarly they lay down that a wife shall honour her husband exceedingly and shall accept his authority and abide by his wishes in all her activities ...

Jewish tradition always stressed that the primary purpose of marriage was to produce and rear children. In the first chapter of *Genesis* the Lord commanded Adam and Eve to 'be fruitful and multiply'. The greatest misfortune that could befall a wife was to be barren, as illustrated by the Old Testament stories of Abraham's wife Sarah, Isaac's wife Rebecca, Jacob's wife Rachel, and Hannah the mother of the prophet Samuel. By Talmudic law (Halachah), a wife who remains childless for ten years can be divorced by her husband on that ground alone.

The wife was legally subordinate to her husband, but extensive protection was given by the Halachah to her person, her property rights and her claims on her husband for cohabitation, maintenance, medical care, and to make provision for her after his death. The husband's obligation to maintain his wife was, however, conditional on her obligation to perform her household duties.

Although subject to her husband's authority, the Jewish wife and mother enjoyed a position of honour and respect, and had a strong influence on family affairs. In the Old Testament, the matriarchs Sarah, Rebecca, Leah and Rachel are treated with deference by their male kinfolk. At the end of the *Book of Proverbs* there is a wonderful acrostic poem lauding the good wife who is 'far more precious than jewels'. The passage describes her manifold activities and says of her:

She looks well to the ways of her household,
and does not eat the bread of idleness.
Her children rise up and call her blessed;
her husband also, and he praises her: . . .
(Prov. 31:27, 28)

Throughout the Diaspora centuries, in conditions of poverty, persecution and migration, the main burden fell on the woman to keep the home and family intact. She was responsible for maintaining the intricate dietary laws and for infusing the home with the luminous spirit of the Sabbath and the festivals. Frequently she shared with her husband the task of bread-winner, especially when he devoted himself to learning.

The memory of the old-fashioned 'Yiddishe mama' has at times been the butt of contemporary Jewish humorists. But she was usually the mainstay of the family in the vanished *shtetl* (small town) of Eastern Europe, or in the desperate immigrant struggle of London's

Whitechapel or New York's Lower East Side.

In traditional Jewish society, the primary role of the woman lay in the home. The synagogue and the study house were a masculine domain. The lay leaders of the community and its religious officials – the rabbi, the cantor, the beadle, the ritual slaughterer, the mohel (circumciser) – were all males as a matter of course, as were both the teachers and the pupils in the talmudic seminaries. Only men were counted for the *minyan*, the prayer quorum of ten. In the synagogue, women were segregated in a gallery or separate section, usually behind a screen.

That was the traditional pattern not only in Judaism, but in early Christianity and Islam as well. It is only today that the pattern is beginning to change under the pressure of the modern movement towards equality of the sexes. Orthodox Jews are naturally more determined to maintain tradition than are the Conservative and Reform movements in the United States and their counterparts elsewhere.

The fifth of the Ten Commandments concerns the duty of children to honour their parents. By Jewish law a grown son is obliged to support his needy parents. On the other hand, the law is remarkably

The Sabbath Meal

The Sabbath starts on Friday evening and ends on Saturday evening. The poorest of families stints itself during the week to have something extra on the Friday night Sabbath table. The food is prepared before the eve of the Sabbath, and the house cleaned.

Shortly before the Sabbath starts, the wife lights the two candles with a special benediction. This custom is not mentioned in the Bible or Talmud and dates back to about the 8th century in Babylonia, during the Gaonic period. In rabbinical writings the Sabbath candles symbolized the duty of a wife and mother to ensure peace and warmth in the house.

The father blesses the children before the meal. In front of his place at table stands a kiddush cup of wine and two *challot* (twisted or plaited loaves of white bread made especially

for the Sabbath) covered by an embroidered cloth. He holds up the cup of wine and recites the prayer for the sanctification of the Sabbath. Another prayer is made over the challot and small pieces are broken from it for everybody at the table.

At the end of the Sabbath comes the ceremony of *havdalah* (separation), marking the transition to the beginning of the working week. Again, a blessing is pronounced over the goblet of wine. A ritual object used in this ceremony is the spice-box or *hadas*. It is made, as a rule, of silver filigree and often takes the form of a tower decorated with the shapes of animals, fish, fruit, or flowers.

Down the ages, the Sabbath has been an interlude when the hardships and dangers of the week are transcended, and each Jewish home seems touched by the divine spirit, the *Shechinah*.

progressive in protecting minors, even to the extent of curbing the authority of the father. A father cannot arbitrarily dispose of a child's property. By marriage-contract husband and wife can renounce or alter the property relations between them, but not to the detriment of their future children. A father is under a legal obligation to teach his son the Torah and a trade or profession; to ensure a good marriage for a daughter; and to provide for unmarried daughters in his will. If there was a divorce, a rabbinical court would decide the custody of a young child according to the interests of the child rather than the claim of the respective parents. As a general rule, illegitimate children have the same status and rights as legitimate ones, and suffer no legal disabilities.

The Jews were unique in the ancient world in hallowing one day a week as a complete rest from toil. The day also served as spiritual refreshment for the individual Jew and an affirmation of the family spirit. The practice is related to the story of the Creation in the *Book of Genesis*:

So God blessed the seventh day and hallowed it, because on it God rested from all his work which he had done in creation.

(Gen. 2:3)

The Hebrew word for 'rested' in this passage is *shavat*, the origin of the name for the Sabbath. Sabbath observance is the second of the Ten Commandments, immediately after the primary injunction to worship a single God. That fact underlines the high degree of sanctity given to the Sabbath from biblical times.

What exactly *is* the work that is forbidden on the Sabbath? This question has exercised the minds of Jewish scholars through the generations, and produced an intricate set of rulings and definitions. For instance, in mediaeval times the limit for walking was set at 2,000 cubits (about half a mile) beyond the walls of a town. A whole array of fresh problems have arisen in a modern technological society. The day of rest applied to the animals on which one rode and Orthodox Jews have extended this to all mechanical transport. They also hold that pressing a switch to set machinery in motion is prohibited on the Sabbath, and automatic devices have been introduced to operate electric lighting and elevators on that day.

Any act involving *pikuach nefesh* (the saving of life) is permitted even if it means breaking the Sabbath laws. It is related in the *Book of Maccabees* that a group of ultra-Orthodox zealots who had joined in the revolt were attacked on the Sabbath, and most of them were killed because they would not take up arms to defend themselves on that day. When the survivors joined the Maccabees, the priest Mattathias, who led the Revolt at the beginning, rejected that rigid interpretation of the Law. From the Talmudic period onward the rabbis applied the principle of *pikuach nefesh* to a wide range of cases.

The Sabbath acquired added significance in the Diaspora, as a means of preserving the spirit of Jewish life under adverse conditions.

The terms *kosher* and *kashrut* are derived from a Hebrew root that means 'fit' or 'proper'. In the post-biblical period they came into use for food that can be eaten in accordance with the Jewish dietary laws.

The distinction between clean and unclean animals is based on the rules in the biblical books of *Leviticus* and *Deuteronomy*. Animals must have cloven hooves and chew the cud. This double requirement excludes, for instance, pigs (who do not chew the cud) and rabbits (who do not have cloven hooves). Fish must have both fins and scales; shellfish and eels are, therefore, excluded. Twenty-four species of birds, practically all kinds of birds of prey or scavengers, are listed as unclean. Even a creature from a clean species is barred if it has died from natural causes or injuries. Methods of ritual slaughter are designed to drain the blood, which was held to contain the life-force.

An elaborate set of rules evolved after the biblical period to keep meat and milk separate in the cooking, serving and consuming of food. Certain types of food, such as fish, eggs, fruit and vegetables, are classified as *parva* – that is, they can be eaten with either meat or milk.

Every housewife in a traditional Jewish home becomes expert in the rules of kashrut. In cases of doubt, it is the rabbi who gives the ruling.

The family ties and the Jewish atmosphere of the home were strengthened by the strict observance of the dietary laws; by the use of certain traditional objects; by the festive ceremonial meals on the Sabbath and the Passover; and by the shared joys and sorrows of family events – circumcisions, bar-mitzvahs, weddings and the mourning for the dead.

Chapter Three

Family Events

Brit Milah (Circumcision)

Circumcision has been practised since prehistoric times in different parts of the world. It was a common religious rite among the peoples of the ancient Middle East. As a rule, the rite was associated with initiation ceremonies of boys at the age of puberty. Only the Jewish faith requires it at the age of eight days.

According to the biblical account, the origin of the custom goes back to the time of Abraham, to whom God said:

> *You shall be circumcised in the flesh of your foreskins, and it shall be a sign of the covenant between me and you. He that is eight days old among you shall be circumcised; every male throughout your generations, whether born in your house, or bought with your money from any foreigner who is not of your offspring. . . .*
> *Any uncircumcised male who is not circumcised in the flesh of his foreskin shall be cut off from his people; he has broken my covenant.*
>
> (Gen. 17:11, 12, 14)

(That passage explains the Hebrew name *brit milah*, which means 'the covenant of circumcision'.)

After God's commandment Abraham circumcised himself (at the age of ninety-nine) together with his son Ishmael and all the males in his household, including slaves. When his wife Sarah gave birth to Isaac the following year, he became the first child to be circumcised on the eighth day.

The custom seems to have lapsed during the forty years the Israelites wandered in the desert after the Exodus from Egypt. When he crossed the river Jordan into the Promised Land, one of Joshua's first acts was to have all the males circumcised with flint knives, thereby renewing the Covenant.

In the 2nd century BC, a ban on circumcision was one of the anti-Jewish measures of the Seleucid (Syrian) ruler Antiochus Epiphanes that precipitated the Maccabean Revolt. A similar ban by the Roman Emperor Hadrian in the 2nd century AD helped to provoke the Bar Kochba Revolt. These two historical episodes indicated that Jews were willing to fight to the death to defend a religious practice that

The Circumcision Ceremony

See colour page 20

This model shows a *mohel* (circumciser) about to perform the operation of the *brit milah*. The infant rests on a pillow placed on the knees of the *sandak* (godfather), an honour usually given to a grandfather or to a senior male member of the family. The sandak is seated in the 'chair of Elijah'. Blessings are said over a goblet of wine, and it is customary to place a few drops in the baby's mouth. He is then given his Hebrew name. The ceremony is followed by a festive meal or refreshments.

By Jewish law, the operation can be performed by any person, including a woman. (Zipporah, the Midianite wife of Moses, circumcised their infant son in the desert.) In practice it is done by a mohel, who is a religious official trained and licensed for the purpose by the rabbinical authorities. The mohel uses a special circumcision knife and a lyre-shaped shield is slipped over the foreskin.

Brit Milah

Right The model shows an infant's older sister sewing and embroidering the swaddling cloth.

One special custom that grew up in mediaeval German communities concerned the linen cloth placed under the infant during the circumcision. It was afterwards cut into four strips that were joined together into a long band. This was then richly embroidered with the name and birth-date of the child and presented to the synagogue when he visited it for the first time. It would later be used as a binding for the Torah scroll at the boy's bar-mitzvah.

symbolized their sacred and individual tie with God.

When the Christian sect was still newborn, a debate took place in its Council of Apostles and Elders in Jerusalem as to whether Gentile converts had to be circumcised. The majority view supported a waiver of the rite in such cases. That decision was a significant step in the turning away of the sect from Judaism.

The Church never actually forbade circumcision for Christians, but it became in practice a mark distinguishing Jews from Gentiles. That was not the case in Moslem lands, for Islam has retained circumcision rites for boys at the age of puberty.

Bar-mitzvah

The Hebrew term *bar-mitzvah* means 'son of the commandment'. It has come to be applied both to the boy and to the ceremony.

The age of thirteen is a turning-point in a Jewish boy's life. From then on he is regarded as having assumed the status and obligations of an adult. This concept crystallized in the post-biblical period, and was clearly established from about the 2nd century AD.

A formal bar-mitzvah ceremony at the age of thirteen became the custom many centuries later, and is not recorded before the 15th century AD. It was adopted by most but not all Diaspora communities – for instance, it was unknown in the Yemen, where the boy becomes a 'man' on the decision of the Rabbi and the community heads.

(continued on page 28)

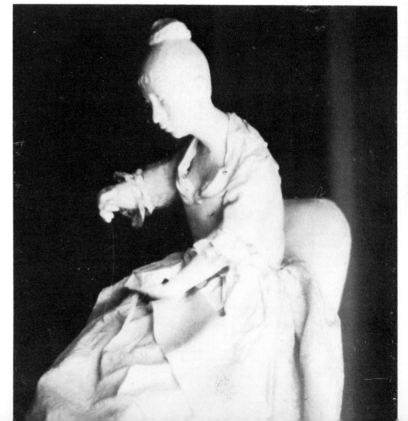

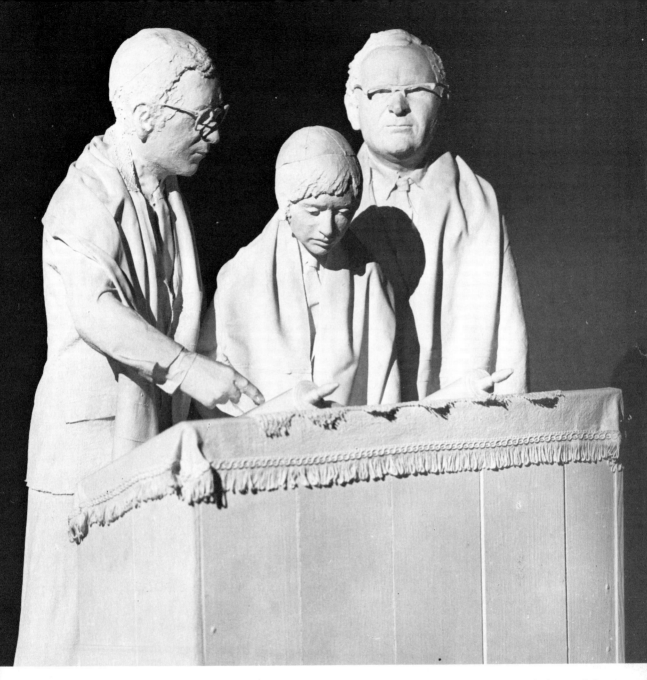

Bar-mitzvah

This model depicts a bar-mitzvah boy appearing in synagogue in contemporary United States, flanked by his father and the Cantor.

On the Sabbath after his thirteenth birthday a boy is called up to the reading of the Torah, in the synagogue. He chants the portion of the Torah reading for that day, and the corresponding portion from the Prophetic Books. He then receives the blessing of the Rabbi, whose address to the congregation stresses the significance of the occasion. At the festive meal that follows, the bar-mitzvah boy is expected to make a speech, which among strictly Orthodox Jews takes the form of a Talmudic discourse on a chosen topic.

After his bar-mitzvah the youth is obliged to carry out the religious duties of an observant Jew, and is counted as one of the ten males eligible to form a minyan, the minimum quorum for communal prayers.

Tefillin *left*
From the date of his bar-mitzvah an observant Jew will regularly lay phylacteries (*tefillin*) with his morning prayers, except on the Sabbath and Holy Days. That practice is based on four similar passages in *Exodus* and *Deuteronomy* which require the words of the Law to be 'as a mark on your hand or frontlets between your eyes' *Ex. 13:16*. The four scriptural passages are inscribed on parchment and inserted into each of two small black leather boxes. The boxes are then tied on with black leather straps, one to the forehead and the other to the left arm above the elbow. In the latter case the strap is wound seven

The notion of marking a Jewish girl's twelfth birthday with a *bat-mitzvah* ('daughter of the commandment') ceremony is of very recent origin. It started in France and Italy in the 19th century and spread to other Western communities. Compared to the *bar-mitzvah*, the emphasis here is more on the family and social aspects than on the assumption of religious responsibilities.

Marriage

The importance Judaism attaches to marriage goes back to the story of Adam and Eve in the Book of Genesis:

> *It is not good that the man should be alone; I will make him a helper fit for him . . .: Therefore a man leaves his father and his mother and cleaves to his wife, and they become one flesh.*
>
> (Gen. 2:18, 24)

The sanctity of the Jewish marriage tie is borne out by the Hebrew word for betrothal, *kiddushin*, which means 'consecration'. At the same time, marriage is not regarded as an indissoluble sacrament as in the Catholic Church, and divorce can be obtained on various grounds.

Though there was no formal prohibition against a man having more than one wife, polygamy became uncommon in post-biblical times. Of the hundreds of Talmudic sages recorded over several centuries, there may have been only one with more than a single wife. In the Jewish communities of mediaeval Europe a ban on polygamy became accepted. It was attributed to Rabbi Gershom of Mainz in Germany (960–1028), the leading Jewish scholar of his time. There was no similar restraint regarding Jews in Moslem lands, although in practice polygamy was the exception. After the State of Israel was established in 1948, a few immigrants from Arab countries came to it with more than one wife. Legislation in Israel has banned polygamy for Jewish citizens.

Orthodox Jews regard early marriage as desirable, with eighteen as a

28

(continued on page 30)

times around the arm between the elbow and the wrist – by custom in a clock-wise direction by Sephardim, and anti-clockwise by Ashkenazim.

A Jewish Wedding

Below *A wedding ceremony in 19th-century Galicia, Poland.*

A Jewish marriage takes place under a decorative canopy (*chuppah*) held up by four poles, the pole-holders being male members of the family or close friends. The chuppah is a symbolic representation of the bridegroom's tent or house, to which the bride was originally brought. The bridegroom, therefore, waits under the canopy for

the bride to be brought in. In some oriental communities there is no canopy. Instead the groom places a prayer-shawl over the bride.

The bride is covered by a veil and stands to the right of the groom. They are flanked by relatives. A group of musicians is often at hand to play the traditional wedding tunes.

Under the canopy the officiating rabbi blesses the couple over a goblet of wine from which the groom and bride then sip. The groom places a ring on the bride's finger and declares: 'By this ring you are hereby betrothed to me according to the law of Moses and Israel.' The *ketubbah*, marriage-contract, is then read out by

the rabbi. That concludes the first or betrothal stage of the ceremony (*kiddushin* or *erusin*). The next stage is the marriage proper (*nissu'in*). Seven marriage benedictions are recited and the groom breaks a glass by stamping his foot on it, as a sign of mourning for the destruction of Jerusalem.

In early centuries the period of betrothal could last up to a year, during which time the parties were subject to certain legal rights and obligations. From about the 12th century it became the general custom to join the two stages in one ceremony.

Some local marriage customs are meant to ward off evil spirits. Thus it

was an Ashkenazi practice to lead the bride seven times round the bridegroom under the canopy, forming a magic circle against bad influences. The breaking of the glass by the groom may also have originated as a device to frighten off demons. In certain Oriental communities, the womenfolk gather the night before at the bride's home and paint her hands with red henna to protect her against evil. In some localities butter and honey were smeared on the doorposts of the groom's house to ensure good fortune.

Local fertility customs have included eating a ceremonial dish of fish, throwing rice, wheat, nuts or confetti over the couple; and having the bride hold a borrowed infant in her arms before the wedding.

The Betrothal Ring

Left *A replica of a betrothal ring from 19th-century Germany surmounted by the model of a house.*

The ring is a token payment for the bride, and her acceptance of it signifies her agreement to the symbolic transaction. Originally a coin could be used for the purpose, and this custom has survived in a few Oriental communities.

The Ketubbah (Marriage Contract)

See colour page 20

The *ketubbah* or marriage contract sets out the obligations the husband assumes towards his wife. It is usually written on parchment in the ancient Aramaic language, with a decorative border painted round the text. A summary is sometimes read out by the rabbi in the language of the country where the wedding is taking place.

suitable age for a young man. In theory the Halachah permits marriage for girls from the age of puberty, but that is not the case in contemporary practice. Israel legislation has fixed a minimum age of seventeen for girls of all creeds. All other civilized countries also have a legal minimum age.

Bereavement

Jewish mourning customs when there is a death in the family go back to ancient times. Various biblical passages refer to rending the garments, wearing sackcloth, fasting, refraining from washing or arranging the hair, sitting or lying down, or partaking of bread and wine as a reaffirmation of life. In the Talmudic period such customs were adapted into a pattern that has remained essentially unchanged to the present. It seeks to ensure both respect for the dead and the easing the grief of the mourners – as the Talmud puts it, 'the dignity of the departed' together with 'the dignity of the living'.

The main requirement is a mourning period of seven days, in which the members of the immediate family *sit Shivah* at home. They refrain from normal personal or business activities and spend each day seated

A funeral procession in Fez, Morocco.

on the floor or on low stools. Relatives and friends come to visit them, and on departing recite the blessing: 'May the Lord comfort you among the other mourners for Zion and Jerusalem.' The men have a tear in their clothes as a token 'rending of garments', wear felt slippers instead of leather shoes, and refrain from shaving. A candle burns continuously, and mirrors are covered or turned to the wall. A *minyan* (the prayer quorum of ten males) gathers for the morning, afternoon and evening services. A close male relative will say the Kaddish, the prayer recited by the mourners. The *Shivah* fulfils the need for the family to come together to express its solidarity when it suffers a loss, and for the community to give a bereaved family its support.

A modified form of mourning is kept up for the *Shloshim*, the rest of the thirty days from the funeral, while certain restrictions last a whole year. Every year thereafter on the anniversary of the death by the Jewish calendar, there is a *yahrzeit*, memorial prayers for the departed, with male survivors saying Kaddish.

The wearing of black mourning clothes or black armbands is frowned upon, since these are regarded as Gentile customs.

Chapter Four

Autonomy

Throughout Diaspora history until modern times, Jews lived in separate communities that exercised autonomy in their internal affairs and kept in close contact with each other. The communities served as the framework for preserving the Jewish faith and way of life. They also provided mutual protection against hostility and attack.

The structure of different communities, and the way of life maintained within them, were by no means uniform. Each community was influenced by the culture, economy, and attitudes of the local society that surrounded it. Despite these variables, the essential features of the Jewish community remained fairly constant down the ages. It occupied segregated quarters (whether voluntary or forced); it had its own internal administration and taxation system; and its network of institutions provided for a wide range of group-needs: religious, educational, legal and social welfare.

As a rule, Jewish autonomy did not run counter to the general pattern in the host countries. An Imperial domain such as the Roman, the Ottoman or the Austro-Hungarian was a mosaic of different peoples and creeds. The rulers had no incentive to interfere in the internal life of subject communities, as long as they were politically docile and paid their taxes. It was actually convenient for rulers to have their Jewish subjects living in organized communities. Their leaders could be the official spokesmen in dealings with the authorities, and could commit communities to collective lump sums in taxes.

After the French Revolution, and the 19th century emancipation of Jews that followed in the Western World, the Jewish community as an autonomous unit, a 'state within a state', declined in importance. As individuals, Jews became citizens of liberal democratic states, with religious freedom, civic rights and equality before the law guaranteed by constitution. In some of these countries, church and state were separated, and the national life had a secular framework. It appeared as if freedom and assimilation might erode the innate strength of the Jewish community where persecution had failed to do so.

But developments in the latter part of the century demonstrated that emancipation was not in itself an answer to the Jewish question. The newly-won freedom of the Jews in Western society provoked a backlash of ugly anti-semitism, with the Dreyfus Affair in France as its most dramatic expression. Even where anti-semitism was not overt,

Autonomy: Mediaeval Spain

Right *The Seal of the mediaeval Jewish community of Seville.*

In general, the Jewish communities in mediaeval Spain were led by their most prominent members – the gifted men who attained high office at the courts of the Moslem and Christian rulers. The outstanding example was Hisdai ibn-Shaprut in the 10th century. He served the Moorish caliphs at Cordoba while protecting his fellow-Jews and promoting their scholarship. Another was Samuel ha-Nagid, who was the chief minister to the Moslem court at Granada in the 11th century, and the acknowledged leader of Spanish Jewry. In Christian Spain, too, the kings tended to appoint Jewish royal counsellors and top officials who at the same time were accepted as the heads of their communities.

The rule of the Spanish-Jewish grandees over their communities caused social tension and discontent among the middle-class and poorer elements, who demanded a greater voice in communal affairs. The class factor is illustrated by the Barcelona Jewish Council set up by royal decree in 1327. The decree divided the community into three 'classes', each of them delegating ten members to the council.

political, economic and social barriers continued to exist. Jews migrating from Eastern Europe flooded into the static Western communities. Against a background of European national movements, the modern Zionist Movement organized itself for a return to the homeland. All these factors, both positive and negative, once more strengthened the sense of identity and peoplehood in the Jewish Diaspora. In Western lands the Jewish communities grew stronger and more organized.

After the First World War the international law concept of minority rights was promoted as a restriction on national sovereignty. At the Versailles Peace Conference in 1919 the Committee of Jewish Delegations spearheaded the campaign for the special minority provisions that were written into the peace treaties with the defeated powers of Austria, Hungary, Bulgaria and Turkey and the successor states of Poland, Czechoslovakia, Rumania, Yugoslavia and Greece. The ethnic, religious, national, cultural and linguistic minorities in these countries (including, of course, the Jewish communities) were guaranteed group rights under international supervision to be exercised through the League of Nations.

These minorities clauses and treaties had, before 1914, been given an ideological basis by the great Russian-Jewish historian Simon

(continued on page 41)

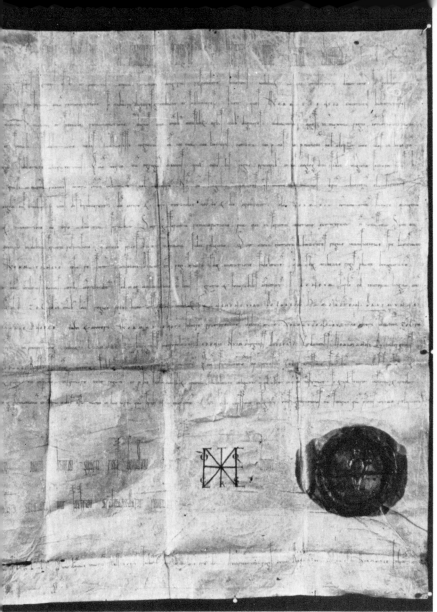

A letter dated 1074 from the Emperor Heinrich IV to the Jews of the German city of Worms, granting them communal rights and the privileges of freedom of trade.

German region would congregate at the great annual trade fairs held in one or other city. From time to time advantage was taken of these gatherings to convene a synod of rabbis and communal leaders, in order to discuss common problems of Jewish life. The conclusions would serve as guidance for local communities. Such synods took place in France, the Rhineland and Italy.

Christian Europe in the Middle Ages was not a monolithic society. It had a corporate structure made up of various contending power-centres: the kings and princes, the great landowning nobles with their serfs and private armies, the Church and monastic Orders, the burgeoning mercantile cities with their privileges gained by royal charter, and the craft guilds. Although the Jews stood outside this feudal framework, they were in a sense another autonomous corporate entity that performed limited but valuable economic functions.

In the absence of an official regional leadership recourse was often had to a *shtadlan* (a person who intercedes). The shtadlan was an individual Jew who had the requisite position, language and connections to deal with the authorities on behalf of his fellow-Jews. He might plead for relief from ruinous taxes and protection from mob violence, anti-Jewish laws, the 'blood-libel' and other fabricated offences against Jews. This one-man lobby was an important device at a time when Jews were at the mercy of rulers and hostile clergy. In Czarist Russia, and other countries with autocratic regimes in Eastern Europe, the shtadlan remained a feature of Jewish communal life until the 19th century.

Autonomy: Ashkenaz (Mediaeval Franco-Germany)

In mediaeval Ashkenaz (Franco-Germany) the autonomous *Kehillah* (local community) emerged as the basis for organized Jewish life. As a rule, all the Jews residing in a particular centre formed a single community under one communal board.

This local unity was disrupted in certain countries in the 16th century, with the influx of Jewish refugees from Spain and Portugal. In Holland and Italy the newcomers tended to set up separate Sephardi congregations, parallel with the existing Ashkenazi ones. (The literal meanings of the Hebrew words Sephardi and Ashkenazi are 'Spanish' and 'German'.)

Jews from all over the Franco-

The Council of the Four Lands meet in Lublin, Poland.

Autonomy: Mediaeval Poland–Lithuania

By the 15th century, Jews migrating eastward from Germany had settled in different parts of Poland, and in the Grand Duchy of Lithuania that came under the Polish crown. They were made welcome and given communal rights by Polish rulers eager to gain their financial and trading skills and their international ties. A regular countrywide institution developed, known as the Council of the Four Lands (Great Poland, Little Poland, Galicia and Volhynia). The Council consisted of thirty delegates – six rabbis and twenty-four lay leaders. It met in two annual sessions, at the spring fair in Lublin and the autumn fair at Jaroslav in Galicia. Its functions included the division among the communities of the annual collective tax imposed on Polish Jewry by the authorities; a special fund to protect Jewish interests; the promotion of Jewish education and welfare; and guidelines regarding business ethics and undue competition. The Council set up a high court of justice that sat at the same time.

While these councils played an essential co-ordinating role, the basic unit of Jewish life in Eastern Europe remained the self-contained local community (Kehillah), with its network of institutions under the democratic control of all its members.

A Rabbi in Salonika.

Above *Bet Din (the Rabbinical Court)* and below *Ritual Slaughter. Details from the 'Sefer ha-Turim', a legal code by Rabbi Jacob ben-Asher appearing in Mantua, Italy, 15th century.*

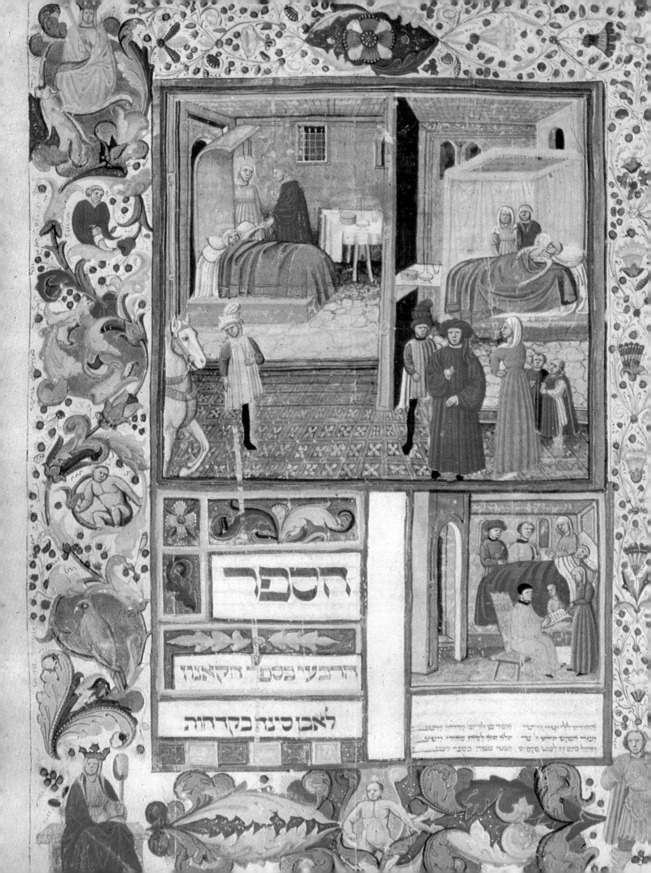

הספר

הרביעי מספר הקאנון

לאבן סינא בקדוח

Above Painted ceiling, Chodorov. A reconstruction of the wooden ceiling of a synagogue.

Left Bikkur Cholim (tending the sick). An illuminated page from the Hebrew translation of the Canon of Medicine of Avicenna, the renowned 11th-century Islamic philosopher and physician.

Below Dura Europos. A reconstruction of the wall-paintings in the synagogue on the Euphrates river in Syria.

Left *A double page from a replica of the Birds Head Haggadah,* AD 1300, *one of the oldest Ashkenazi illuminated manuscripts of the Haggadah that survives.*

Below *'Days of Awe' (High Holy Days). A representation taken from a painting by Maurycy Gottlieb.*

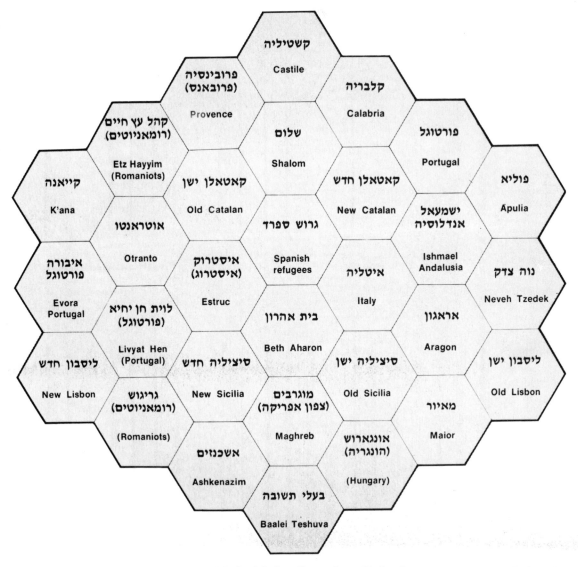

Dubnow, who developed the concept of Galut Nationalism, also called Autonomism. Dubnow maintained that the existing European Jewish communities in the Diaspora had become a permanent national entity, with Yiddish as the cornerstone of its national culture. However, the minorities treaties were poorly implemented between the two World Wars, and faded away with the demise of the League of Nations.

In the Western world Jews are free citizens of the countries where they live, but remain strongly organized in communities, on the basis of voluntary affiliation. The outstanding example is the United States, where an organized Jewry with millions of members fits comfortably into a highly pluralistic society. On the local level, communities continue to be centred on their synagogues and Reform temples with a network of ancillary institutions: community centres, parochial

Autonomy: The Salonika Community

This is a diagram of the congregations that made up the Salonika Jewish Community in the 17th century. As the names indicate, these congregations are formed according to the places of origin of their members, and thus roughly correspond to the *landsmanshaften* (country-of-origin associations) set up by European immigrants to the United States and elsewhere.

schools, youth organizations, charitable and fund-raising agencies, social and recreation facilities. On the national level there are a large number of Jewish bodies but no single organization that speaks for American Jewry as a whole.

In Britain, France and other Western countries, the pattern of voluntary organizations is similar. In each of these countries there is a single representative body on the national level, such as the Board of Deputies of British Jews.

After the Bolshevik revolution of 1917, the huge Jewish community in Soviet Russia was virtually cut off from the rest of the Jewish world. Soviet policy towards the Jewish minority was self-contradictory. The anti-Jewish restrictions of the Czarist era were abolished. The Jews were officially recognized as one of the many different nationalities within the Soviet Union. Since each of the others had a territorial base, an Autonomous Jewish Region was set up in Birobidjan, in the Far Eastern region of the Soviet Union. This experiment proved a dismal failure. Less than one per cent of Soviet Jews live there, and those that do constitute a small minority of the local population. At the same time the distinctive features of Jewish group identity – religion, language, culture, ties with Jewish communities elsewhere, Zionist sentiments – were discouraged and suppressed by the Soviet authorities. In these conditions, Jewish communal life virtually ceased in Russia and declined in the Baltic States of Lithuania, Latvia, Esthonia and other territories annexed by the Soviet Union at the beginning of the Second World War.

Autonomy: The Ottoman Empire

In the Ottoman Empire, what was called the 'millet system' gave non-Moslem religious groups the right to organize their communal lives, practise their own faiths and apply their religious laws in their own courts in matters of personal status. The overall structure of the Ottoman Jewish community was fragmented. In Constantinople, the capital, the pattern resembled that in Salonika. There were about forty congregations established according to localities of origin, each with its own synagogue, officials and institutions, but with little co-ordination between them. Only as late as 1865 was a law adopted that set up central organs representing all the Jews of the Ottoman Empire. A Chief Rabbi (*Haham Bashi*) was to be appointed by the Sultan, with extensive powers. In addition there was to be a General Council of eighty members, with two committees, one rabbinical and one secular.

Chapter Five

Communal Institutions

The internal structure of local communities has varied. In some areas communal leadership has been exercised by an aristocracy of scholars, notables and influential families. That has been the general pattern in the Moslem world. In the Western world, from the Middle Ages, the system of a community administration was a mixture of democracy and oligarchy. Sometimes decisions were taken by a majority vote, sometimes by lot, sometimes by a few individuals. The assembly elects a communal board (*kahal*) presided over by the elected president of the community (*parnass*). The other important honorary officer is the treasurer (*gabbai*) who is also the senior warden for charitable funds. The board administers the affairs of the community and appoints its officials.

The central institution of a community has always been the synagogue. Its primary function is worship, but the building and its courtyard have also served as a meeting place and as a venue for bar-mitzvahs and weddings. Other institutions, like the law court (*bet din*), the study house (*bet midrash*) and the ritual bath-house (*mikveh*), have usually been clustered round it. Next to the synagogue, the essential communal property is the burial ground, for Jews have to be buried in consecrated soil.

The most important community official is the rabbi. In Judaism there is no clerical hierarchy, as, for instance, in the Catholic Church. Each rabbi is responsible only to God's law and to the community that engaged him. The practise of formally ordaining a rabbi goes back to mediaeval Germany. Among other officials are the cantor (*chazzan*) who leads the prayers in synagogues; the beadle (*shamash*) and the ritual slaughterer (*shochet*).

In traditional Jewish society elementary education took place in a *cheder* (schoolroom) where boys from three to thirteen were taught religious subjects by rote. After his bar-mitzvah a boy would move to a *yeshivah* (Talmudic academy) until he was seventeen or eighteen. The closed system of religious education started breaking down from the beginning of the 19th century, with the demand for more general secular studies. Until modern times the education of Jewish girls was virtually confined to reading and reciting the prayers; more serious study was regarded as a male preserve.

(continued on page 45)

The Shulhof Complex

The Shulhof was an imposing example of the traditional role of the
synagogue as the focal point of community activities. There were some
twenty small synagogues and other
institutions round the courtyard, as
well as the main synagogue. The
complex was founded in 1572, and
twenty years later the street passing
the main entrance gates was officially
named the 'Street of the Jews'.

On the left-hand side of the model
is the academy bearing the name of
the Vilna Gaon, Rabbi Elijah ben-
Solomon Zalman (1720–97), the most
renowned Jewish scholar of his day.

On the right-hand side of the
model are the Great Synagogue and a
Jewish public library.

Bet Din

See colour page 37

The *Bet Din* is usually presided over
by the community rabbi aided by two
or more *dayanim* (judges of a rabbinical court). In larger centres of
population the Bet Din might have
city-wide or regional jurisdiction,
serving a group of communities.

The general pattern of Jewish
autonomy in Diaspora lands included
the administration of Jewish law
through an internal court system.
The extent of the jurisdiction permitted to these courts varied. Everywhere they dealt with ritual matters, as
well as with questions of family and
personal status, including marriage,
divorce, guardianship and inheritance. Usually the Bet Din could also
hear civil cases where both parties
were Jews. As a rule it could not try
criminal cases, though in mediaeval
Spain that was one of the privileges
granted by the kings.

Charity has always been regarded as a supreme virtue, which would gain merit in the world to come. The Hebrew word for charity, *tzedakah*, means righteousness, which stresses that it was a religious duty for the well-off to take care of the needy. In the local community the mechanism for relief services was the charity fund (*kuppah*) to which each member of the congregation contributed according to his means. It was administered by three elected charity wardens. The fund provided money, food and clothing to the indigent, dowries for poor brides, burial of paupers and ransom money for captives. The remarkable record of modern Jewish philanthropy is in the direct tradition of *tzedakah*.

Among the charitable features of the community were the duty to visit and help the sick (*bikkur cholim*) and the maintenance of a poorhouse-infirmary (*hekdesh*) and a soup kitchen (*tamchui*). As a rule the hekdesh was used for transients, since families within the

Left A reconstructed model of part of the Shulhof synagogue complex in Vilna, Lithuania, destroyed by the Nazis in the Second World War.

Below Bikkur Cholim (tending the sick). A detail from the Canon of Medicine of Avicenna.

Bikkur Cholim

See colour page 38 and detail right

A special act of piety in a Jewish community was *bikkur cholim* (visiting the sick). The visitors were required to attend to the wants of the invalid and the disabled, to cheer them up, and to pray for their recovery. The sages gave detailed guidance how to avoid untimely, protracted or depressing visits. A special point was made of fulfilling this duty in cases where the sick person was poor, for 'many go to a rich man to pay him honour'.

Ritual Slaughter

See colour page 37 and detail right

One of the basic services rendered by the community has been to ensure a regular supply of kosher meat. From early times communities have arranged for the ritual slaughter (*shechitah*) of animals and birds under the supervision of the rabbinical authorities. The fees paid for this service have been a major source of revenue for the community.

By Jewish law, any adult sufficiently versed in the dietary laws can perform the ritual act. But from the Middle Ages, it has always been done by a professional *shochet* (slaughterer) who has been licensed after passing an examination. In small communities this task was often combined with other paid communal offices, such as cantor or teacher.

The ritual method makes the death of the animal as instantaneous and painless as possible. The essence of the method is the slitting of the throat in a single stroke with an extremely sharp knife. The carcase is drained of blood, which by Jewish belief contains the life-force and should not be consumed. In modern times the method has been questioned by animal welfare bodies but the weight of scientific and medical opinion has endorsed it, and it is expressly legalized in the United States, Britain and elsewhere.

Distorted accounts of Jewish ritual slaughter have featured in antisemitic literature, and it was banned by the Nazis in all the territories they occupied.

Ritual Slaughter, a detail from the 'Sefer ha-Turim'.

community would generally look after members who needed help.

A characteristic of Jewish communal life was the *chevrah*, a society under the general control of the community board, and often subsidized from community funds. These societies served various charitable and social purposes. The most influential was the *Chevrah Kaddisha* (burial society) that attended to funerals and cemeteries. *Bikkur Cholim* societies also operated as voluntary sick funds.

With its elaborate system of religious, educational and charitable agencies, the Jewish community functioned as a social welfare state in miniature.

Chapter Six

The Synagogue

The form of public worship embodied in the synagogue was, like monotheism itself, a unique Jewish concept in the ancient world. It was in due course taken over and adapted by the two later monotheistic faiths, Christianity and Islam.

The roots of the synagogue lie in the Babylonian captivity after the destruction of the kingdom of Judah and the First Temple, in 586 BC. As the Jewish exiles settled down on the alien soil of Babylonia, they clung to their Mosaic creed and sacred Books, and developed local meeting-places for prayer and study. After the disaster that had uprooted them, they had to be reassured that God had not abandoned them. The answer came through the great prophet of the Exile, Ezekiel. 'Thus says the Lord God: Though I removed them far off among the nations, and though I scattered them among the countries, yet I have been a sanctuary to them for a while in the countries where they have gone.' (*Ezek. 11:16*) In a later age the Talmudic sages interpreted this passage to mean that the Divine Presence had remained with the exiles in the houses of worship that formed the early synagogues.

Certainly the synagogue was a well-established institution, both in the Land of Israel and in the Diaspora, long before the destruction of the Second Temple in AD 70. The New Testament mentions those synagogues where Jesus preached and those elsewhere in the Roman Empire where St Paul preached. From inscriptions and archaeological remains, it is estimated that hundreds of synagogues co-existed with the Second Temple. The synagogue, however, was not a small local replica of the Temple. There were profound differences between the two institutions.

The mystic act of sacrifice could only be carried out at the central sanctuary, the Temple. The rituals there, including the sacrifices and benedictions, were performed by a hereditary caste of priests. Psalms of thanksgiving and praise to the Lord were sung to musical instruments by professional choirs of Levites. The services took place outside the Temple, with the worshippers gathered in the courtyard. Only the priests had access to the sanctuary itself, and only the High Priest had access to the Holy of Holies, once a year on the Day of Atonement. The building was not only a house of worship – it was also God's dwelling-place.

In the case of a synagogue, the congregation assembled inside the building. (The Greek work 'synagogue' and the Hebrew equivalent *bet knesset* have the meaning of 'a meeting-house'.) There were no sacrifices, and in fact sacrifices ceased altogether to be a feature of Jewish worship when the Temple went out of existence. The synagogue service rested on collective prayers and Scripture readings. A quorum (minyan) of ten or more males over the age of thirteen constituted a congregation for public worship at any place, and any person able to do so could conduct the service, without the need for a priest.

These three elements of the service – the order of prayers, Scripture readings and the sermon – were already regular features of the synagogue by the time the Second Temple was destroyed and the synagogue became the major institution of Jewish life everywhere. Since the Temple priesthood no longer existed, authority in religious matters lay informally with the learned sages and scholars whom their pupils called by the title *rabbi*, meaning 'my teacher'. They had no official standing in the congregations; it was at a much later stage that communities appointed paid rabbis.

The synagogue did retain or adapt certain Temple customs. The times and names of the daily services corresponded to those of the daily Temple sacrifices: morning (*shacharit*) and afternoon (*minchah*). To these were added the evening service (*ma'ariv*) and an additional service (*mussaf*). The priestly blessing from the Temple was repeated in the synagogue by members of the congregation who were descendants of the priestly families (*Cohanim*). Men and women were separated in the synagogue, as they had been at the Temple, where

Sardis, Turkey, *above*.

Originally built as a secular basilica, this edifice became a synagogue from the late 2nd century AD. The model has been constructed on the basis of archaeological excavations.

Prague, Czechoslovakia,

right.

The 'Altneuschul' is the oldest synagogue in Europe still in use. It was built in the 13th–14th centuries, and influenced by the Gothic church architecture of the period. Although restrictions were imposed by the authorities at that time on the height of synagogues, the Altneuschul dominates the surrounding houses, as it is located in the heart of the old Jewish quarter of Prague.

(continued on page 51)

Kai-Feng Fu, China, *above*.

A community of Chinese Jews was at Kai-Feng-Fu, capital of the Honan province of Central China. It was established at the beginning of the 12th century by Jews from Persia or India, engaged in the production of cotton fabrics. The synagogue was built in 1163, and after being destroyed by flood, was rebuilt in 1653, through the efforts of a Jewish mandarin. The community fell into decay and had assimilated by the 19th century. The first report about them to reach Europe came from an Italian Jesuit missionary in the 18th century.

Dura-Europos

See colour page 39

The synagogue of Dura-Europos, on the Euphrates River in Syria, was built in AD 245. It was excavated in 1932 and moved to the National Museum in Damascus.

The four inside walls of the synagogue were entirely covered by coloured frescoes, in a style that is a fusion of Hellenist and Persian art. The murals include scenes from the *Pentateuch*, the *Prophets* and the *Book of Esther*. The subjects of some of the paintings have not been definitely identified. Certain ones may be derived from legends that have been lost.

This model of a 17th-century wooden synagogue represents the type of synagogue building common in the small towns of Eastern Europe in the 17th and 18th centuries. Over a hundred of them still existed in Poland, Lithuania and the Ukraine at the outbreak of the Second World War. All of them were destroyed by the Nazis during the War.

there was a special Women's Court. The eternal light (*Ner Tamid*) before the Ark in the synagogue represented the great menorah in the Temple. A degree of the holiness attached to the Temple precincts was transferred to the synagogue building.

By the period of the Mishnah (2nd-3rd century AD), the basic order of prayers in the synagogue liturgy had already become fixed. In the course of time variations developed in different Jewish centres, mainly by the addition of liturgical poems (*piyyutim*) for the Sabbath, festivals and High Holy Days. Thus there were differences between the Palestinian and Babylonian rites (*minhagim*) that eventually evolved into the Ashkenazi and Sephardi variants in the liturgy.

In its external aspect, the synagogue has had no special Jewish style, and its architecture has been influenced by that prevailing in different countries and periods of Diaspora life. Jewish law and tradition are much concerned with the interior functions of the synagogue, but have had little to say about its outward appearance.

In Christian Europe synagogues were apt to be targets of hostility or mob violence, so the tendency was to place them in the heart of the Jewish quarter or ghetto and to make them outwardly plain and inconspicuous, even where the interior was lavishly decorated. One restriction imposed by the Church was that a synagogue had to be lower than any churches in the vicinity; as a result, it became customary for the ground floor to be sunk below street level, so as to afford more height inside.

Early synagogues, to about the 8th century AD, generally conformed to the rectangular design of the Roman basilica. That was the case both in the Land of Israel and in the Diaspora.

In mediaeval Europe synagogues were built in the successive styles of Romanesque and Gothic, and later, Renaissance and Baroque. However, in Spain the synagogues were strongly influenced by Moorish architecture, with its courtyards and colonnades. After the Expulsion from Spain, the new synagogues built by the Spanish and Portuguese congregations in Holland and Britain were modelled on the Protestant churches in those countries.

The wooden synagogues that appeared all over Poland in the 17th and early 18th century developed a distinctive character. The painted ceilings in some of these synagogues were an expression of an authentic Jewish folk-art.

In 17th-century Eastern Europe some synagogues were of the fortress type, designed to withstand attack from raiding bands of Cossacks and Tartars.

The Chassidic movement that sprang up in Eastern Europe in the 18th century had a modest and austere attitude towards the synagogue. It was usually a small room known as a *shtiebl*, furnished with tables and benches rather than pews. The services were informal and full of fervour.

In 19th-century Western Europe and America, Jewish emancipation and growing wealth produced a great number of large synagogues in an eclectic mixture of styles – Egyptian, Moorish, Renaissance or neo-classical – and many of them with exuberant ornamentation. Particularly noticeable was a revival of the Moorish idiom of mediaeval Spain, reflected in fanciful domes.

Contemporary synagogue architecture, particularly in the United States, shows a complete break with the past. The stress is on the functional aspect of modern architecture with its new technology, its use of concrete and glass, and its austere appearance. Wealthy American congregations, especially of the Reform trend, engage the leading architects of the day to design their great new temples – including Erich Mendelsohn, Percival Goodman, Louis Cahn and Frank Lloyd Wright. In general these buildings provide for multiple community functions: halls for social occasions, classrooms, and recreation and sport facilities. The sanctuary within such a complex can be expanded for the High Holy Days by opening the partition dividing it from the large social hall.

The interior design of every synagogue down the ages has had two focal points: the Ark and the *bimah*.

The Ark is the cabinet containing the parchment Scrolls of the Law, the most sacred objects in the synagogue. (The Ashkenazi name for it is *Aron Kodesh* and the Sephardi one is *Heichal*.) It is always placed on the wall facing in the direction of Jerusalem, which in the Western world would be the East wall. From the late Middle Ages the Ark was usually built into the wall and was of elaborate design, with an embroidered or velvet curtain hanging in front of it. A representation of the twin tablets of the Law is often set as a decorative motif above the Ark. The congregation stands facing the Ark when it is opened for

Fez, Morocco, *above right.*

The Danan synagogue was built in the mid-17th century and renovated in its present form at the end of the 19th century. A distinctive feature is the Arks. The platform, set in the western wall, is surmounted by a crown, and on it stands the Chair of Elijah used for circumcision ceremonies.

Cochin, India, *below right.*

Model of the Paradesi ('foreigners') synagogue of the 'White Jews' of Cochin – so-called because they originated from Syria, Spain, Holland and Germany and had fairer skins than the native Cochinis who were called 'Black Jews'. The synagogue was built in 1568 and enlarged in 1761. The present structure shows European influence.

Painted Ceiling, Chodorov

See colour page 39

A reconstructed segment on a reduced scale of the painted ceiling of the synagogue in Chodorov, near Lvov in Poland. Dating from 1651, this was the oldest wooden synagogue in Europe.

In the centre is a double-headed eagle enclosed in a circle and surrounded by smaller circles containing the signs of the Zodiac. The rest of the ceiling is filled with animals, birds, plants and biblical and Talmudic verses.

This type of painted ceiling was found in a number of the Polish synagogues that were destroyed during the Nazi occupation.

The Tallit

The *tallit* was originally a mantle or gown of wool or linen worn by men as an outer garment. In the Dispersion it evolved into a prayer-shawl worn in the synagogue over the shoulders (sometimes over the head) during the morning service, and all day on the Day of Atonement.

There are two main types of tallit. The ordinary one is of white wool, linen or cotton, with blue or black horizontal stripes at either end. The type worn by rabbis, cantors and important members of the congregation is of cream-coloured wool with black stripes. Round the edge that rests on the neck an extra strip is sewn called the *atarah* (diadem), decorated with silver or gold thread.

At the four corners of the tallit are tassels (*tsitsiot*) made of threads inserted through holes and tied together with knots. This fringe fulfills the biblical commandment in the Books of *Numbers* and *Deuteronomy* to make tassels on the corners of garments, as a reminder to observe religious duties. A tallit is carried to synagogue in a decorated bag.

An Orthodox Jew also wears under his outer garment a rectangle of white cloth with a similar fringe hanging from the corners, in such a way that it is visible. This garment is known as a 'small tallit' (*tallit katan*).

the Scrolls to be taken out and brought to the bimah for reading and when they are returned, or when certain prayers are recited.

The bimah is a raised platform used primarily for reading the Torah Scrolls that are unrolled on a table or desk. In Sephardi communities it is known as a *tevah*, the Hebrew word for a box. Traditionally the bimah is in the centre of the synagogue. In one type of early mediaeval synagogue, the vaulted ceiling was supported by two columns, with the bimah between them in the centre. Later, in the 17th century, there evolved in Central and Eastern Europe a design with the bimah between four central pillars, thereby stressing its importance. This tradition was so strong that some later wooden synagogues retained four wooden posts round the bimah though they were not required structurally to support the roof span.

Italian synagogues of the 16th and 17th centuries departed from the centrality of the bimah by placing it at the end of the synagogue opposite the Ark, thus creating a bi-polar design. The 18th-century Reform Movement went the opposite way. The bimah was linked to the Ark with a platform in front of it facing the congregation seated in rows. This break with tradition was strongly attacked by the Orthodox authorities, who went as far as to declare the arrangement a violation of the Halachah, the religious law. Nevertheless this has become the regular design in Reform and Conservative synagogues. Orthodox synagogues usually have a reading desk apart from the bimah and in front of the Ark, for the use of the cantor and for the rabbi's sermon.

The bimah has had different shapes – square, round, curved or octagonal. It usually has a low railing round it. In mediaeval Spain the bimah was a wooden platform raised high above the ground on columns.

The traditional place for women in a synagogue is in an upper gallery. Where the architectural design did not allow for a gallery, the women would sit on the same level as the men but separated from them by a lattice division (*mechitzah*) or in an adjoining chamber. In Reform temples the segregation between the sexes has been abolished. In Conservative synagogues men and women either sit together or sit on opposite sides of an aisle with no screen between them.

Under the Nazi regime the destruction of synagogues was carried out as a deliberate and planned operation. In the Kristalnacht (Crystal night) of 1938, 280 of them were demolished in a single night in Germany alone. As the Nazi occupation spread across Europe, thousands of synagogues were burnt down by special squads, and in some recorded cases the congregations were locked inside and burnt alive. Altogether, 33,914 European Jewish communities with their synagogues were wiped out by the Nazis.

Chapter Seven

Festivals

Traditional Jewish life has always been regulated by the Hebrew calendar. It is based on the lunar cycle and is adjusted to the solar year by the device of the leap year – except that the lunar year adds a month and not merely a day. There are seven such leap years in each nineteen-year period, so that a Hebrew date and its corresponding secular date will coincide once every nineteen years. For example, the State of Israel was proclaimed on 15 May 1948, which was the fifth day of the Hebrew month of Iyar. Since Israel Independence Day is celebrated according to the Hebrew date, it again occurred on 15 May in 1967, and will do so next time after a further nineteen years, in 1986.

The Christian calendar is reckoned from the putative year when Jesus was circumcised; the Jewish calendar from the putative year of the Creation. The year AD 1980 corresponds to the Jewish year 5740.

For traditional Jewry the pivotal dates of the year have always been the festivals that punctuate the Jewish calendar. The most ancient of the festivals are those that are laid down in the Torah (Pentateuch). They fall into two groups. The first is the New Year (*Rosh ha-Shanah*) that ushers in ten days of penitence culminating in the Day of Atonement (*Yom Kippur*). This is the most solemn religious interlude in the year, known traditionally as the 'Days of Awe' and called in the Western world by the term High Holy Days.

The second group are the three 'pilgrim festivals', Passover (*Pesach*) in the Spring, the Feast of Weeks (*Shavuot*) in the early summer, and the Feast of Booths (*Succot*) in the autumn. (Succot is followed immediately by the festive day of *Simchat Torah*, the Rejoicing of the Law.) On these occasions the farming population used to bring their offerings to the Temple in Jerusalem and mingle with crowds of pilgrims from the Diaspora communities. These three festivals originate in the agricultural cycle of the year in the Land of Israel.

In whatever climate Jews find themselves – even in the southern hemisphere where the seasons are reversed – Pesach, Shavuot and Succot are celebrated at times and with rites that are directly related to farm life in the ancient homeland. Each of these festivals has also acquired an historical context related to the great national and religious experience of the Exodus.

In the Diaspora a 'Second Day' is added in the observance of the

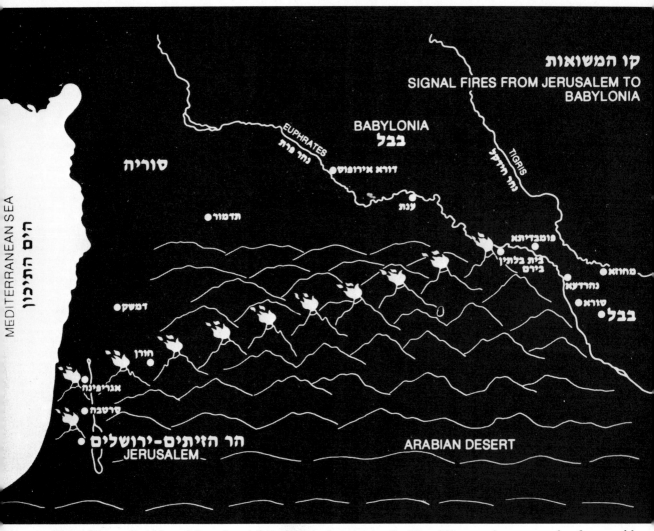

קו המשואות
SIGNAL FIRES FROM JERUSALEM TO BABYLONIA

Signalling the New Month

The map shows a chain of bonfires on high points stretching from the Mount of Olives in Jerusalem across the desert to Babylonia. When two witnesses reported to the religious leaders in Jerusalem that they had sighted the new moon, this indicated the start of the lunar month. That fact was communicated to Diaspora communities by the speediest means possible, so that their calendar could be kept in line with that in the Land of Israel. The line of beacons was used to 'telegraph' that signal to Babylonia.

biblical festivals – except for Yom Kippur, since a two-day fast would be too onerous; and for the New Year, which came to be celebrated for two days in the Land of Israel as well. In the case of Passover, the *Seder* is repeated on the second evening in the Diaspora.

The reason for the extra Diaspora day is to ensure that at least one of them will be the correct one. In ancient times, it was the Sanhedrin in Jerusalem who determined the opening day of each Hebrew month by reporting the time of the new moon, and passing the word to the Diaspora communities. Communications were uncertain, and increasing one day to two reduced the risk of getting the date wrong.

Other festivals are of later origin, and are 'minor' in the sense that they do not have the same degree of sanctity as the Torah festivals. *Purim*, in early spring (March) is connected with an episode at the Persian court, related in the *Book of Esther*. The Feast of Dedication (*Chanukkah*) occurs about the same time as Christmas and is post-

(continued on page 59)

Passover (Pesach)

This model depicts a family sitting down to the Passover meal (*Seder*) in 15th-century Spain.

Passover (*Pesach*) is the most festive and important family occasion of the Jewish year. It originated in ancient times as the Spring festival in the Land of Israel, marking the end of the rainy season and the beginning of the grain harvest. During the Temple period Pesach was one of the three great pilgrimage festivals, when farmers brought their offerings to the Temple, and Jerusalem was crowded with thousands of pilgrims from the Diaspora communities.

Passover commemorates a central event in the biblical story, the Exodus from Egypt and God's deliverance of the Children of Israel from bondage:

'And when your children say to you, 'What do you mean by this service?' you shall say, 'It is the sacrifice of the Lord's passover, for he passed over the houses of the people of Israel in Egypt, when he slew the Egyptians but spared our houses. (Ex. 12:26,27)

In Israel the festival lasts seven days, with the ceremonial family meal (*Seder*) on the first evening. The first and last days are holidays while those in between, though festive, are days when work is permitted. In the Diaspora there are eight days of Passover, with the Seder repeated on the second evening as well.

Before the start of the festival, every scrap of leaven (*chametz*) must be collected and destroyed – bread, pastry, and any foodstuffs such as porridge or beer made from grain. The Ashkenazim, but not the Sephardim, include rice in the ban. Cooking utensils, dishes and cutlery must be cleansed by boiling or heating, though many households keep duplicate sets just for Passover use. From then until the end of the Passover, *matzah* (unleavened bread) is eaten instead of bread, in accordance with the passage in the *Book of Exodus*: 'And they baked unleavened cakes of the dough which they had brought out of Egypt ... because they were thrust out of Egypt and could not tarry ...' (*Ex. 12:39*)

On the festive Seder table are a number of items that have a symbolic use during the evening. Three cakes of matzot are placed one above the other, and covered by an ornamental cloth. On a special Seder dish, usually painted with quotations and scenes from the Haggadah, the following are set out in a prescribed order:

a shank bone of lamb, to recall the paschal lamb sacrificed by each family at the Temple of Jerusalem.

a roasted egg symbolizing the burnt offering at the Temple (it may have been an ancient Spring fertility symbol).

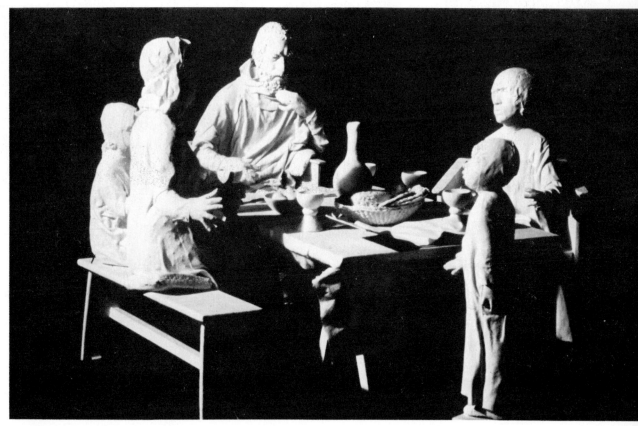

a dish of salt water symbolizing the Israelite tears.

lettuce, parsley or celery (*karpas*) dipped into the salt water and eaten.

bitter herbs (*maror*), usually horse-radish, symbolizes the bitter lot of the Israelites under the yoke of the Egyptians.

charoset, a sweet paste made from grated apples, almonds and wine as a symbol of the mortar used by the Israelites when laying bricks during their Egyptian bondage.

The Seder evening is devoted to the reading of the Haggadah. The reading is interrupted for the meal and resumed afterwards. Woven through the Haggadah are a series of ritual acts: partaking of the karpas, bitter herbs, and charoset, drinking four cups of wine (two before the meal and two after), the various blessings, and the washing of the hands. At the outset the middle one of the three cakes of matzot is broken into two and one piece, called the *afikoman*, is hidden by the head of the family, to be ransomed with a gift when the children find it.

A full cup of wine called 'Elijah's cup' stands on the table. As the Prophet Elijah will herald the coming of the Messiah, it symbolizes the hopes for a final redemption. Towards the end of the service the front door is opened to indicate that all Jews are awaiting the arrival of Elijah.

The Haggadah's theme, the Exodus from Egypt, must have had ominous overtones for a 15th-century Spanish-Jewish family such as that depicted in the model. The Golden Age of the Jews in Spain was over, and the clouds of persecution were gathering over their heads. Already some of their number had accepted formal baptism as New Christians, while continuing to practise the Jewish faith in secret. Towards the end of that century, in 1492, all the Jews would be expelled from Spain.

'Days of Awe' (High Holy Days)

See colour page 40

Jews at prayer on the Day of Atonement – representation taken from a painting by Maurycy Gottlieb, dated 1878. Gottlieb (1856–79) was an outstanding Polish-Jewish artist who died at the age of twenty-three. Many of his paintings are on Jewish themes. His younger brother Leopold (1883–1934), also a painter, became a well-known member of the Paris school.

The 'Days of Awe' (or High Holy Days) are the most solemn period of the Jewish religious year. The New Year (*Rosh ha-Shanah*) is the beginning of ten days of penitence that reach their climax on the Day of Atonement.

Unlike the other holidays, the High Holy Days are neither agricultural in origin nor do they commemorate any significant episode in the national history. They concern the individual Jew and his relationship with God and his fellow men.

According to Jewish belief, the New Year ushers in the period of ten days when the conduct of each person during the preceding year will be judged by God, and it will be decreed who shall be inscribed in the 'Book of Life' and who in the 'Book of Death'. The key rite in the synagogue service on Rosh ha-Shanah is the blowing of the ram's horn (*Shofar*), in a fixed series of notes.

The rituals of the High Holy Days give central importance to the concept of repentance. God is not only just but merciful, and the remorseful sinner can gain divine forgiveness and a suspended sentence. That is why the first ten days of the New Year must be set aside as a period of penitence, and the Day of Atonement, when the verdict is 'signed', devoted entirely to prayer and fasting. The spirit of this, the holiest day of the year, is reflected in the passage in *Leviticus* that '. . . on this day shall atonement be made for you, to cleanse you; from all your sins you shall be clean before the Lord. It is a sabbath of solemn rest to you, and you shall afflict yourselves; . . .' (*Lev. 16:30–31*)

A confession covering a long list of sins is recited ten times during the day's service, which is concluded with the blowing of the Shofar.

The most celebrated prayer in the Yom Kippur liturgy is the *Kol Nidre* ('all vows') sung to an ancient melody on the eve of the Holy day. It is a formula in Aramaic for the annulment of all personal vows and oaths made unwittingly and not affecting other persons. The tradition goes back to about the 9th century AD.

Pesach: The Haggadah

See colour page 40

The *Haggadah* has been the most popular and the most profusely illustrated Jewish religious work in Diaspora history. The Birds Head Haggadah is one of a number of beautiful illuminated versions that have survived from the Middle Ages. One of the earliest and most sumptuous Sephardi ones is the 14th-century Golden Haggadah, now in the British Museum. Haggadot started to be printed in the 15th century. Since then there have been thousands of different examples, many of them illustrated with quaint woodcuts.

The Haggadah is a collection of benedictions, biblical and talmudic references, commentaries, stories and folk songs. Its central theme is an account of the Exodus and a discussion of its meaning. The recital is introduced by a young child asking four set questions that concern the difference between that particular night and all other nights. The explanations that follow expand on the Haggadah injunction that 'in every generation each Jew should regard himself as though he personally went forth from Egypt'.

biblical. It commemorates the deliverance of the Temple during the Maccabean Revolt in the 2nd century BC. Various memorial days were added in the course of time. The ninth day of the month of Av (*Tish'a be'Av*) was accepted as the day of mourning and fast for the destruction of the First Temple in 586 BC and the Second Temple in AD 70. In the present generation, Holocaust Day was established in 1951 by the Israel Parliament (*Knesset*) as a national day of remembrance for victims of the Nazis. It coincided with the date of the Warsaw Ghetto uprising in 1943. It is suitably marked by Diaspora communities.

Israel's Independence Day in May is also celebrated throughout the Jewish world.

Pesach Seder Plate

Above *A replica of a German Seder plate of engraved pewter c.1800, with a scene of a group celebrating the Passover.*

The Seder plate has taken a variety of forms. Some European Ashkenazi communities have used a three-tiered stand for the three cakes of matzot. The Sephardim as a rule have a large platter or flat basket with the matzot in the centre and the other items around it.

Pesach: The 'Four Sons'

Above *A replica of a gilded silver wine goblet for Pesach from 17th-century Germany. It is decorated with the figures of the 'Four Sons' from the Haggadah.*

The Haggadah interprets four passages from the Bible as the reaction of four sons attending the Passover ceremony: one wise, one foolish, one simple and one who does not know enough to ask any questions.

Shavu'ot

Above right *Moses on Mount Sinai holding the Tablets of the Law. A miniature from the Sarajevo Haggadah, Spain, 14th century.*

Shavu'ot, the Feast of Weeks, is one of the three 'pilgrimage festivals', the other two being Passover and Succot (the Feast of Booths). In ancient Israel, it was an agricultural festival in early summer, marking the end of the barley harvest and the beginning of the wheat harvest. Its name is derived from the passage in *Leviticus* stating that seven weeks must be counted from the second day after Passover, and on the following day an offering of new grain must be brought to the Temple. The festival is also known in the Bible as 'the Harvest Feast' and as 'the Festival of the First Fruits'.

Shavu'ot commemorates the date on which the Law was given to Moses on Mount Sinai, and Orthodox Jews often spend the whole night of the festival reading and discussing scriptural and other passages.

On this festival it is customary to read the *Book of Ruth* in the synagogue. The setting for that idyllic story is harvest time in the Judean hills.

Succot

Right *A blessing over the four species at the Western Wall.*

The festival of *Succot* (Booths or Tabernacles) occurs in the autumn and lasts for seven days. Like the other two biblical pilgrimage festivals, Passover and the Feast of Weeks, Succot has a double dimen-

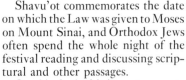

Simchat Torah *in the Great Synagogue, Moscow, in the 1960s.*

sion: the first is the agricultural aspect, denoting the season of the autumn harvest (it is also called 'the feast of harvest' in the *Book of Exodus*). The second significance is historical, recalling the sojourn of the Children of Israel in the desert after the Exodus. The two distinctive customs of Succot are the booths and the Four Species.

The booths are constructed adjacent to the house, on a porch or in a yard. They are roofed with branches, and decorated inside with fruit and gay curtains or wall hangings. The members of the family eat their meals in the booth during the week of the

festival, thereby identifying themselves with the nomadic life of their ancestors in the wilderness, and also with their former ancestors in ancient Israel who erected booths in the fields at harvest time to provide shade while guarding the crops.

The 'four species' carried in procession in synagogue are a citron (*etrog*), and a palm branch bound with twigs of myrtle and willow (called the *lulav*).

Throughout every teeming ghetto and shtetl, Succot with the booths and plant species would bring alive the nostalgic folk-memory of the rural life in the homeland.

Simchat Torah

Simchat Torah (the Rejoicing of the Law) is celebrated in Eretz Israel on the eighth day from the beginning of Succot, and on the ninth day in the Diaspora.

The Torah (*Pentateuch*) is read in its entirety in the synagogue services during the course of one year. On Simchat Torah the cycle is completed and re-started, when one worshipper reads the last portion of *Deuteronomy* and another the first portion of *Genesis*.

It is a joyful occasion. All the Torah Scrolls are taken out of the Ark and carried seven times in procession

Lighting the Chanukkah lights in the synagogue. A drawing by Wilhelm Thielmann, Germany, 1898.

round the synagogue to the loud singing of prayers. By tradition, the children get gifts of candy, nuts and raisins.

Discouraged from giving public expression to their Jewish identity, many Russian Jews nevertheless do so by congregating inside and outside synagogues on special occasions such as Simchat Torah. Tens of thousands gather in Moscow, marking the revival of Jewish sentiment in the Soviet Union.

Chanukkah

Chanukkah (Dedication) is the latecomer among important Jewish festivals, and came into existence in the post-biblical period. It is both national and religious in essence, marking the successful revolt of the Maccabees in the 2nd century BC, and their re-dedication of the Temple in Jerusalem. According to legend, a miracle occurred when the sacred lamp that had only enough purified oil for one day went on burning for eight. It is, therefore, also called the Feast of Lights, and its emblem is the eight-branched candelabrum (*chanukkiah*). In every Jewish home a candle is lit the first evening and an additional candle is lit each evening thereafter for the eight days of the festival.

Chanukkah occurs in late December, usually about the time of Christmas. It is a time for parties and gifts for the children.

Actors in a Purim *play. A woodcut from the 'Sefer ha-Minhagim' ('Book of Customs'), Italy, 1400.*

Purim

The early spring festival of *Purim* is the merriest event in the Jewish calendar of festivals. By tradition it has a carnival atmosphere, with folk-dancing, the children decked out in fancy-dress, the performance of Purim plays and the consumption of triangular buns stuffed with poppy seed, called 'Haman's ears'.

The background for the celebration is set out in the biblical *Scroll of Esther*, which is read out in synagogue on the festival. The Diaspora episode it describes is supposed to have taken place in Persia during the reign of the monarch Xerxes I (486–65 BC), who is called Ahasuerus in Hebrew. The massacre planned by his wicked chief minister Haman was foiled by the beautiful Queen Esther and her sagacious relative Mordecai. The word 'purim' refers to the lots cast by Haman to pick a propitious day for the evil deed.

It is strange that the Scroll of Esther should have been among the works included in the Writings, the last group of books in the Old Testament. It has no religious aspect, and God is not even mentioned in it. It was probably written about the 2nd century BC by an unknown author, and it is questionable whether the events described in it actually took place – at any rate, there is no corroboration of them in Persian records. Yet the story has had a strong hold on Jewish sentiment down the centuries. It stands for a rare victory against the evil forces arrayed against the Jewish people. Hitler was in direct descent from Haman, with a long line of persecutors in between. In the bloody context of Jewish history, a pogrom that did *not* take place is indeed a cause for celebration.

64

Chapter Eight

The World of the Talmud

The ancient Hebrews drew no clear distinction between legal, moral and religious precepts. All laws came from God and were sacred, whether they dealt with forms of worship, family relations, property, criminal offences or any other aspect of daily life. God's commandments appear in all the Books of the Torah (Pentateuch). Together, these biblical precepts formed the Written Law or Mosaic Code.

After the text of the Torah took its final form, its legal provisions continued to be discussed, interpreted and adjusted to changing conditions and needs by succeeding generations of Jewish sages and scholars. Not only did moral and social ideas alter and external circumstances change, but in the Mosaic Code itself there were gaps to be filled and obscurities to be clarified. For instance, very little was laid down concerning so basic and complicated a subject as marriage and divorce.

The continuous process of interpretation of the Written Law produced a vast body of rulings and opinions known as the Oral Law. However, the terms 'Written' and 'Oral' are somewhat misleading. The Torah itself was derived from centuries of oral traditions that began to be written down about the 10th century BC, several centuries after Moses received the Ten Commandments on Mount Sinai. On the other hand, the Oral Law was in due course compiled in written form, in the *Mishnah* and then in the expanded Talmud.

A modern secular analogy for the relationship between Written and Oral Law is that between statutes passed by parliament and the case law that comes into being as the courts interpret and apply the statutes.

The Oral Law came to be accepted as having virtually equal validity with the Written Law. Both are regarded as having divine authority, and by tradition the origin of both is attributed to Moses the great Lawgiver. There is one essential difference between the two. The provisions of the Written Law are fixed and immutable in the Scriptures. Yet by its very nature, the Oral Law can never be given final form. Its development is an open-ended process that has gone on for 2,000 years and will go on as long as the Jewish people remains a living entity.

The development of the Oral Law was well advanced before AD 70. By the reign of the Hasmonean ruler John Hyrcanus I (134–104 BC),

(continued on page 68)

Ten Topics from the Talmud

1   *A man is responsible for damage caused by his property. One of the four main categories of damages is that caused by a goring ox.*

2   *A bill of divorce is handed over. Detailed discussions in the Talmud are devoted to the form of marriage and divorce documents, their legal formulation, the method of handing them over, and how they are witnessed.*

3   *Two men have found a garment and both claim it. The Talmud deals with ways to establish ownership of goods in case of such disputes.*

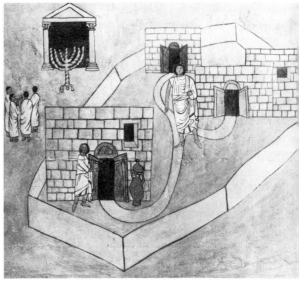

4   *'A Sabbath of Sabbaths Holy to the Lord.' The synagogue prayer for Sabbath eve was instituted in Babylonia. The existence of synagogues outside the towns made it necessary to lay down special regulations for attending the services without violating the Sabbath.*

5　In the picture, an emissary of the rabbinical court comes to Rabbi Huna and asks him to judge a case. Since he gets no payment the rabbi agrees, provided arrangements are made for someone to pick his fruit while he is away. Many outstanding rabbis were engaged in agriculture.

6　Babylonian Jews, especially the more distinguished, brought their dead to the Land of Israel for burial. The seven days of mourning began when the body left the city.

7　Sabbath desecration. The Jewish inhabitants of a village in Babylonia went out on the Sabbath to collect fish which had been washed up into a field from a flooded pond. The sages excommunicated them.

8　Purification is an important subject in the Talmud. The ritual bath is a basic requirement.

9　The Talmud says that a scholar who brings his produce to the market has a right to offer it for sale first. The question is, who is a scholar? One rabbi brought his figs by boat to sell, but a local scholar examined his erudition and failed him. The figs were a dead loss.

10　A man who owns property along the river is not allowed to cultivate it right up to the bank but he must leave a path for people to walk along, or for the use of animals pulling boats along the towpath.

two conflicting trends and parties existed in Eretz Israel: the Sadducees and the Pharisees. The Sadducees represented an Establishment that included the palace, the Temple priesthood and an affluent upper class. It was natural for this privileged group to be conservative in its outlook. The Sadducees took their religious stand on the diligent performance of Temple rituals and sacrifices, and on the literal adherence to the Mosaic Code as set out in the Old Testament.

The Pharisees were a party that appealed to the artisans, the petty traders and the peasant farmers. They wanted the Law to be expounded directly to the people, as Ezra the Scribe had started doing when he came to Jerusalem from Babylon several centuries earlier. They asserted that this could be done by any scholar who was learned in the Law, outside the ranks of the Temple priesthood. The Pharisees interpreted the Scriptures in a flexible manner, and adjusted them to changing ideas. The liberal attitude of Hillel, the leading Pharisee sage in the 1st century BC, is illustrated by an oft-quoted remark. When a Gentile convert challenged him to expound the basic tenets of Judaism while standing on one foot, he answered: 'What is hateful to you, do not unto your neighbour; this is the entire Torah, all the rest is commentary.'

According to the Pharisees, the Oral Law had equal validity with the Written Law, and both originated with Moses. During the reign of Herod the Great (37–4 BC) the Pharisaic movement had produced two great schools of law, headed, respectively, by Hillel and Shammai, the leaders of the *Sanhedrin* (Supreme Religious Council). It is related that when Shammai was asked by a puzzled Gentile, 'How many Torahs do you have?', he replied, 'Two – one written and one oral.'

After the fall of Jerusalem in AD 70, the bulk of the Palestinian Jewish community (*Yishuv* in Hebrew) remained intact in the rest of the country, under Roman rule. With the monarchy and the Temple priesthood swept away, the leadership of the community passed exclusively to an aristocracy of learning – the sages and teachers who expounded and applied the Torah. One of the eminent rabbis, Yochanan ben-Zakkai, had gained permission from Titus, the Roman commander, to leave the doomed city of Jerusalem and start an academy at the small town of Yavneh in the coastal plain (near present-day Rehovot). Legend has it that he was carried out of the city in a coffin borne by two of his disciples. Other scholars gathered around Rabbi Yochanan. The Sanhedrin, which had been the highest council in the State, was reconstituted with the leading Yavneh sages as its members. Rabbi Gamaliel, a respected scholar who was a direct descendant of the great Hillel, succeeded Yochanan ben-Zakkai and became President (*Nasi*) of the Sanhedrin. The office was to remain an hereditary one for the next few centuries. The Nasi was accepted by the Roman authorities as the Patriarch or official head of Palestinian Jewry, and he was accepted by the Diaspora Jewish communities as their spiritual leader.

A major measure of consolidation taken at Yavneh, about AD 90, was to finalize the canon of the Old Testament. It consisted of twenty-four books, grouped into three sections: *The Torah* or *Five Books of Moses* (*Pentateuch*); *The Prophets* (including the historical *Books of Joshua, Samuel* and *Kings*); and *The Writings*. This Canon was to remain fixed throughout the ages. It may be said that at Yavneh the Jewish religious heritage was preserved after the great disaster.

Jewish national sentiment continued to smoulder in Palestine and burst into flames again with the Bar Kochba Revolt of AD 132. At first it was successful. The Roman garrisons were driven out of southern Judea, Jerusalem was recaptured, and new coins were struck to mark the liberation. But within three years the emperor Hadrian had brutally crushed the insurrection. The southern half of the country was left devastated and almost denuded of its population. Jerusalem was barred to Jews and on its ruins Hadrian built a Roman garrison town called Aelia Capitolina. The embers of national resistance had been stamped out. The Jews from now on were a minority in their own land.

Akiba was the foremost Jewish sage in the early part of the 2nd century AD, with his school located at Bnai Brak. He devoted himself to the arduous task of bringing order into the Oral Law, sorting it out according to subjects and relating it to the biblical text. Akiba supported the Bar Kochba Revolt, and when it was crushed he was arrested and tortured to death by the Roman authorities.

Akiba's outstanding pupil **Rabbi Meir** established his own school at Tiberias, and continued the collation of the Oral Law.

Judah ha-Nasi was the most erudite Jewish teacher of the late 2nd and early 3rd centuries AD, and head of the rabbinical court. His prestige was such that in the later Talmudic literature he is referred to simply as 'Rabbi'. As *Nasi* (Patriarch), he was the official leader of Palestinian Jewry. At that time the centre of Jewish life in the country had shifted to the Galilee, in the wake of the Bar Kochba tragedy.

Judah's historic achievement was the editing of the Mishnah. He organized a panel of the most eminent Jewish scholars to work with him on the systematic codification of the Oral Law. The project took over half a century.

The Aramaic word *Tannaim* (teachers) was applied to the five generations of Palestinian scholars between the deaths of Hillel and Shammai (AD 10 and AD 30 respectively) and the completion of the Mishnah. Some 140 individual Tannaim can be listed from various sources. The key figures among them were Rabbis Jochanan ben-Zakkai, Akiba, Meir and Judah ha-Nasi.

In compiling the Mishnah, the teachings of the Tannaim were collated, and on disputed points the opinions were quoted of the Hillel and Shammai schools and of other leading authorities. The work already done by Akiba and Meir provided a point of departure. The Code was completed about AD 210, but it is uncertain whether it was reduced to writing at that time or at a later date.

The Mishnah was divided into six Orders; each Order was sub-divided into tractates dealing with specific topics (63 in all) and each tractate into chapters. The six Orders were:

1 'Seeds' (*Zera'im*) – laws relating to agriculture;
2 'Seasons' (*Mo'ed*) – laws relating to the Sabbath and Jewish festivals;
3 'Women' (*Nashim*) – laws relating to marriage, divorce and kindred family topics;
4 'Damages' (*Nezikin*) – laws relating to civil claims and criminal offences;
5 'Holy things' (*Kodashim*) – laws relating to Temple sacrifices and rituals. (Though the Temple was destroyed, it was felt necessary to preserve its regulations for the future.)
6 'Purities' (*Tohorot*) – laws concerning ritual purity and impurity.

Amora is an Aramaic word meaning a spokesman or an interpreter. The primary function of an amora was to repeat in a loud, clear voice

The Spread of the Talmud

Above *One of four rabbinical scholars, captured by Moslem pirates at sea, being ransomed by the leaders of the Jewish community of Kairouan, North Africa (modern Tunisia).*

The story of the Four Captives was current in mediaeval Spain and was preserved in the important work *Sefer ha-Kabbalah* (the 'Book of Tradition'), written by the Spanish-Jewish philosopher, physician and astronomer Abraham ibn-Daud (1110–80). According to this account, four rabbis from Babylonia set sail from Bari in southern Italy on a mission to raise funds for charity. When they were captured and sold into slavery, they were redeemed by the Jewish communities in Kairouan, Alexandria and Cordoba in Spain, and were instrumental in establishing new Talmudic academies in these cities.

Although the story is of doubtful authenticity, it can be seen as a parable for the decline in the paramount authority of the Babylonian academies in the Jewish world, and the rise of new centres of learning in North Africa and Spain, based on the Babylonian Talmud.

The Karaite Movement

See colour page 105

This diorama shows the Sabbath being observed without lights, one of the practices of the Karaite sect of Judaism that sprang up in the 8th century AD.

It is accepted that the founder of the Karaite movement was Anan ben-David. It is said that he was aggrieved at having been passed over in the succession to the hereditary post of exilarch, the titular head of the Babylonian community. Whether that was so or not, Anan came out against the pre-eminence of Talmudic scholarship, and in favour of a return to the biblical source of authority. His followers called themselves *Karaites* ('Scripturalists') as opposed to the Rabbanites, who clung to the Oral Law expounded by the rabbis.

Karaism became a popular movement in revolt against the complexities of the Talmud and the intellectual sophistication of the scholars. As usually happens with a breakaway movement, it attracted to itself elements of social protest among the under-privileged. Developing its own literature, it spread rapidly from Babylonia through the rest of the Islamic world, including Palestine, Egypt and Spain.

Karaism might well have become the dominant ideology of Jewish religious life, except for one single but very powerful opponent. He was Saadyah ben-Joseph (AD 882–942), a brilliant Egyptian-born scholar who was appointed head of the academy of Sura and therefore one of the two Geonim of Babylonia – the other being the head of the academy of Pumbedita. As the foremost Jewish

the words of a rabbi teaching a large class, or to repeat a Hebrew lesson in Aramaic, a Semitic language akin to Hebrew, that was the colloquial daily tongue of the Jews in that era. The term came to be used in a wider sense, for the scholars who interpreted and expounded the law during the three centuries between the Mishnah and the conclusion of the Talmud. This work went on in two centres, the Palestinian and the Babylonian, with a constant interchange of scholars and opinions between them.

From Talmudic quotations and references, over two thousand Amoraim can be identified by name. The titles they were given differed in the two centres. The Palestinian scholars were called *rabbi* (my teacher), with some of the most distinguished given the more ceremonious form of *rabban*. The Babylonian sages were given the title of *rav* or *mar*, both meaning 'master' (*Mar* has survived in modern Hebrew as the equivalent of 'Mr'.)

By Jewish tradition, religious teaching and study were an unpaid profession. Those teachers who were unable to support themselves by other work, such as traders or artisans, were helped by donations from the well-to-do or by scholarship funds available to the academies.

The Hebrew word *Talmud* means 'teaching' and is used for each of the two great compilations of the Oral Law, the Palestinian (or Jerusalem) Talmud and the Babylonian Talmud.

The two centuries of expounding the Mishnah that produced the Jerusalem Talmud was carried out mainly in the Palestinian academies of Sepphoris and Tiberias in the Galilee, and Caesarea and Lydda on the coastal plain. By about AD 400 this scholarly impetus petered out as the Palestinian community declined under Roman rule. The Jerusalem Talmud has survived only in an incomplete form and came to be overshadowed by the much larger and more comprehensive Babylonian Talmud.

From the 3rd century, the centre of Jewish scholarship moved eastwards from Palestine to Babylonia (Mesopotamia). The two pioneers of the new centre were Abba the Tall (simply known as Rav) and Mar Samuel. **Rav** was sent from Babylon to Palestine to study under Judah ha-Nasi and was his most brilliant pupil. On returning to his adopted land, he founded a new school at Sura. It soon became the most popular one in the country, and was to last for 800 years. Rav's contemporary, **Mar Samuel**, a noted scholar, physician and astronomer, headed the academy at Nehardea, the principal Jewish settlement in Babylonia at that time. After the city was sacked by an invading force in the 3rd century, another school founded at Pumbedita came to rival Sura in importance. A modern historian has termed these two academies 'the Oxford and Cambridge of Babylonian Jewry'.

The main compiler of the Babylonian Talmud was **Rav Ashi**, head of the Sura academy in the 4th century. During his fifty-two years in this post he sifted and arranged the bulk of the commentary that had grown up round the Mishnah. The vast accumulation of material was

(continued on page 74)

intellect of his time, Saadyah Gaon launched a powerful counter-attack on the Karaite movement. At the same time, his own positive achievements undermined the validity of their protests. He championed traditional Judaism, gave it a philosophical basis in his book *Beliefs and Opinions*, compiled a prayer book, founded the scientific study of Hebrew, translated the whole of the Old Testament into colloquial Arabic, and gave a fresh emphasis to biblical study.

With so formidable a champion of the scholastic establishment, the growth of the Karaite movement was arrested. From then on it declined steadily in numbers and influence. Before the Second World War, there were about 10,000 members of the sect in Russia, mostly in the Crimea, and 2,000 elsewhere, mostly in Egypt.

The Burning of the Talmud

See colour pages 108 and 109

This diorama shows cartloads of Talmudic literature being collected in 1242 in the square in front of the Notre Dame Cathedral, Paris, before being fed into a nearby bonfire. Twenty-four cartloads were destroyed on that occasion.

The attack on the Talmud was one aspect of the persecution of the Jews in mediaeval Europe. It figures in the public disputations that took place during this period between Christian churchmen and Jewish rabbis. These unequal contests, designed to 'prove' the error of Judaism, were usually promoted by the Dominican Order that served the Church as a heresy-hunting agency. The witnesses for the church were as a rule Jewish apostates, eager to vindicate their change of faith. One such apostate was Nicholas Donin, who had become a Dominican monk. In AD 1239, he submitted to Pope Gregory a formal denunciation of the Talmud as containing blasphemous and immoral material, with a list of thirty-five alleged examples. The Pope decreed that all copies of the Talmud should be seized, pending a public investigation. The kings of England

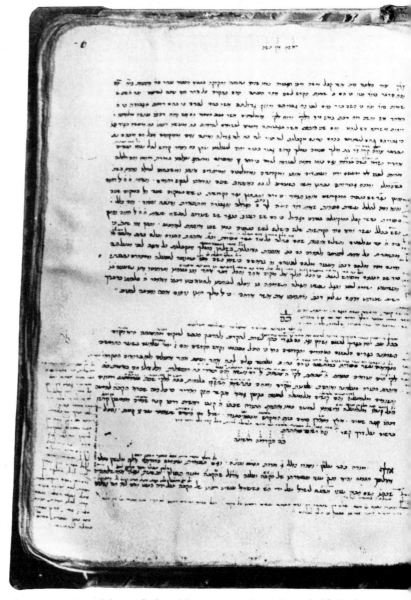

A representation of the ten Sefirot (divine emanations) from the 'Sefer ha-Zohar' ('The Book of Splendour'), Italy, 1400.

and Spain ignored the decree, but in France it was carried out by the pious King Louis IX (afterwards canonized as St Louis). At his order, Jewish institutions in Paris were raided on a Sabbath and a large number of copies of the Talmud and other sacred books were impounded.

The public 'case' took place before a panel of bishops and Dominican friars, in the presence of the Queen Mother. The case against the Talmud was presented by Donin. Appearing for the defence were four eminent Jewish scholars, whose refutation of the charges fell on deaf ears. What is more, the scholars were obliged to speak in Latin, a tongue less familiar

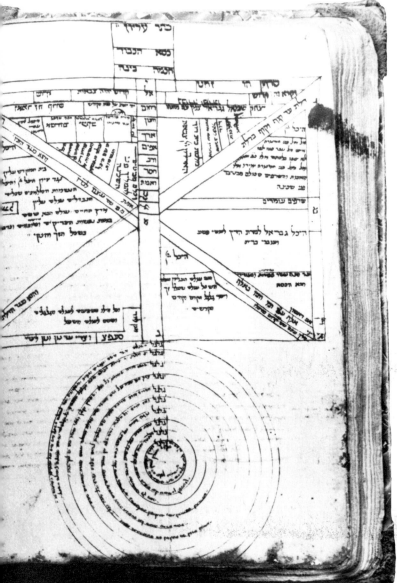

example followed elsewhere in Italy.

In 1757 hundreds of volumes of the Talmud were burnt in Poland by order of the ecclesiastical authorities, after the fierce controversies that broke out between the rabbis and the Frankists, a mystical sect founded by the pseudo-messiah Jacob Frank (1726–91). When the sect was excommunicated by the rabbinical authorities it gained the protection of the local bishop by renouncing the Talmud and accepting the concept of the Holy Trinity.

The Kabbalah

Left *The ten Sefirot.*

The ordinary meaning of the Hebrew word Kabbalah is tradition. In the religious context it denotes the mystical trend that has existed in the Jewish faith since antiquity. The subject matter included the attributes of God, the mysteries of Creation, the future Messianic redemption, the hidden meanings in biblical verses and the powers latent in certain combinations of letters and numbers.

Kabbalah was the preoccupation of small coteries of scholars, whose mystical frame of mind was usually attained by fasting and intense meditation. As a branch of Jewish lore, it came to a climax in the appearance in 13th-century Spain of the *Zohar* or *Book of Splendour*. This was said to have been written by a 2nd-century Jewish sage. The *Zohar* was the basis for all later Kabbalistic documents. Translated into Latin, it also had an influence on some mediaeval Christian churchmen.

After the expulsion of the Jews from Spain at the end of the 15th century, the leading Kabbalists settled in Safad in the Galilee, one of the four Jewish holy cities in Palestine. The most important personality among them was Isaac Luria, later known by his acronym *Ha'Ari* ('the Lion'). His teachings, written down by his disciples, gave Kabbalah a widespread impact on the Jewish world. They were eagerly studied by the Baal Shem Tov and were absorbed into the beliefs of the Chassidic movement.

to them than to the Christian clergy. The verdict was a foregone conclusion: the rigged court condemned the Talmud and ordered all copies to be destroyed by fire. The order was carried out in Paris two years later, in 1242. Talmud burning then spread to other parts of France.

A similar step was taken in Italy three centuries later. The Renaissance popes had been tolerant towards the Jews, until the Catholic Counter-Reformation brought about a revival of mediaeval anti-Jewish bigotry. In the middle of the 16th century, Pope Paul IV banned the use of the Talmud and ordered copies to be burnt. A vast pile of Talmudic and rabbinical works was destroyed in Rome on 9 September 1553 – an

reduced to writing by the end of the 5th century. The final editing of
the text was carried out during the next half-century by a succession of
scholars known as the *Saboraim* (Reasoners).

The Babylonian Talmud is a gigantic work, running to some $2\frac{1}{2}$
million words on nearly 6,000 folio pages. An English translation, the
Soncino Talmud, has been published in thirty-five volumes.

In the Talmud each short extract from the Mishnah was followed
by the rabbinical discussion on it, known as the *Gemara*, an Aramaic
word meaning 'completion'. All printed editions of the Talmud since
the 16th century have added, on either side of the text, further
explanatory notes from later commentaries, chiefly Rashi, the 11th-
century French scholar and his pupils.

The lay-out and pagination of each page of the Talmud was
standardized in the first printed edition, made by a non-Jewish
printer, Daniel Bomberg of Venice, in AD 1520–3.

While the Mishnah itself is straightforward and concise, the
Gemara commentary is not easy to read. The contents of the Talmud
were not originally devised as a written document. It is really a
synopsis of the verbal discussions that went on in the academies for
several centuries. That fact accounts for the discursive style, the
frequent digressions from one topic to another, the detours into
byways of anecdote and homily, and the raising of points that to a
modern mind may seem trivial and irrelevant. The language is not
Hebrew but colloquial Aramaic.

There are actually two different categories of material. Woven into
the Halachah, the exposition of religious law, is the Aggadah – a
miscellany of non-legal elements: legends about biblical figures,
sayings and reminiscences of the Talmudic sages, moral instruction,
philosophical discourse, parables and prayers. Roughly a quarter of
the total text of the Babylonian Talmud consists of Aggadic material.

What emerges strongly in the Talmud is the interplay between
critical intellects trained to dialectic methods of a specialized kind,
probing and testing all possible answers to Halachic problems. The
Talmud has aptly been compared to an ocean – somewhat formless,
full of cross-currents, and so vast that few men can swim across it in
their life's span.

Because of its bulk, its discursive style, and its method of reflecting
diverse opinions on a single issue, the Talmud was not a convenient
source of guidance. The post-Talmudic centuries saw a continuing
stream of rulings on specific problems and learned treatises on
individual tractates. In the mediaeval period there were several
important efforts to clarify the general body of the Halachah.
Outstanding among them were the works of Rashi, Maimonides and
Joseph Caro.

Rashi (1040–1105) – the initials in Hebrew for Rav Solomon ben-
Isaac – compiled a set of concise and lucid notes on the Talmud that
have remained the accepted key for later studies. Rashi had no sons of
his own, but his learned sons-in-law and grandsons, as well as his

The Opponents of Chassidim

Above *At the main gate of the
Shulhof, the synagogue complex in
Vilna, two Chassidim seek an
audience with the Vilna Gaon but are
turned away by one of his aides.*

Rabbi Elijah ben-Solomon Zalman,
the Vilna Gaon (1720–97) was the
Talmudic genius of his age. He led the
fight against the Chassidic movement, and the world of traditional
Jewish scholarship rallied behind
him. The anti-Chassidic groups
were known as the *Mitnagdim*
('Opponents').

The Chassidim were accused of rejecting the values and traditions of Talmudic study, of adopting superstitious practices, and of building up around their 'tzaddikim' a personality cult that almost amounted to idolatry. Feeling against the new sect ran so high that in 1772, and again in 1781, the established leadership issued a ban against it. The edict read: 'They must leave our communities with their wives and children . . . and they should not be given a night's lodging; their ritual slaughter is forbidden; it is forbidden to do business with them, to inter-marry with them, or to assist at their burial.'

pupils and his pupils' pupils, added important supplements known as *Tosephot* (additions), to his commentary. Later editions of the Talmud incorporated Rashi's notes and sometimes passages from the Tosephot, alongside the Talmudic text.

The **Rambam** (the initials stand for Rabbi Moses ben-Maimon) who lived in 12th-century Egypt, was the commanding figure of the mediaeval Jewish world. He is commonly known by the Greek form of his name, Maimonides. Among his major works was the *Mishneh Torah*, a detailed, clear and systematic exposition of the Halachic law. He produced it, as he wrote to a friend, 'to save himself in his advanced age the trouble of consulting the Talmud on every occasion.'

In 16th-century Safad in the Galilee, the scholar and mystic **Joseph Caro** produced the *Shulchan Aruch* (the Arranged Table) as a practical manual of Talmudic Law. It remained the accepted guide for daily Jewish life. The domination of Jewish life by the Oral Law, as compiled in the Talmud, did not go unchallenged. The strong hold of rabbinic learning was twice shaken by movements of dissent – the Karaite schism in the 8th century, and Chassidism in the 18th century.

From early times, the evolution of Judaism was marked by two contending trends. There were the rabbis and teachers who developed the Oral Law as a living, organic and flexible tradition, derived from Holy Writ but adapting it to changing needs. Against that was a more fundamentalist approach that thought the Scriptures must be taken literally and not be subject to interpretation. In the latter part of the Second Temple period, before the destruction in AD 70, this difference was already reflected in the conflict between the Pharisees and the Sadducees. It came to the surface again nearly a thousand years later in Babylonia, with the Karaite movement that sprang up in the 8th century. It spread rapidly and caused a major upheaval in Jewish life at the time. But the movement faded out again, and left little permanent impact.

The mainstream of Jewish religious life once again faced a major challenge in the Chassidic revivalist movement that originated in 18th-century Ukraine. Its founder was Israel ben-Eliezer (AD 1700–60). He was not a learned man, and earned a modest living as a digger of lime. But he seems to have been one of the natural holy men that have arisen from time to time in different faiths and have strongly affected their course. He was given to solitary communion in the countryside, to visions and revelations, and to an intense absorption in the esoteric doctrines of the Kabbalah, the Jewish mysticism that had spread from its centre at Safad in the Galilee. Among simple Jews in Eliezer's native province of Podolia, his reputation spread as a faith-healer of the sick and the afflicted. As a result of the miraculous powers attributed to him, he became known as the **Baal Shem Tov** (the 'Good Wonder Worker'). The facts of his life are little known and are obscured by the legends that afterwards clustered round his memory.

The background to the rise of Chassidism was a period of upheaval and bloodshed in the life of Eastern European Jewry, with the Chmelnicki massacres of 1648 as its grim highlight. During the century that followed conditions remained disturbed in the area, with the Jews subjected to local pogroms, blood-libel accusations and other harassments. A steady stream of refugees moved into Western Europe and the Ottoman empire.

The mood of despair among the Jews aroused the Messianic longings that are embedded in Jewish tradition, and accounted for the extraordinary episode of the false messiah Shabbetai Zevi (AD 1626–76). The belief swept through Jewry that the long-awaited redemption and the Return to the Holy Land were at hand. The hopes collapsed with Shabbetai Zevi's conversion to Islam.

These troubled events left the Jewish masses in Eastern Europe groping for a brand of faith more emotionally satisfying than the sophisticated Talmudic scholarship. The movement that sprang up

The Chassidic Way of Life

See previous page

As a doctrinal system, Chassidism held that the whole universe was a manifestation or 'garment' of God, and the separate existence of living things was an illusion. Through piety and fervent prayer any Jew, however lowly, could attain a state of exultation in which he could experience personal communion with God. In order to do so he had to try to eliminate his own ego. Since everything that existed partook of the divine essence there was no room in life for melancholy or despair. A Jew had to feel joy and a 'burning enthusiasm', expressed not only in prayer but in group singing and dancing.

The Chassidic pattern of life was dominated by the special role of the *tzaddik* ('righteous one'), the religious leader of the group. He was regarded as having a mystical relationship with God, and as able to use the power this gave him in order to bring his disciples closer to their Creator. The tzaddik was venerated by his disciples and had absolute authority over them, even in their personal and business affairs. They maintained him and his court, where they attended on him at the Sabbath meal and came on pilgrimage from afar on the High Holy Days.

from the personality and teaching of the Baal Shem Tov spread rapidly through the communities in the region. Its progress was accelerated by the missionary zeal of the Baal Shem Tov's disciple and successor Dov Baer, the *Maggid* ('the Great Preacher'). The adherents called themselves Chassidim ('the pious ones').

The movement was bitterly fought by the traditional leadership, the so-called *Mitnagdim* ('Opponents'). They rallied behind the great Vilna Gaon, the leading Talmudic scholar of the age. The struggle raged for a generation, up to the Napoleonic Wars, but then gradually died down as the two camps moved into middle ground. The Chassidic movement regained respect for systematic study of the Bible and injected new life into the study of the Talmud. For its part, the rational world of rabbinical law regained some of the emotional elements that lie at the subconscious roots of all religion. Chassidism became part of the Orthodox establishment, while retaining its distinctive ways and beliefs. It was the first dissident movement, since the fall of Jerusalem in AD 70, to win acceptance in the mainstream of Jewish religious life.

Chassidism never evolved into a single cohesive movement with a central leadership. It was divided into a number of local centres, each a self-contained community under its own independent Tzaddik. In some cases these acquired a family dynasty of leaders descended from their original spiritual heads.

In the 20th century the Russian revolution and the Nazi Holocaust eliminated all the Chassidic centres in Europe, just as they eliminated so much else in Jewish life. Some of the survivors of the Chassidic sects re-established themselves in the United States and other Western countries as well as in the State of Israel. For instance, the Williamsburg district of New York is the seat of various Chassidic sects of which the largest is the Satmar dynasty ruled by the Teitelbaum dynasty. Like traditional Chassidic groups elsewhere, they resist the inroads of modern secular life and cling to the traditional and now vanished ways of Eastern European Jewry.

The literature produced by the Chassidic movement has consisted mainly of anthologies of stories and sayings about the Baal Shem Tov and the later masters. A well-known 20th-century collection is the *Tales of the Chassidim* compiled by the celebrated philosopher Martin Buber. The basic tenets of Chassidism had a strong impact on Buber's semi-mystical doctrine of a direct encounter, an 'I-Thou' relationship, between Man and God.

Chapter Nine

Jewish Religious Culture

A gifted nation leaves its own distinctive mark on human culture. The roots of Western civilization go back to two small peoples in the ancient Mediterranean world – the Greeks and the Hebrews. The Greeks were brilliant innovators in philosophy, the natural sciences, democratic institutions, drama, architecture, sculpture and athletics. The Hebrews excelled in none of these fields. Their special genius lay in religious thought and its literary expression. They originated the concept of a single and universal God, and in the course of its development transmitted it to two daughter faiths, Christianity and Islam. They evolved the Mosaic Code, embodying ethical and social values far ahead of their age, with the Ten Commandments as its focus. The sublime message of the Hebrew prophets still reverberates down the corridors of time. And, in the Old Testament, the ancient Hebrews produced a thousand-year anthology of sacred literature that has been without parallel in the story of man.

For millennia after the biblical period, the Jews remained the People of the Book. As a dispersed nation they clung to their unique God-centered culture, with the written and spoken word as its medium. The stream of religious discourse and writings flowed on from century to century. In its course it shaped the contours of the Diaspora way of life.

Religious learning was the most revered activity open to Jews, and it engaged the best minds of each generation. Indeed, study of the sacred books ranked with prayer as a way to serve God. Moses, through whom God transmitted the Torah to his people, is customarily referred to as Moshe Rabbenu – that is, Moses our Teacher. The central cultural achievement of the Diaspora was the immense accumulation of law, morality and story in the Babylonian Talmud, and the layer upon layer of commentary that derived from it.

There were times of despair when the intricate logic of the Halachah and the discipline of the study-house seemed somehow arid and unsatisfactory. Jews then turned for emotional nourishment to the mysticism of the Kabbalah, to the wild hopes raised by false messiahs, or to the fervour of the Chassidic movement with its holy Tzaddikim and its ecstatic group dances and tunes. But the powerful intellectual thrust of Jewish culture always reasserted itself. In modern times, it

The Torah Scribe

The Torah Scribe belongs to an honourable profession that goes back to biblical times. He spends his life writing Scrolls of the Law, also the inscriptions used in *tefillin* (phylacteries) and in the mezuzot affixed to doorposts.

Meticulous rules are laid down for the scribe. He writes with a feather quill held in an upright position, in indelible ink, and along straight lines on specially prepared parchment. Since he is engaged in setting down God's word, he must be a strictly observant Jew and is expected to approach his task in a reverent spirit and must purify himself by immersion in a ritual bath – a *mikveh*.

The oldest extant edition of the Old Testament in Hebrew is that of the Masoretic (traditional) text written in Tiberias in the 10th century AD. This shows the care and devotion the scribes have traditionally brought to bear on their work.

has projected itself outwards into a wealth of secular books, plays and newspapers, subconsciously inspired by the traditional reverence for the Word.

In every Diaspora community, high priority was given to the education of boys. Elementary education took place in a *cheder*. The ordinary meaning of this Hebrew word is 'room', but in this context it was a schoolroom attached to a synagogue or a room in the home of the teacher. In either case, the *melamed* (teacher) was paid by the parents and not by the community.

The children in a cheder were roughly divided into three age groups: 3–5, 6–7, 8–13. No secular subjects were taught in the traditional cheder. The three 'classes' would concentrate on learning to read the prayers, then the Bible with the help of Rashi's commentary, and finally elements of Talmud. The teaching method concentrated on memory and repetition. After their bar-mitzvah, some boys would move to an academy or yeshivah, where they would plunge into more advanced Talmudic study until they were seventeen or eighteen years old. The sons of poor families were taught in a free elementary school which was maintained out of the community funds; if it was necessary, provision was made for the pupils' food and clothing as well.

From the beginning of the Enlightenment movement (Haskalah)

The Yeshivah

Right Rav Ashi (AD 352–427), head of the famous Talmudic academy of Sura in Babylonia, giving a public lecture during what was called the kallah month.

In a Palestinian or Babylonian academy of that period, the main lecture was given daily by the head of the school. If he appeared before a large class, one of his assistants would repeat his words in a loud voice (a kind of public address system) or simultaneously translate them from Hebrew into Aramaic, the spoken language of the time. The students were encouraged to ask questions, to express their own opinions or even to argue with their teachers. The pedagogic aim was to develop their critical faculties and enable them to apply their knowledge to practical problems.

A unique practice in Babylonia was the kallah months. Twice a year scholars would assemble from all over the country at one of the main academies for a month-long seminar on a prescribed chapter of the Mishnah. At the public lectures the first seven rows in the hall were reserved for the most respected scholars.

During the fifty-six years Rav Ashi headed the Sura Academy, he was responsible for arranging and editing the vast accumulation of material that formed the Babylonian Talmud.

towards the end of the 18th century, the closed system of Jewish religious schools started to break down and the demand grew for a more general secular education. Today, in a modern community, Jewish day-schools prepare their pupils for the general examinations of the country, while at the same time giving them a grounding in Hebrew and in Jewish subjects. Those Jewish children who attend general schools can get some Jewish knowledge in Sunday schools and other part-time educational institutions run by the community. In all but the most extreme Orthodox circles, practically as much educational attention is given today to girls as to boys.

For over 2,000 years religious learning has been concentrated in a type of regular academy known as a *yeshivah*, from the Hebrew word for 'sitting'.

Before the destruction of AD 70, there were noted schools of religious law in Jerusalem. The central one was attached to the Temple. It had jurisdiction to settle disputed questions by a majority vote of its members, to appoint local judges and to examine the credentials of priests. The most eminent sages had their own schools, including Hillel, Shammai, Jochanan ben-Zakkai and Gamaliel – with whom St Paul studied as a youth.

After the destruction of Jerusalem and the Temple the academies became of vital importance as instruments for preserving and developing the distinctive laws and traditions of Judaism. Starting with that founded by Jochanan ben-Zakkai at Yavneh, some ten schools sprang up during the next two generations on the coastal plain and in the Galilee. They prepared the ground for the classic codification of the Oral Law in the Mishnah, completed at the beginning of the 3rd century. As Palestinian scholarship declined after that, the Babylonian academies became the new centres of learning. By the 4th century those at Sura and Pumbedita held a commanding position in the Jewish world.

From the 11th century onwards, as the dominant role of the Babylonian community receded, academies were established in the new Diaspora centres emerging to the west – in the Islamic lands of Egypt, North Africa and Moorish Spain, and the Christian lands of Northern Spain, Italy, France and Germany. Some of these schools attracted students from far and wide because of the fame of the scholars that headed them.

As European Jews migrated eastward into Poland and Lithuania, they carried the torch of learning with them. During the next four centuries, yeshivot flourished in many large Jewish communities in Eastern Europe.

The expulsion from Spain dispersed great Spanish-Jewish scholars through the Mediterranean lands. Talmudic academies flourished in the Ottoman Empire, particularly in Constantinople, Salonika, and Safad in the Galilee.

From the Middle Ages, yeshivot served as professional schools for the training of rabbis and other religious officials, but their basic function remained learning for learning's sake. Students ranged from young boys of bar-mitzvah age to elderly men with a lifelong commitment to study. Yeshivah students who went on to earn their living in secular occupations would continue to read and discuss the sacred books in their spare time. It was said that 'the yeshivah has an entrance but no exit.' In the mediaeval world it was only among the Jews that the ordinary man was not an illiterate.

It is hard to exaggerate the prestige that Jews attached to traditional learning. In the Jewish scale of values, the learned man had a status superior to that of the man of property. A merchant was proud to have his daughter marry a poor but promising student, and was willing to support his son-in-law so that he could go on studying. Private households of even modest means would gladly share their food with needy students, under a rotation system called in Yiddish *essen-tag* ('eating-days').

The Eastern European yeshivot, especially in Poland, evolved a

The Cheder. *A singing lesson at a school in the Warsaw Ghetto, May 1940. Even under Holocaust conditions, with the doomed Jews herded together inside Nazi-built walls, they stubbornly persisted with the education of their children.*

method of Talmudic argument called *pilpul* from the Hebrew for 'pepper'. It involved an intricate chain of logic in order to link apparently unrelated or contradictory passages in the Torah or the Talmud. Pilpulistic skill became much admired, though some eminent scholars, including the great Vilna Gaon, dismissed it as a hair-splitting exercise that did not bring real understanding of the texts. However, the method of pilpul undoubtedly helped to develop the remarkable keenness and subtlety of the Jewish intellect.

From the late 18th century onwards, the closed world of the yeshivah was threatened by the Haskalah (Enlightenment) movement. The object of Haskalah was to inject a knowledge of Western secular culture into Jewish life. In spite of opposition by the Orthodox leadership, Haskalah did stimulate change in some types of yeshivot. Their curriculum was broadened to cover general Jewish studies, Hebrew as a modern language and secular subjects like science and mathematics. Ultra-Orthodox yeshivot concentrated only on Talmudic studies.

The yeshivot in Soviet Russia were closed down after the Revolution. Those in Poland, Lithuania and elsewhere in Europe were wiped out during the Nazi occupation. Since then, however, there has been a rapid spread of yeshivot in the United States and some Western countries, and in the State of Israel. Some of these were founded by the displaced remnants of famous Eastern European academies. Different types of contemporary yeshivot evolved, ranging from high-school level to the *kolel* – an adult group engaged in advanced religious study. As an institution, the yeshivah thus continues to survive and even prosper in the markedly secular Jewish world of today.

In periods of repression Jewish cultural and intellectual life turned inwards, and entrenched itself behind the fortress walls of tradition. But there were more relaxed periods when particular Diaspora communities participated freely in the society and culture of their environment. In such cases Jewish intellectuals faced the problem of

(continued on page 85)

Right: Woman preparing for the Sabbath, *an oil painting by Reuben Rubin, 1920. See also colour pages 106 and 107.*

Modern Ideological Pluralism

The twenty-two Jews appearing in this composite picture (in roughly chronological order), have all lived in the modern era, from the beginning of the 18th century. They personify some of the religious and political trends that reflect the ideological pluralism of Jewish life during that period.

Israel Baal Shem Tov (1700–60). Founder in Poland of the Chassidic revivalist movement.

Elijah Ben-Solomon Zalman, the Vilna Gaon (1720–97). The greatest Talmudic sage of his time, and the main opponent of Chassidism.

Hayyim Joseph David Azulai (1724–1806). Renowned Kabbalist and bibliographer from Hebron.

Moses Mendelssohn (1729–86). Brilliant German-Jewish philosopher and writer and leading spokesman for Jewish emancipation and the Haskalah (Enlightenment).

Shalom Sharabi (1720–77). Yemenite rabbi in Jerusalem revered as miracle-worker and exponent of Kabbalism (mystical doctrines).

Leopold Zunz (1794–1886). German-Jewish scholar and pioneer of modern scientific Jewish studies.

Samson Raphael Hirsch (1808–88). Frankfurt rabbi and leader of German neo-Orthodoxy, who combined strict adherence to traditional Judaism with European culture.

Judah Alkalai (1798–1878). Sephardi rabbi in Serbia who promoted the idea of Jewish colonization in Palestine and paved the way for religious acceptance of Zionism.

Ahad Ha'am (Asher Ginsberg) (1856–1927). Hebrew writer and Zionist from Odessa, whose *Cultural Zionism* called for renewal of the inner creative forces of the Jewish people through the national centre in Palestine.

Abraham Isaac Kook (1865–1935). Important religious thinker and Ashkenazi Chief Rabbi of Palestine, who sought understanding between religious and secular elements in Jewry.

Simon Dubnow (1860–1941). Leading Russian-Jewish historian of his time, who advocated national and cultural autonomy for Jewish minorities in the Diaspora.

Vladimir Medem (1879–1923). Russian-Jewish socialist and the leading figure in the Bund, a Jewish workers' party in Eastern Europe, that combined socialist doctrines with a claim for cultural Jewish autonomy in Eastern European countries.

Theodore Herzl (1860–1904). The founder of the World Zionist Organization, launched at the First Zionist Congress in 1897, and the father of political Zionism.

Dov Ber Borochow (1881–1917). Russian Zionist and socialist who helped found the Poale Zion, the first Zionist workers' party.

Aharon David Gordon (1856–1922). Russian Zionist philosopher whose teaching and personal example promoted the ideals of Jewish labour and cultivation of the soil in Palestine.

84

Martin Buber (1878–1965). Religious philosopher. In his books, religious faith was presented as a dialogue between man and God, and biblical history as a dialogue between the people of Israel and God.

Chaim Weizmann (1874–1952). Zionist leader and first President of Israel. A research chemist, his pragmatic attitude to Zionist ideology called for a synthesis between political activity, cultural revival and practical colonization.

Joseph Dov Soloveitchik (1903–). Talmudist and philosopher, professor of Talmud and Jewish philosophy at Yeshiva University, New York, and the leading exponent today of enlightened Orthodox Judaism.

Vladimir (Ze'ev) Jabotinsky (1880–1940). Russian-Jewish Zionist leader, orator and writer, and founder of the militant Revisionist Party in opposition to the official leadership of the Movement.

Berl Katzenelson (1887–1944). A leader and ideologist of the Jewish Labour movement in Israel.

David Ben-Gurion (1886–1973). Coming to Palestine as a young Zionist pioneer, he helped found the Israel Labour Party and the Histadrut (Labour Federation). He was the central figure in Israel's struggle for independence and became its first Prime Minister.

Menachem Mendel Shneersohn (1902–). The present head of the family dynasty that rules over the Lubavitcher Chassidic sect that has its headquarters in New York.

bridging two worlds, of absorbing outside culture without losing their own. In the nature of things such a synthesis was never stable for an indefinite period.

A situation of this kind existed in ancient Alexandria, where the Jewish community tried to maintain its own faith and identity in a Hellenist (Greek) environment. The cultural dualism is reflected in the writings of the community's foremost intellectual, Philo (20 BC – AD 40). A devout Jew, he read the Old Testament in Greek translation, and his philosophical ideas sought to combine Jewish monotheism with Greek rationalism.

Another remarkable chapter in cultural synthesis was the Jewish-Arab relationship from the 10th century onwards. The most famous work of Spanish-born Maimonides, his *Guide of the Perplexed*, was written in Egypt in Judeo-Arabic, and its exposition of Judaism was influenced by the Arab philosophers. At the same time, Moorish Spain was one of the most creative and flourishing periods in the history of Jewish religious culture in spite of the Jewish involvement with Arab culture.

In the modern era the hold of the traditional religious culture and way of life has weakened, and ideological trends have developed in many directions. There were those who saw the solution to the Jewish problem in the disappearance of the Jewish people, either through assimilation or in the classless and atheist society of the Marxist dream. But even those who remained within the Jewish frame of reference and had a common desire to preserve the Jewish identity in a changing world, differed sharply about the answers. There were diverse currents in Judaism, diverse approaches to Zionism, and abortive attempts to gain a national and cultural minority status in the Diaspora.

From the beginning of the 18th century to the present there has been a greater ferment of ideas in Jewish life than ever before. The most striking fact about the modern Jewish age has been its ideological and cultural pluralism.

In traditional Jewish life, art was not pursued for art's sake. The visual arts served as the handmaiden of the faith. Their chief outlets were in synagogue architecture and decoration; the diversity in style of ceremonial objects (Torah scrolls, kiddush cups, Chanukkah lamps, Passover dishes, havdalah spice boxes, prayerbook covers and betrothal rings); and the illumination and adornment of books and manuscripts (religious commentaries, Passover haggadot, marriage-contracts and the like). In modern life there have been notable Jewish artists, but strictly speaking their works can be categorized as Jewish art only when they depict Jewish subjects.

Chapter Ten

Jewish Languages

The letter *Aleph*, the first letter of the Hebrew alphabet, symbolizes Jewish literacy, and the continuity of the Hebrew language from biblical times to the present. It is remarkable that an Israeli schoolboy of today can read and understand the Dead Sea Scrolls written 2,000 years ago. Jews also used the Hebrew alphabet for other languages they absorbed in the Diaspora. Hebrew throughout Diaspora history has remained the sacred tongue (*leshon ha-kodesh*) for prayer and literature.

Aramaic was a Semitic language closely akin to Hebrew and used the same alphabet. From about the 6th century BC onwards, it served in the Middle East as a lingua franca for diplomatic and commercial intercourse between the countries of the region. Its use by the Palestinian and Mesopotamian Jews as their daily tongue accounts for the fact that the Talmud is mostly written in Aramaic, while some of the familiar Jewish prayers (notably the Kaddish, the mourner's prayer) have survived only in that language. Aramaic fell into disuse by the time of the Arab Conquest in the 7th century AD.

In general, Diaspora communities adopted the languages of the countries where they were settled. That was so, for instance, with the Greek-speaking Jews in ancient Egypt, a country of Hellenist (Greek) culture after its conquest by Alexander the Great.

In later centuries 'Jewish' versions evolved of a number of local languages. These versions had two characteristics in common: they were written in Hebrew script; and they had an infusion of Hebrew-Aramaic elements transposed from the religious literature – the Bible, the Talmud, and the prayer-book. In the lands conquered by the Arabs, from Mesopotamia to Spain, the language of the Jewish communities was Ladino. In mediaeval Europe there were Jewish versions of Spanish, Portuguese, French, Italian, German, Greek and a number of other local languages. Only two of these survived on a substantial scale in modern times: Ladino and Yiddish (Judeo-German).

Yiddish has been by far the most important and widespread Jewish language to emerge in the Diaspora. It evolved in early mediaeval Germany as an amalgam of local German dialects, mixed with Hebrew-Aramaic and elements of the Romance languages. As the

'Aleph'. On the letter are the ten commandments.

Yiddish Writers

See illustrations overleaf

Yiddish literature began in the 16th century. In its early phase it consisted mainly of collections of tales based on the narrative books of the Bible or on Talmudic fables and popular folk-tales, and written in the form of verse epics. In the latter half of the 19th century, under the influence of the Haskalah (Enlightenment) movement in Eastern Europe, a modern secular literature emerged at the same time in Yiddish and Hebrew. The leading Yiddish authors of the period wrote in both languages.

The first modern master of Yiddish was **Mendele Mocher Seforim** (1835–1917). The name means Mendele the Bookseller, and was a pseudonym for S.J. Abramowitz. His fiction depicted Russian-Jewish life with a mixture of satire and sentiment. He also collaborated in translating the Torah into Yiddish.

Shalom Aleichem ('Peace upon you'), the standard greeting in Hebrew) was the pen-name of Shalom Rabinowitz (1859–1916), the most popular Jewish writer of all time. His stories and sketches created a galaxy of characters, like Tevye the dairyman in the modern musical *Fiddler on the Roof* who is based on the central character in a lengthy series of stories. Tevye exemplified the wry humour, hardship and resilience of the Jews in the Russian Pale of Settlement. Like Dickens, whom Shalom Aleichem greatly admired, his works came out in instalments over many years, and he travelled around giving public recitals from them, including two journeys to the United States.

The third of the classic Yiddish writers was **Isaac Leib Peretz** (1852–1915), known for his short stories and plays. Peretz popularized the mystical tales that emerged from the Chassidic movement.

A Yiddish writer of the next generation was **Shalom Asch** (1880–1957) who achieved international standing as a novelist in the wider European tradition. His historical trilogy on the life and period of Jesus made him a

Jews migrated eastward into Poland and Lithuania, the Yiddish they carried with them gathered Slavic elements and moved further away from its German origins. Regional dialects developed, particularly in the pronunciation of certain vowel sounds. By their Yiddish speech a Lithuanian Jew in the north could easily be distinguished from a Polish Jew in the centre, and both of them from a Rumanian Jew in the south.

In the 19th century the Yiddish-speaking Jews of Eastern Europe expanded rapidly in numbers, and from 1880 onwards a great wave of them moved into Western Europe and onwards to the New World beyond the seas: the United States and Canada, Latin America, South Africa and Australia. On the eve of the Second World War there were an estimated eleven million Jews who spoke Yiddish or had a Yiddish-speaking background. They constituted two-thirds of all the Jews in the world at that time.

Yiddish is a highly expressive tongue. It became saturated with the intellectual subtlety, the sardonic wit, the faith and fortitude, the poverty and insecurity, the love of stories, the humour, sentiment and pathos that marked the life of the Jewish masses in Eastern Europe. These traits were mirrored in the works of the great Yiddish writers.

Modern Hebrew literature started with the Haskalah movement in Prussia towards the end of the 18th century. The movement aimed at breaking down the ghetto isolation of the Yiddish-speaking Jewish community, and drawing it into the mainstream of European culture. It was felt that Yiddish was not intellectually respectable and Hebrew could serve as a transition stage for Jews who did not yet know German. The German Haskalah lasted for half a century, roughly from 1780 to 1830. It faded out as the emerging Jewish middle class became increasingly assimilated into German life.

Meanwhile the Haskalah movement had spread to Polish Galicia, then a part of the Austro-Hungarian empire with a dense Jewish population. Between 1820 and 1860 a network of Hebrew schools developed. There was also the beginning of scientific Hebrew studies under the leadership of the scholar and philosopher Nachman Krochmal (1785–1840). His major work was the *Guide of the Perplexed of the Time*, a title that deliberately echoed Maimonides'.

The Lithuanian city of Vilna was the major centre for the early Russian Haskalah up to about 1880. After that the focus of Hebrew letters in Russia shifted to the Ukrainian port-city of Odessa.

The modern revival of spoken Hebrew was stimulated by the rise of the Zionist movement. The aim of making the biblical tongue the national language of the restored Jewish homeland had a strong historical and emotional appeal. But at first the concept seemed unrealistic. There was opposition from several Jewish quarters. Religious Jews objected to using the sacred tongue for secular purposes. The champions of Yiddish claimed that it had become the *mamme loshen* (mother-tongue) of the majority of Jews, and should be preserved as such. The sceptics maintained that an ancient

(continued on page 90)

A portrait of Shalom Rabinowitz, whose pen-name was 'Shalom Aleichem'.

controversial figure in the Jewish press.

In the first decades after the Russian Revolution, a new generation of Yiddish writers, poets and playwrights arose in the Soviet Union; and so did an active Yiddish theatre. But Yiddish culture was suppressed during the Stalinist purges, and some of the Jewish writers were liquidated. The Soviet drive against the so-called 'cosmopolitan' tendencies of Jewish intellectuals was savagely renewed in the last years of Stalin's life, culminating in the execution on 12 August 1952 of the leading Jewish writers. Yiddish literature in the Soviet Union never fully recovered.

Yiddish writing continued to flourish in Poland between the two

The Khaliastre ('The Gang'). Left to right Mendl Elkin, Peretz Hirschbein, Uri Zvi Greenberg, Peretz Markish, Melech Ravitch and Israel Joshua Singer in Warsaw, 1922.

World Wars, only to be wiped out in the Holocaust, together with so much else.

Meanwhile the United States, and especially New York, had become a major Yiddish centre. But Yiddish culture declined there as the children of the immigrants became Americanized, moved up the social and economic ladder and often dispersed into middle class urban suburbs.

On receiving the Nobel Prize for Literature in 1978, the Yiddish novelist **Isaac Bashevis Singer** (1904–   ), *right*, who emigrated to America from Poland, sadly suggested that the award was a last tribute to a dying language and culture.

Isaac Bashevis Singer, the Nobel prize winner.

language not spoken for 2,000 years was unsuited to the complexities of modern life.

Fresh impetus was given to the Hebrew-speaking movement by the early Zionist pioneers who arrived in Palestine from Russia and Poland in the decade before the First World War. A major breakthrough was achieved in 1922, when the new British Mandatory Administration made Hebrew together with English and Arabic the official languages of the country.

Today, in the State of Israel, Hebrew is the firmly established medium for all aspects of the nation's life: the educational system from

kindergarten to university, politics, business, public services, the armed forces, the press and media, science and technology, recreation and sport. The language is also being learnt to an increasing extent by Jews elsewhere, as a living link with Israel. Hebrew is the only case of an ancient tongue that has successfully been revived in the modern age.

In the last half-century a Hebrew literature of great range and vitality has emerged in Eretz Israel. For the most part its themes have been insular, reflecting Israeli life before and after independent statehood – the hardships and dreams of the early pioneers on the land; immigrant absorption; the Jewish-Arab conflict; war experiences; and the self-critical mood of a younger Israeli generation.

The Yiddish Theatre

The father of the modern Yiddish theatre was **Abraham Goldfaden**. He founded his own touring company in Rumania and Russia and wrote, directed and acted in a large number of Yiddish plays and operettas. Yiddish theatre companies sprang up all over Eastern Europe. Prominent among them were the Vilna Troupe, the Moscow Yiddish Theatre and, after the Second World War, the Jewish State Theatre in Poland, headed by **Ida Kaminska**.

Nowhere did the Yiddish theatre flourish more than among the dense concentration of immigrant Jews on the Lower East Side of New York. At one time about twenty Yiddish companies were performing in New York City. The most prolific playwright was **Jacob Gordin**, whose 100 plays included such popular favourites as *Mirele Efros* and *The Yiddish King Lear*. The repertoires of these theatres contained original plays by Gordin and others, works adapted from the great Yiddish story-writers, and after the First World War, translations into Yiddish of plays by Shakespeare, Molière, Shaw and Brecht. The outstanding actor at that time was **Maurice Schwartz**, whose full-blooded renderings of Shylock or King Lear delighted his audiences. The lively New York Yiddish theatre has long vanished together with its immigrant audience, who had flocked to the performances.

Abraham Goldfaden (1840–1908), father of the Yiddish theatre.

Left *Maurice Schwartz (1890–1960) was the most celebrated actor on the New York Yiddish stage. He is shown here as Rab Melech in a 1933 production of I. J. Singer's play* Yoshe Kalb.

Right *Ida Kaminska (1899–1980) as* Mother Courage *in the play of that name by Berthold Brecht, in the Jewish State Theatre, 1957. She was the head of the Jewish State Theatre of Poland.*

Below The Dybbuk *by S. An-Ski, performed by the Habimah in Hebrew in Moscow.*

ספר הנהגת החיים

[Hebrew/Ladino title page of Il Regimiento della Vida, Salonika, 1564]

The Modern Hebrew Language

The struggle to revive Hebrew as a modern colloquial tongue was led by **Eliezer Ben-Yehuda** (1850–1922). He arrived in Palestine from Lithuania, via Paris, in 1881, and devoted his life to this objective with single-minded zeal. For years his home was the only one where nothing but Hebrew was spoken, and his children were the first in modern times to be reared in that language. He ran a weekly Hebrew newspaper, set up a Hebrew Language Council and worked on a monumental dictionary that ultimately filled seventeen volumes.

The main problem facing Ben-Yehuda and his successors was to fill out the vocabulary. Hebrew, it is true, had not remained static since biblical times. The religious laws that were developed in the Mishnah and in later rabbinical commentaries and rulings, had stretched the language to meet the comprehensive needs of Jewish family and community life. In mediaeval Spain, Jewish intellectuals had used Hebrew in such secular fields as poetry, philosophy, medicine and mathematics, and a range of Arabic literature had been translated into Hebrew. Nevertheless the lexicon was woefully inadequate for modern life. Ben-Yehuda complained that he and his family 'felt every moment a lack of words without which living speech cannot take place'.

In evolving present-day Hebrew thousands of new words have been coined, old words have acquired new meanings, and technological terms have been absorbed from international usage (such as 'telephone' and 'autobus').

Ladino

Above *A Ladino text*, Il Regimiento della Vida *by Moses Almosnino, Salonika, 1564.*

After the Expulsion from Spain at the end of the 15th century, Ladino (Judeo-Spanish) was carried by Jewish refugees eastward into the Balkans and Turkey. At the beginning of the 20th century there were about 250,000 Jews speaking Ladino in the eastern Mediterranean area.

An extensive Ladino literature developed. The Bible and several other ethical books were given a Ladino translation. Original writing included poetry and works of mysticism. The best-known work is *Me-Am Lo'ez* (*From a People of Strange Language*, Psalm 114:1), a religious encyclopaedia begun by the 18th-century writer Jacob Culi (*c.*1685–1732). In the 19th century secular Ladino writing included novels, drama and an active press. With the virtual extinction of many of these communities during the Second World War, and the absorption of their remnants into Israel, Ladino is today fading out as a living language.

Eliezer Ben-Yehuda, the father of modern Hebrew, c.*1912.*

Chaim Nahman Bialik (1873–1934).

Modern Hebrew Writers

In the second half of the 19th century the dominant figures in the Vilna school of Hebrew letters was the poet **Judah Leib Gordon** (1831–92). At home in both European culture and traditional Jewish learning, he evolved a precise and realistic Hebrew style. Among his many translations were the Pentateuch from Hebrew into Russian and the poems of Byron into Hebrew. Gordon summed up his Haskalah anti-isolationist philosophy in the saying, 'Live as a Jew at home and a man in the street'.

Lithuania also produced the first Hebrew novelist, **Abraham Mapu** (1808–67). His two most popular works were historical romances with biblical settings – Judah under King Hezekiah and Samaria under King Ahab.

Towards the end of the century the focus of Hebrew writing shifted to Odessa in the Ukraine. The mentor of this literary circle was the great Yiddish writer **Mendele Mocher Seforim**. From 1886 onwards he switched from Yiddish to Hebrew, which he wrote in a simple and colloquial-sounding style, although it had not yet become a spoken language in his time. He produced a three-volume national history in Hebrew, grappling with the lack of an adequate scientific vocabulary.

In the generation after Mendele two major Hebrew writers came to the fore in Odessa: the essayist Asher Ginsberg (1856–1927) who wrote under the name of **Ahad Ha'am** ('One of the People'), and the poet **Chaim Nachman Bialik**.

Ahad Ha'am was the father of the modern Hebrew essay, to which he brought an analytic mind and a lucid style. He expounded the concept of Judaism as a nation-society with an organic system of ideas, laws, and mores. The spiritual genius of the nation would be revived through the return to the ancestral soil, but Ahad Ha'am was sceptical of Herzl's hopes for a political charter for Palestine and mass migration to it. Ahad Ha'am's *Cultural Zionism* had a potent influence over the movement's intellectuals.

Bialik was the greatest Jewish poet of modern times, and the outstanding literary figure in the Hebrew national renaissance. In his hands Hebrew was a pliable modern instrument that yet

Shmuel Yosef Agnon (1888–1970), receiving the Nobel Prize for Literature in Stockholm in 1966. On the left King Gustav VI of Sweden is seen applauding. (Nellie Sachs can be seen in the centre of the picture.)

echoed the idioms and rhythms of the Bible. The themes of his poems were wrath at the persecution of the Russian Jews; the hope of Zionist redemption; the tension between traditional Judaism and the secular modern world; and a lyrical nostalgia for the countryside of his childhood. Bialik also excelled as an essayist, a writer of short stories, a literary editor and a lecturer. In 1924 he settled in Palestine, where he became president of the Hebrew Language Academy and head of the Hebrew Writers Association.

The poet **Saul Tchernichowsky**

(1875–1943), a younger contemporary of Bialik in Odessa, was the most 'European' of the Hebrew national writers. He mastered a number of modern and classical languages and translated into Hebrew works of Homer, Sophocles, Shakespeare, Molière and Goethe. Traditional Jewish circles were offended by Tchernichowsky's agnostic tendencies and his somewhat pagan attitude to life and nature. However, the brilliance of his poetry and his ardent Zionist commitment gained him a wide following. Like Bialik, he settled in Palestine in later life.

The one modern Israeli writer to gain international recognition was **S.Y. Agnon**, who in 1966 shared the Nobel Prize for Literature with the poet Nellie Sachs, a Jewish refugee from Nazi Germany. Agnon came to Palestine from Galicia at the age of nineteen. His novels straddle two worlds – the Eastern European *shtetl* ('small town') and the Israel scene, especially in Jerusalem. His style is highly individualistic, blending biblical and Talmudic elements with modern Hebrew, and filled with echoes of the folklore, Chassidic tales and symbols of the Jewish past.

The Jewish Press

In modern times the Jewish press has been a basic ingredient of Diaspora cultural activity. It has mirrored every event of contemporary Jewish history, and expressed every ideological, social and literary trend in the Jewish world. The Jew read his daily newspaper with the same avid concentration that his forefathers gave to a page of the Talmud.

The first two Jewish papers in any language appeared in 17th-century Amsterdam. They were the *Gazeta de Amsterdam* (1672) in Ladino, and the *Dienstagishe Kurant* (1686) in the Western European dialect of Yiddish. The first journals in Hebrew appeared in Prussia (1858) and Odessa (1860). The first Yiddish periodical was published in Odessa in 1861.

From that time on a wide-ranging press developed in Yiddish, Hebrew and Ladino. In addition, hundreds of Jewish papers have been printed in the local languages of the Diaspora countries. The London *Jewish Chronicle*, a weekly in English, goes back to 1841, making it the oldest Jewish paper still in existence.

In the 1970's it was estimated that 629 Jewish dailies and periodicals (weeklies, monthlies and quarterlies) were appearing in Diaspora communities.

An American Jewish press developed from about 1840. At first it appeared in German and English, but with the mass immigration of Eastern European Jews after 1880, Yiddish became the dominant language. There were some small periodicals in Hebrew, and in the early 20th century also in Ladino, introduced by immigrants from the Balkan countries.

The Yiddish daily press in New York reached hundreds of thousands of readers. The two major dailies were the *Jewish Daily Forward* and the *Jewish Morning Journal*. They vied fiercely with each other for circulation, advertising and talent, and provided their readers with a lively mixture of news, politics, fiction and magazine features. During the First World War, the subscriptions to all the New York Yiddish dailies rose to the staggering figure of half a million. In the post-war years there was a steady decline, since the US immigration law of 1924 cut the flow of Yiddish-speaking immigrants, and a new American-born generation moved over to the English-language general press.

Top left Ghetto Politicians, *a painting by Lazar Krestin, 1904.*

Top right *The* Gazeta de Amsterdam, *12 September 1672.*

Above *The first issue of* Olam Katan, *an illustrated children's weekly published in Warsaw and Vienna, 1901.*

100TH BIRTHDAY NUMBER

The Jewish Chronicle

THE ORGAN OF BRITISH JEWRY  INCORPORATING THE "JEWISH WORLD"

One Hundred and First Year   Established November 1841

No. 3,788
REGD. AS A NEWSPAPER   Friday, November 14, 1941 — Marcheshvan 24, 5702   Price : 4d.

CENTENARY OF THE JEWISH CHRONICLE

Messages from State and Religious Leaders

From THE PRIME MINISTER

(The Right Hon. Winston S. Churchill)

On the occasion of the centenary of THE JEWISH CHRONICLE, a landmark in the history of British Jewry, I send a message of good cheer to Jewish people in this and other lands. None has suffered more cruelly than the Jew the unspeakable evils wrought on the bodies and spirits of men by Hitler and his vile regime. The Jew bore the brunt of the Nazis' first onslaught upon the citadels of freedom and human dignity. He has borne and continued to bear a burden that might have seemed to be beyond endurance. He has not allowed it to break his spirit; he has never lost the will to resist. Assuredly in the day of victory the Jew's sufferings and his part in the struggle will not be forgotten. Once again, at the appointed time, he will see vindicated those principles of righteousness which it was the glory of his fathers to proclaim to the world. Once again it will be shown that, though the mills of God grind slowly, yet they grind exceeding small.

Winston S. Churchill

From THE CHIEF RABBI:

This is the first time that a Jewish religious journal anywhere has lived to celebrate its centenary. Jewry would, in gladness, have taken note of such a landmark in our latter-day history, but for the appalling contrast between Israel's position and outlook in 1841 and the heart-breaking situation that confronts us a hundred years after.

THE JEWISH CHRONICLE was founded one year after the Jews of the Old and the New World had united, under the leadership of Sir Moses Montefiore, for their successful protest against the Damascus Blood Libel. This moral triumph was followed within a generation by the removal of every Jewish disability in England, and Jewish enfranchisement in the Central Empires and

been hurled into the abyss of defamation and misery, and are facing annihilation.

All the changes in the fortunes of the Jew, his hopes and fears, during these eventful decades are faithfully mirrored in the columns of THE JEWISH CHRONICLE. It has from the very first been a wise defender of Jewry against dangers from without, and a fearless mentor of failings within, Pan-Jewish in its cultural consciousness, it has opposed every form of spiritual self-obliteration or revolution in religion; but given its utmost support to all movements that stood for Jewish life and the deepening of Jewish self-respect. It has aimed to be the voice both of our Unknown Warriors and of the architects of Israel's future; and that noble aim has been crowned with a gratifying measure of success.

" Each age is a dream that is dying, or one that is

From THE ARCHBISHOP OF CANTERBURY:

I congratulate THE JEWISH CHRONICLE on having reached its centenary year. That it should have been issued regularly for these 100 years is a striking proof of the security which British Jewry have had in this country, in contrast with the cruel treatment to which their brethren in other lands have been subjected, especially in recent years. In this country we regard them as in every sense our fellow-citizens. In the present struggle the Jewish people have given abundant proof of their wholehearted association with the British Commonwealth and its Allies. I have always admired the remarkable generosity with which British Jewry have done their utmost to alleviate the lot of their brethren who, in other lands, have been so cruelly

The message of encouragement from Winston Churchill on the first page of the centenary number of the Jewish Chronicle, *14 November 1941.*

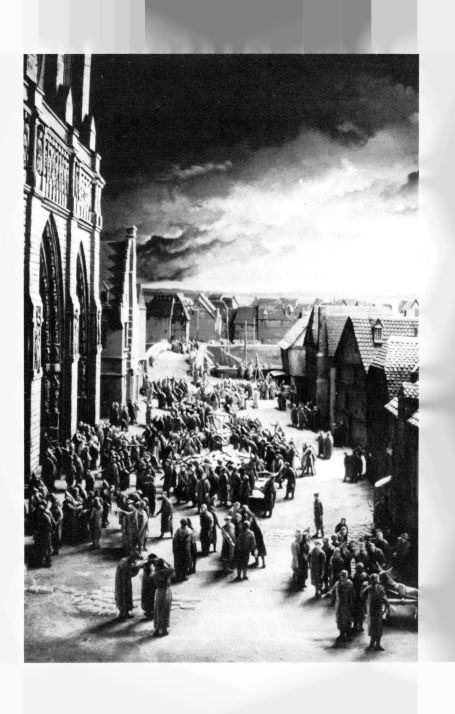

Part Two

Jews Among the Nations

The burning of the Talmud. A diorama of the square before Notre Dame, 1242. See pages 72 and 73.

Chapter Eleven

The Ancient Middle East

The Biblical Period

After King Solomon's death in 922 BC, the United Monarchy split into two. The southern kingdom, Judah, contained the tribe of that name and the tribe of Simeon in the Negev, already absorbed into Judah. The rest of the twelve Israelite tribes seceded and established the northern kingdom of Israel. (In theory Israel included ten tribes; actually, they were nine plus a part of Benjamin, the other part of Benjamin being incorporated into Judah.)

The kingdom of Israel lasted for just two centuries. In 722 BC it was overrun by an Assyrian army and its capital, Samaria, was sacked. All but the lowliest of the citizens were carried away into captivity in Assyria, at that time the dominant Near Eastern power. They were resettled in Mesopotamia – according to the Bible, in 'Halah, and on the Habor, the river of Gozan, and in the cities of the Medes' (*2 Kings 17:6*). From that time they disappeared from history. But the belief persisted among Jews that their brethren of the Lost Ten Tribes had survived and would one day return home. That faith was echoed in the visions of great Hebrew prophets like Isaiah and Ezekiel.

The legend kept recurring in the Diaspora after the end of the Second Temple. The 12th-century Jewish traveller Benjamin of Tudela recorded reports that the Lost Ten Tribes were living in Persia and in Arabia. In 1650 the celebrated Amsterdam rabbi Manasseh Ben-Israel published his book *The Hope of Israel*, which discussed the supposed discovery of the Tribes in South America.

From the 19th century, nations in different parts of the world have been 'identified' as the descendants of the Lost Ten Tribes, on ingenious but flimsy grounds. These include the British, the North American Indians and the Japanese.

One of the Jewish sages, the redoubtable Rabbi Akiba in the 2nd century AD had had the courage to state bluntly that 'The ten tribes shall not return again'. That must be regarded as the verdict of history.

The Assyrian liquidation of the kingdom of Israel in 722 BC did not produce an opening chapter in the history of the Jewish Diaspora. The first experiment in Diaspora life came with the Babylonian Exile. In 598 BC, the troops of Nebuchadnezzar besieged and took Jerusalem

The Biblical Period: Assyria and the Hebrew Kingdoms

These Jewish captives are being presented to the Assyrian monarch Sennacherib (reigned 705–681 BC). The detail is from the wall-relief in the excavated royal palace at Nineveh, the Assyrian capital.

Sennacherib's father, Sargon II, had captured Samaria and destroyed the northern Hebrew kingdom of Israel in 722 BC. He carried away a large number of captives who gave rise to the legends of the Lost Ten Tribes.

Under Sennacherib the Assyrian empire continued to expand southward into Egypt. In 701 BC he led a victorious army in a sweep down the coastal plain of Syria and Palestine and defeated an Egyptian force that tried to stem his advance. According to the account of this campaign among the palace records at Nineveh, he captured 66 cities in the southern Hebrew kingdom of Judah, took 200,150 Jewish prisoners of war and exacted from King Hezekiah a heavy tribute in gold and silver.

Assyria lay along the Upper Tigris river in the north-eastern part of Mesopotamia. Obsessed with war and conquest, they were a ruthless 'herrenvolk' that built up the strongest military machine seen in the world until then and dominated the Near East for centuries. Their empire finally collapsed with the fall of Nineveh in 612 BC.

It was Assyrian policy to uproot the populations of the territories they conquered by interchanging them. Thus, Sargon deported some of the Hebrews from the vanquished kingdom of Israel to the north-western part of his empire, and transferred the peoples of that territory to what had been Israel. The newcomers merged with the remaining Israelite inhabitants, and the mixture became known to later history as the Samaritans, who practised their own form of Judaism. A small number of them still exist.

and plundered the Temple. The young king of Judah, Jehoiachin, the leading citizens and most of the merchants and artisans were taken off as captives. The king's uncle, Zedekiah, was installed as a puppet ruler in his stead. Eleven years later he led a revolt, but was quickly crushed and cruelly punished, by Nebuchadnezzar who now, in 586 BC put an end to the southern Hebrew kingdom, Judah. He sacked Jerusalem, destroyed the Temple – known as the First (Solomon's) Temple – and sent into Babylonian captivity the bulk of the survivors. The Bible states that the Babylonian commander 'left some of the poorest in the land to be vine-dressers and ploughmen.' *2 Kings 25:12*

Groups of refugees, including the prophet Jeremiah, found their way to Egypt. The Bible does not state where they settled. It is known that a Jewish settlement already existed in the garrison town on the island of Elephantine (Yeb), on the Nile in Upper Egypt.

It is remarkable that the small Judean people, crushed and largely uprooted, did not at this point fade out of history, as their brethren in the northern Hebrew kingdom had done. The disaster was not only political and physical; it was also religious. For four centuries the nation had been taught to put its faith in Divine protection. Since God had made a promise to King David ensuring that his dynasty would occupy the throne forever, how could the kingdom go under? Since God's Presence was in the Holy of Holies, how could the Temple be destroyed? It now appeared as if God had turned against His Chosen People. The *Book of Lamentations* is filled with a sense of bitter betrayal:

> The Lord has become like an enemy,
>   he has destroyed Israel; ...
> the Lord has brought to an end in Zion
>   appointed feast and sabbath,
> and in his fierce indignation has spurned
>   king and priest.
> The Lord has scorned his altar,
>   disowned his sanctuary;
>
>   Lam. 2:5,6,7

The agony of exile cried out in the words of Psalm 137:

> By the waters of Babylon,
>   there we sat down and wept,
>   when we remembered Zion. ...
> How shall we sing the Lord's song
>   in a foreign land?
>
>   Psalm 137:1,4

The Babylonian Exile

This copy of a cuneiform tablet is from the archive of Murashu's Sons, a prominent Jewish banking and commercial family in the Babylonian city of Nippur in the 5th century BC.

Above *The Karaite movement. A diorama of the Karaite Sabbath in darkness.* Below *The Jewish Revolt of* AD *115–17. The Great Synagogue goes up in flames during the suppression of the revolt.*

Right '*At the Gates of Jerusalem*', part of a triptych by
Mordechai Ardon, 1967.

Left '*Jew in Bright Red*' by Marc Chagall, 1914–15.

Below '*Fire in Water*' sculpture by Ya'acov Agam,
1969–71.

Left *The Burning of the Talmud. A diorama of the square before Notre Dame.*

Overleaf *Battles for Jerusalem. Jerusalem was conquered by three successive invaders: Persian (AD 614), Byzantine (AD 629) and Arab (AD 638).*

Jewish occupations in Egypt. This mural depicts the Egyptians harvesting, tending their animals and weaving.

But in time they settled down in their new home. Writing from Jerusalem to the first group of deportees, the prophet Jeremiah gave them some pragmatic advice:

> *Build houses and live in them; plant gardens and eat their produce. Take wives and have sons and daughters. ... But seek the welfare of the city where I have sent you into exile, and pray to the Lord on its behalf, for in its welfare you will find your welfare.*
>
> Jer. 29:5–7

Little is known about the life of the exiles for the next sixty years. They maintained their group identity, clung to their distinctive faith, language and traditions, developed organized communities, and presumably resumed their occupations as farmers, artisans and merchants. Instead of the elaborate sacrificial rituals of the Jerusalem Temple, now lying in ruins, they came together in regular meeting-places for prayer and study, thus creating the prototype of the synagogue. According to the Old Testament, the captive king of Judah, Jehoiachin was released on the accession to the Babylonian throne of Evil-Merodach in 561 BC; and in the records of the excavated royal palace in Babylon it is mentioned that Jehoiachin, his family and other Judean captives were maintained from the king's own stores.

The survival of Judaism in the Babylonian captivity was helped by two earlier developments that were to be of the greatest importance in

The Elephantine Community

This island in the River Nile, near Aswan in Upper Egypt, was known in Greek as Elephantine and in Aramaic as Yeb. In ancient times the island was important as a military outpost guarding the southern frontier of Egypt against raids from Nubia (modern Sudan), further to the south. Even before the destruction of Jerusalem by the Babylonians in 587 BC, the army garrison of Elephantine included units of Jewish mercenaries. They lived here with their families, and were later joined by Jewish civilian settlers. The small community prospered, partly from the trade in ivory from Nubia. A temple was built for 'Yahu' and sacrifices were made. The settlement continued under Persian occupation, from 525 BC onwards.

Light has been shed on the life of this isolated community by the discovery at the beginning of the 20th century of a collection of documents by them in Aramaic, known as the Elephantine Papyri. Some of them deal with such legal matters as marriage, divorce, inheritance and transfers of immovable property. One document quotes a decree in 419 BC from the Persian monarch Darius II to the local Persian governor providing for the observance of the Passover (including the use of unleavened bread) by the Jewish trooops stationed in Elephantine. It is unclear why an internal Jewish festival should have required royal authority. One explanation may be that pressure was being exerted by the priesthood of the Egyptian god Khnub, to whom Elephantine was sacred. At all events, in 411 BC the Jewish temple there was destroyed, apparently at the instigation of the Egyptian priests. A later papyrus refers to an appeal from the Jewish community to the Persian governor of Judea, Bigvai, for assistance in reconstructing their temple.

After the Persian occupation ended at the end of the 4th century BC, Elephantine declined as an inhabited town. However, the Ptolemaic rulers of Egypt during the 3rd century BC seem to have revived the use of a Jewish force brought from Judea to guard the southern frontier of Egypt.

later Diaspora history – indeed, in the spiritual history of mankind. One was the emergence of a written Torah; the other was the Hebrew prophetic movement.

The process of compiling the Torah from oral traditions started in the kingdom of Judah in the 10th century BC and in the kingdom of Israel in the 9th to 8th centuries BC. The *Book of the Law* discovered in the Temple during the reign of the good king Josiah (640–609 BC) was probably an early version of *Deuteronomy*. The Babylonian conquerors had carried away with them as booty the sacred gold and silver vessels from the Temple. The Judean captives carried away with them even more precious baggage: their Scriptures.

During the Exile the biblical works were further edited and expanded by the Hebrew priests. About a century and a half later Ezra the Scribe came from Babylon on a mission to Jerusalem, bearing with him 'the book of the Law of Moses which the Lord had given to Israel'. (*Neh. 8:1*) He assembled the whole community in the public square and read the sacred scroll out to them.

Even before the Exile the great Hebrew prophets had warned their people that God's covenant with them could not be taken for granted: unless the nation purged itself of moral corruption, it would be brought to judgment. But they also held out hope for the future. The disaster, when it came, would not end the national destiny. The first of the classical prophets, Amos, ends his message on this note of rebirth:

I will restore the fortunes of my people Israel
and they shall rebuild the ruined cities and inhabit them.
Amos 9:14

Isaiah speaks of the remnant that will return to Zion, and of the Messianic kingdom to come. Jeremiah even predicted that the Return would take place after seventy years of exile. Two of the greatest prophets emerged in the Babylonian captivity, and reaffirmed the message of hope. One was Ezekiel, whose visions created for his fellow-exiles a detailed blueprint for the restored kingdom and the rebuilt Temple. His powerful symbol for the resurrection was the valley of dry bones brought to life again. The identity of the other sublime exilic prophet is unknown, and he is simply called the Second Isaiah, or Deutero-Isaiah. To him is attributed the latter part of the *Book of Isaiah*, opening with the words:

Comfort, comfort my people,
says your God.
Speak tenderly to Jerusalem,
and cry to her
that her warfare is ended,
that her iniquity is pardoned,
that she has received from the
Lord's hand.
Double for all her sins.
Isa. 40:1–2

In 539 BC the Persian ruler Cyrus the Great took Babylon. In the following year he issued his famous Edict, permitting the return of the Jews to their homeland, and the rebuilding of the Temple in Jerusalem. Only a minority went back. The rest preferred to remain in what had become an established Diaspora community, and to support the first 'Zionist' venture with funds.

The Hellenist-Roman World

In the last three centuries before AD 70 the Babylonian community remained quietly under Persian rule, on the fringe of recorded Jewish history. During this period Jews spread throughout the Hellenist-Roman Mediterranean world.

By the beginning of the Christian era a chain of Jewish communities stretched through the Near East and Southern Europe and along sections of the North African coast. Jewish trading posts sprang up in the wake of the Roman legions as far as Spain and Gaul.

The New Testament accounts of the missionary journeys of St Paul in the middle of the 1st century AD throw some light on the Jewish dispersion at that time. He was born into a Diaspora Jewish community, that of Tarsus in Asia Minor, and given the name Saul. His father, a devout Pharisee, sent the youth to study Torah with the renowned Rabbi Gamaliel in Jerusalem. After his mystic experience on the road to Damascus, he tried to persuade his fellow-Jews that the advent of Jesus was the fulfilment of the Messianic prophesies in the Old Testament. Among the synagogues in which he preached during the decade from AD 48 were those in Damascus, Cyprus, Tarsus, Antioch and Ephesus in Asia Minor; Thessalonica and Beroea in Macedonia; and Athens and Corinth in Greece. When Saul, now called Paul, was arrested and taken to Rome, there was already an established Jewish community there.

How large was the total Jewish population at the beginning of the Christian era? There are no reliable statistics, and any estimate can at best be very tentative. Scholars generally agree, however, that the number was relatively large, more than five million; that the majority lived in the Diaspora communities outside Palestine; and that the Jews were at least ten per cent of the general population in the Mediterranean-Middle East world. One noted modern authority, in the *Encyclopaedia Judaica*, suggests that the total was at least eight million, including about two and a half million in Eretz Israel, and over a million in each of four other areas: Egypt, Syria, Mesopotamia (Babylonia) and Asia Minor. Writing in the first century BC, the famous Greek geographer Strabo commented:'It is not easy to find a region in the whole world where this people has not been accepted, and where it has not assumed a leading position.' That was an exaggerated view, but it does indicate that the Jewish presence was generally felt in the ancient world by the first century AD.

Wherever Jews lived they maintained their ties with the homeland. Eretz Israel was the national and spiritual centre of their people even

A Document from Elephantine

A photostat of one of the papyri in Aramaic found at Elephantine. This document is a contract of sale of a house to Hananiah ben-Azariah, in the year 437 BC.

through it had come into the orbit of imperial Rome. Diaspora Jews travelled the long overland caravan routes or risked storms and pirates at sea to congregate in Jerusalem for the great pilgrimage festivals. Each community sent its annual tribute for the upkeep of the Temple, based on a voluntary tax of a half-shekel per person. Bright young men came to study Torah in the academies. By correspondence or special emissaries, authoritative rulings were requested on knotty problems of Jewish Law. Whether near or distant, communities were dependent on Jerusalem for determining the beginning of the Jewish calendar months. It was in the Palestinian centre, too, that major trends in religious life were taking shape that would profoundly affect the Diaspora future – particularly the crystallization of the biblical text, the evolution of the Oral Law – and the beginning of the Christian sect.

The disaster of AD 70 left the Diaspora like the circumference of a wheel with its hub smashed. It is at this point that 'Dispersion' once more became 'Exile', as it had been with the Babylonian captivity over six centuries earlier.

Alexandria: (1st–2nd centuries AD)

When Egypt was occupied by the Romans in 30 BC, it had a Jewish population estimated at one million. The Jews had entered every sphere of life. There was an affluent and cultured middle class of merchants, bankers, scholars, officials and army officers. The bulk of the community formed a working class of peasant farmers, skilled artisans, soldiers, seamen, port-workers and peddlers. *See colour page 112.*

For 300 years before the Roman advent, Egypt had been ruled by the Greek Ptolemaic dynasty, founded by one of the generals of Alexander the Great. Alexandria had become not only the leading port in the Mediterranean but also the major centre of Hellenic (Greek) culture. Of the Jewish inhabitants of Egypt at that time, a majority lived in Alexandria. They occupied two of its five wards, and were prominent in its business and artistic life. They were organized as an autonomous entity under an ethnarch (the head of a separate ethnic community) with a council of elders and a network of institutions.

The Jews of Alexandria adhered faithfully to their own religion and identity. Their neighbourhood synagogues were the centres of communal life. They sent their offerings to the Temple in Jerusalem and many of them went there on pilgrimage. At the same time, they were strongly influenced by Hellenism. They spoke Greek, had Greek names and wore Greek dress. The Hebrew Bible was translated into Greek for their use – the Septuagint version.

Relations between the Jewish and Greek communities in Alexandria were anything but harmonious. One reason for this was competition among the merchants, sharpened by the business slump that followed the Roman occupation. Another issue concerned civil rights. The Roman authorities had confirmed the existing rights of the

Jewish Literature in Alexandria

The Jewish intellectuals and writers of ancient Alexandria produced a body of literature that sought to bridge two cultures. They wanted to familiarize their fellow-Jews in Alexandria, as well as their Greek neighbours, with the Old Testament and Jewish history; to extol the basic values of Judaism; and to show that these values were not in conflict with the ideas of classical Greek philosophy. Some of their writings are among the Apocrypha, the additional works included in the Septuagint but not in the Hebrew Bible. One of these works is the *Wisdom of Solomon*; another is *Ecclesiasticus* or the *Wisdom of Ben Sirach* (the latter actually a Greek translation from a Hebrew original). Both of them praise the Hebrew concept of Wisdom as the guide to a good life, and uphold the validity of Jewish traditions as compared with pagan beliefs. Another Apocryphal work in Greek, the *Second Book of Maccabees*, is a summary of a fervently nationalist and pious account of the Maccabean Revolt in the 2nd century BC.

An interesting survival from that period is a fragmentary verse-play by Ezekiel, an Alexandrian Jew described as 'a writer of tragedies'. In form and style it is a typical Greek play, but its theme is biblical – the Exodus from Egypt.

In the Hellenist-Jewish literature of the period one can sense the urge of a minority group to explain and justify its different religion and outlook to the dominant majority. That is apparent in the works of the philosopher Philo Judaeus (20 BC–AD 45), the outstanding Jewish intellectual to emerge in Alexandria. He came from a wealthy and assimilated family, and his education was mainly Hellenist. In his writings the Alexandrian synthesis between Jewish beliefs and Greek learning found its most articulate expression. Philo's complex philosophic system contained both Hebrew and Greek elements. It maintained that God's concern with human affairs was remote and indirect, that man had a dual nature (body and soul), and that the Scriptures were to be understood in their allegorical rather than their literal meaning. Such abstract concepts were more akin to Greek than to Hebrew modes of thought; Judaism has always been more concerned with moral conduct than with formal intellectual systems. Philo had virtually no impact on the subsequent development of rabbinic Judaism. But he was to have an influence on the new Christian creed founded by two of his Jewish contemporaries, Jesus of Nazareth and Saul of Tarsus (St Paul).

A model of a seated Jew engaged in discussion with an Alexandrian Hellenist, whose son is listening.

Jewish community to practise its own religion and to regulate its own internal affairs. But the privilege of citizenship, which also carried with it certain tax exemptions, was restricted to the Greeks, who fiercely opposed the Jewish claim to equal status. The animosity of the Greeks was increased because under the Romans they were not the ruling establishment, as they had been under the Ptolemaic dynasty.

These mingled resentments bred the kind of ugly anti-semitism that would later become chronic in Europe. In 1st-century Alexandria the crude anti-Jewish smears were made intellectually respectable when repeated by scholars. One of them was Chaeremon, an historian and priest who was invited to Rome as a tutor to the young Nero. His version of the Exodus was that the Jews were descended from a band of lepers expelled from Egypt, and had remained an unclean race. The most scurrilous writer of the time was Apion, a demagogue who roused

(continued on page 120)

In the port of Alexandria, the leaders of the Jewish community await the return of the delegation led by Philo Judaeus to Rome, in AD 40.

The Delegation to Rome

In AD 38 the inter-communal tension in Alexandria burst out in Greek mob violence against the Jews. A number of them were killed or injured, and the community was penned up in one quarter of the city. Their homes and businesses were plundered, their synagogues were polluted and statues of the emperor were set up in them. Flaccus, the Roman prefect in Egypt, did nothing to protect the Jews. Among other things, he would not order the offending statues to be removed from Jewish places of worship. The deranged Caligula had

mounted the imperial throne in Rome the previous year and was demanding that his subjects worship him as a god. (His order to install a golden statue of himself in the Jerusalem Temple would have provoked an insurrection if his representatives in the field had not stalled off its implementation.)

A delegation of Alexandrian Jews headed by Philo travelled to Rome to plead with the emperor, but they were repulsed with derision. Soon afterwards, Caligula was assassinated. The Jews of Alexandria armed themselves and counter-attacked the Greek quarters. The disturbances were suppressed by Roman troops.

The new emperor, Claudius, tried to damp down the conflict by a compromise decree. He restored to the Jews all the rights that had been taken from them during the riots; but he appeased the Greeks by rejecting the Jewish claim to citizenship. The relations between the Alexandrian Jews and their Roman masters remained brittle.

a livelihood for himself and the members of his family.

(The waving of the flag as a signal for the responses was required because the cantor's voice could not be clearly heard by everyone in the huge hall.)

After the Jewish War in Judea had ended in the national calamity of AD 70, feelings of bitterness continued to simmer in the Diaspora communities against their Roman masters. In Alexandria the disaffection was fed by zealot refugees from Judea, and by the Messianic expectations running through the Jewish world at the time. Revolt flared up in AD 115. The Roman emperor Trajan had launched a large-scale campaign on the Eastern frontier against the rival Parthian power. The Roman army temporarily occupied Mesopotamia, and brutally suppressed local Jewish elements that had taken up arms against them. The Jews of Alexandria rebelled, but were ruthlessly put down. The burning of the Great Synagogue in Alexandria marked the end of an era in that city.

The uprising spread to other Jewish communities – the rural towns and villages of Upper Egypt; Cyrene, Egypt's neighbour westward along the African coast; and the island of Cyprus. At one stage a force of Jewish militia from Cyrene actually penetrated into Egypt. It took two years of bloody and destructive fighting over a wide area before the Roman legions put out the flames of Jewish revolt.

The Jewish Revolt of AD 115–17

See colour page 105

The Great Synagogue was the largest and most splendid in the ancient diaspora, and symbolized the size and wealth of the Alexandrian community. A colourful description appears in the Talmud, attributed to Judah ha-Nasi (late 2nd century AD):

He who has not seen the double stoa of Alexandria in Egypt has never seen the glory of Israel. It was said that it was like a huge basilica, one stoa within another, and it sometimes held twice the number of people that went forth into Egypt. There were in it seventy-one cathedras of gold, corresponding to the seventy-one elders of the Great Sanhedrin, not one of them containing less than twenty-one talents of gold, and a wooden platform in the middle upon which the attendant of the synagogue stood with a flag in his hand. When the time came to answer Amen he waved his flag and all the congregation duly responded. They moreover did not occupy their seats indiscriminately, but goldsmiths sat separately, silversmiths separately, blacksmiths separately, metalworkers separately and weavers separately, so that when a poor man entered the place he recognized the members of his craft and on applying to that quarter obtained

the Greek rabble in Alexandria against the Jews. One of his allegations was that Jewish religious rites called for the human sacrifice of non-Jews – the first appearance of the blood-libel that would recur for the next eighteen centuries. Towards the end of that century the Jewish historian Flavius Josephus, in a book written in Rome and entitled *Against Apion*, set himself the task of refuting the anti-semitic propaganda.

In AD 66 the revolt against Rome in Judea produced anti-Roman disturbances among the Jews in Alexandria. The prefect of Egypt at the time was Tiberius Julius Alexander, the Jewish philosopher Philo's able and ambitious nephew, who had joined the Roman military service as a young man and turned away from his Jewish background. He had served a term as procurator of Judea, and in the Jewish War would become chief-of-staff to Titus. At the outset of the war he used the Roman garrison in Alexandria to smash the resistance of the community into which he had been born. Josephus later wrote that 50,000 Jews were killed in these troubles, but that figure may have been exaggerated.

The AD 115–17 revolt of the Jews in the Roman Empire left the Egyptian community decimated, and its economic life in ruins. The once proud and prosperous Jewry of Alexandria would fade from the Jewish scene for centuries to come.

Babylonia (2nd–7th centuries AD)

At the time of the destruction of Jerusalem in AD 70, the Babylonian Jews had lived for 200 years under Parthian rule. The homeland of the Parthians was the mountainous region south-east of the Caspian Sea (now in northern Iran). Noted for their martial skill as horsemen and archers, they had swept through Persia and Mesopotamia and established a new empire. When Rome moved into the Near East during the 1st century BC, and occupied Palestine and Syria, its further expansion eastward was blocked by the Parthians. The Jews found themselves on both sides of the imperial power-struggle, but the Babylonian community maintained its close links with the Land of Israel.

In AD 226 Parthian rule was ended by a new Persian dynasty, that of the Sassanids. The autonomy of the Jewish community in Babylonia remained intact, under its Exilarch, known in Jewish records by the Aramaic title of 'Resh Galuta', which means Head of the Exile. Numbering at least a million, the community ran its own internal affairs and was free to develop its religious and cultural traditions. By the 4th century it had taken over from the declining Palestinian community the spiritual leadership of the Jewish world.

The economic base of the Babylonian community was a wide one, and there were no legal limits imposed on its range of occupations. There was an upper stratum of merchants and property-owners; a medium stratum of Jewish artisans in every skilled craft; while Jewish peasant farmers laboured in the humid heat along the irrigation canals

(continued on page 122)

Jewish Occupations in Babylonia

Left A rural scene in Babylonia in the style of Dura-Europos. Jews are seen in various agricultural occupations.

The majority of the Jews in Babylonia were cultivators of the soil. From time immemorial Mesopotamia had been a river civilization based on watering the flat plain through a network of canals from the Tigris and Euphrates rivers. Since the intricate irrigation system required centralized control, there was no room for small, independent farm holdings. The land belonged legally to the State, and in practice was controlled by absentee landlords. The peasants, Jewish and non-Jewish alike, were tenant farmers, share-croppers or day labourers, kept on a subsistence level by the burden of taxes exacted from them by the landlords and the government.

Urban occupations had a stronger base. Much of the trade was in Jewish hands, and some of the merchants became affluent from the export of wool, flax, grain and wine, the import of metals and gems and the passing trade in silk from China. Jewish artisans worked in many crafts, and in some of them had a reputation extending far beyond the borders of the country. They were weavers and dyers of cloth, sailors, fishermen and boat-builders, blacksmiths, carpenters and porters.

The marked disparity in living standards between the rich and the poor, especially between the urban merchants and property owners and the rural cultivators, caused resentment and social tension in the Babylonian Jewish community.

The Exilarch

See colour page 177

For over a thousand years, from the 2nd to the 13th centuries AD, the Exilarch was the official head of the Babylonian community. It was a hereditary office, with its incumbents claiming descent from King David. The Exilarchs lived in princely style,

wore the ornamental sash of a high official and had an honoured position at the courts of the rulers. Their functions included the collection of taxes from the Jews, the appointment of judges to Jewish courts and the appointment of market inspectors. In religious matters, however, authority lay with leading scholars, and later was concentrated in the heads of the two major academies of learning at Sura and Pumbedita.

The Sassanid Period

The neo-Persian dynasty of the Sassanids ruled over Babylonia from AD 226 to the conquest of the country by the Arab followers of Mohammed in AD 642. On the whole, the attitude of the regime to its Jewish subjects was benign, and it did not interfere in the internal affairs of the community. But at the outset of the Sassanid period the Babylonian Jews encountered religious intolerance for the first time. The new regime had revived the fire-worshipping Persian creed of Zoroastrianism that dated back to the 6th century BC. It now became the state religion, and its zealous 'magi' (priests) tried to force other faiths to conform.

One particularly sensitive issue concerned the disposal of the dead. The Zoroastrian custom was to expose corpses where they would be consumed by vultures and wild animals. (This is still done by the Parsees in India, a surviving Zoroastrian sect.) The Jewish community was shaken by incidents of bodies being exhumed in the cemeteries and synagogues being desecrated, and by the banning of some Jewish rituals.

The position improved with the second Sassanid ruler, the tolerant Shapur I. He had a great esteem for Mar Samuel, the leading Jewish scholar in Babylon at that time. The Talmud gives a resume of the discussions between the two men. As a result, religious coercion was stopped. An understanding was also reached in the legal sphere. While maintaining its internal jurisdiction in religious and family matters, the

King Chosroes I of Persia (559–531 BC), seated on his throne.

and carted their produce to the weekly markets in the towns and cities.

The Babylonian community adjusted to its non-Jewish environment in a manner that differed from that of the Alexandrian Jews. The latter had tried to achieve a synthesis between their Jewish heritage and the dominant Hellenist culture. The Babylonian Jews felt no similar need to reconcile their Judaism with Persian culture. All their intellectual and spiritual energies were funnelled into the task of developing and enriching the Jewish legacy they had received from the Land of Israel. The mainstream of the Oral Law, of Talmudic and rabbinic Judaism, passed through Babylonia and from there spread throughout the Jewish world. That process was facilitated by the Arab conquest, one of the turning-points of human history.

community agreed to abide by the laws of the state on such general subjects as land tenure and taxation. Mar Samuel summed this up by stating that 'the law of the land is law', a dictum that was to be of fundamental importance in the future relations between Diaspora communities and their host countries.

The king may also have been influenced by factors other than friendship for Samuel and benevolence towards his Jewish subjects. He had embarked on a military campaign against the Roman border provinces to the west, and needed both the financial support of his own Jews and the goodwill (at least tacit) of their fellow-Jews living under Roman rule in Galilee and elsewhere.

The community did not again experience religious persecution until the 5th century AD. In circumstances of political disorder and economic decline at that time, the Jews were cast in the familiar role of scapegoat. The Exilarch and other leading Jews were executed. A good part of the local community in the city of Isfahan was wiped out on the allegation that they had killed two priests. Many Jewish children were forcibly converted to the Zoroastrian faith. The climate of insecurity induced by these events reinforced the urge to reduce to writing three centuries of learned discussion in the academies, in order to preserve the record for the future. That decision gave birth to the Babylonian Talmud.

Important Events

The Biblical Period

BC

722   Destruction of Samaria and the end of the Hebrew
        Kingdom of Israel. Origin of the legend of the
        Lost Ten Tribes.

598   Beginning of the Babylonian captivity.

587   Destruction of Jerusalem and the First Temple and the
        end of the Hebrew Kingdom of Judah.

538   The Edict of Cyrus and the beginning of the Return.

520–15   Temple rebuilt.

458(?)   Mission of Ezra to Jerusalem.

445   Walls of Jerusalem reconstructed under Nehemiah.

The Hellenist-Roman Period

334–1   Conquests of Alexander the Great.

167   Beginning of Maccabean Revolt.

19   Herod the Great rebuilds Temple.

AD

48–58   Missionary journeys of St Paul.

66–70   Five-year war in Judea.

70   Titus sacks Jerusalem and destroys Temple. End of
        Second Jewish Commonwealth.

c.210   Completion of Mishnah.

c.390   Jerusalem Talmud completed.

Alexandria (*1st century* BC–*2nd century* AD)

BC

30   Roman occupation of Egypt.

AD

38   Anti-Jewish riots in Alexandria.

40   Philo Judaeus heads delegation to Rome.

66   Romans crush Jewish disorders.

115–17   Jewish Revolt in Egypt, Cyrene and Cyprus.

Babylonia (*2nd–6th centuries* AD)

226   End of Parthian rule. Beginning of Sassanid (neo-
        Persian) rule.

c.500   Babylonian Talmud completed.

589   Beginning of Gaonate period.

Chapter Twelve

In the Shadow of the Cross

Byzantium: 4th–15th centuries AD

From the middle of the 2nd century AD Jewish life in the pagan Roman empire had become relatively secure and peaceful. The Edict of 212 AD, that extended Roman citizenship to all free inhabitants of the empire, applied to the Jews as well. Their religion was officially recognized and they were not required to make sacrifices to the Roman gods. There was no interference with the internal autonomy of the Jewish communities, including the right to settle disputes between Jews. Jewish citizens were exempt from military service. There were no occupational restrictions on them, whether as tillers of the soil, traders or artisans. They could live and work anywhere – except in Jerusalem, which was still closed to Jews. The only financial imposition on them was the *fiscus judaicus*, the head tax all Jews had to pay to the imperial treasury.

This tolerable situation started changing for the worse during the reign (306–37) of the emperor Constantine the Great. By his time Christianity was a pervasive force throughout the Roman world. He sought Christian support in his long power-struggle to become sole ruler of the Empire. In AD 313 he issued the Edict of Milan, extending freedom of worship to all Roman citizens. For the Jews, the decree confirmed the existing status quo. For the Christians, it marked a sudden change from official repression to official recognition. Due to imperial patronage, Christianity soon became the dominant faith in the Empire.

In little more than three centuries an obscure Jewish sect in Judea had expanded to become a major power. That turning point in history boded ill for the Jewish citizens of the Roman Empire – for Christianity, the daughter religion of Judaism, had set in a mould of hostility to its parent.

The early Church Fathers had given this hostility a doctrinal framework: the advent of Jesus Christ was regarded as a direct fulfilment of the messianic prophecies in the Old Testament (a thesis argued by St Paul in his Epistle to the Hebrews, where Jesus is called a High Priest and 'the mediator of a new Covenant'); after their rejection of Jesus, the Jews had ceased to be God's Chosen People, while the

Medallions with the heads of Constantine the Great (top) *and Julian the Apostate* (below).

The Byzantine Emperors and the Jews

See colour page 177

In the reign of Constantine the Great (AD 306–37) Christianity became the official religion of the Roman Empire (though the Emperor was only baptized on his deathbed).

(continued on page 126)

In AD 325 the Church Council of Nicaea was convened by Constantine to deal with the deep doctrinal schism in Christianity. Among other matters the Council called for the 'seclusion and humiliation' of the Jews. This was followed by a number of anti-Jewish imperial edicts by Constantine and his successors. The death penalty would be incurred by Christians who converted to Judaism, and by Jews who obstructed the conversion of other Jews to Christianity. Intermarriage was proscribed. Jews could not hold public office. They were not allowed to own Christian slaves, and later even pagan slaves – a serious economic blow, since slave-labour was the only available man-power for agriculture or industry.

There was a brief respite for the Jews during the reign of the emperor Julian the Apostate (361–3), who tried to turn the wheel back from Christianity to the old pagan gods. He was well disposed to the Jews, even promising to restore them to Jerusalem and to rebuild the Temple. After his death official policy relapsed into religious intolerance.

In 529 Emperor Justinian began to publish his famous legal Code, the *Corpus Juris Civiles*. In the chapters devoted to the status of the Jews, it amplified the provisions in the earlier Code of the emperor Theodosius II (408–50).

Certain specific topics were also dealt with in *Novellae* (Imperial Directives) issued by Justinian.

Justinian's Code fixed the legal status of the Jews in Byzantine society for the next seven centuries. Of special import was his *Novella 146* of the year 553. For the first time a Christian ruler had interfered in the internal religious practices of his Jewish subjects. The *Novella* forbade the Jewish practice of reading the Sacred Books in synagogue exclusively in the original Hebrew text, and it insisted that translations in other languages, such as Greek and Latin, be used. The Mishnah and other rabbinic interpretations of the Old Testament were banned, on the ground that they had no divine authority but were purely the handiwork of man and were responsible for spreading error. This *Novella* anticipated by many centuries the Talmud burnings of mediaeval Europe. The effect of Justinian's legislation was to make the Jews 'second-class citizens', with their religion tolerated but their lives severely restricted.

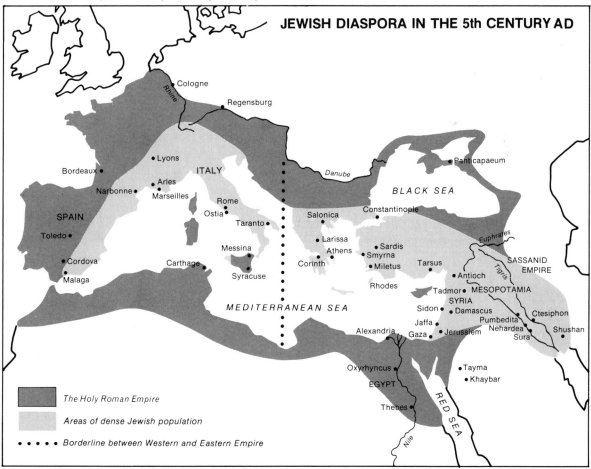

JEWISH DIASPORA IN THE 5th CENTURY AD

The Holy Roman Empire

Areas of dense Jewish population

• • • • Borderline between Western and Eastern Empire

(continued on page 128)

Church had become 'Israel according to the spirit'; the Jews had been kept in existence only to serve as living witnesses to the truth of the new faith; they should suffer punishment and humiliation to make them admit their error and embrace Christianity.

The Christian charge against the Jews was not just that they had rejected Jesus, but that they were collectively responsible for his death. The Gospels were written long after the events they described, at a time when the Jewish Revolt of AD 66–70 had been crushed by the military power of Rome. While there are discrepancies in the four Gospels, their writers had a common urge to shift the blame for the Crucifixion from the Roman authorities to the Jewish religious leaders. The stigma of 'Christ-killers' was cast on all Jews in subsequent ages; it would not be modified by the Church until 1965, at the Second Vatican Council convened by Pope John XXIII.

In AD 330 the emperor Constantine established his new capital in the town of Byzantine on the Bosphorus and renamed it Constantinople after himself. Sixty-five years later the Roman empire permanently split into two. During the 5th century the Western

Separating the Two Faiths

Above *The Christian preacher John Chrysostom, which means 'Golden-mouthed' (AD 345–407), eventually became the Bishop of Constantinople. Here he is shown appearing near the synagogue at Antioch in Syria and railing against 'Jewish Christians' who still attended synagogue services, brought their disputes to Jewish courts or consulted Jewish doctors.*

The early Church was concerned about the fact that the dividing line between the old religion and the new remained blurred. There were still many Jewish Christians – Jews who were influenced by the tenets of the new creed but had not cut themselves off from their synagogues and their ancestral traditions. Moreover, there

The Late Byzantine Empire

The *Chronicle of Ahimaaz* – Ahimaaz was the son of Paltiel – was compiled in 1054 in the southern Italian town of Oria. The work sets out the author's family history from the 9th century, covering different communities in Italy and North Africa. It shows that the active religious, cultural and economic activities of the Jews in southern Italy continued uninterrupted under Byzantine rule.

The actual conditions of Jewish life in the Byzantine Empire were less oppressive than official decrees might suggest, and the Jews adjusted themselves to discrimination with all their ingrained resilience. Established communities maintained their synagogues, institutions and culture in Constantinople; on the islands of Cyprus and Rhodes; at Bari, Oria, Brindisi and Otranto in the 'heel' of Italy; at Salonika and Corinth in Greece; and at Izmir (Smyrna) and other places along the coast of Asia Minor. Regular contact was maintained with Eretz Israel.

Many of the Jews were traders, some of them prosperous. Others were engaged in the distinctive Jewish crafts of cloth dyeing, silk weaving and tanning. In certain areas Jewish peasants still tilled the soil. Soon after the Byzantine empire ended in the 15th century and was replaced by the Ottoman Empire, the Jewish population in that area was solid enough to absorb a wave of refugees from Spain and Portugal.

Massacre in Jerusalem

See colour pages 110 and 111
Not all later Byzantine emperors respected even the limited status given the Jews in Justinian's Code. The emperor Heraclius (610–41) tried to forbid the practice of Judaism and to force baptism on the Jews. In 614 the Jews in the Holy Land assisted an invading Persian force to capture Jerusalem. When Heraclius regained the city fifteen years later, he had its Jewish inhabitants massacred or expelled in revenge. Within less than a decade Byzantium lost the Holy Land again, this time to the emergent power of Islam.

In addition to the Holy Land, the

Rabbi Shephatiah sails to Constantinople and enters into a disputation with Basil, who recognizes Shephatiah's superior wisdom but does not cancel his edicts. From the Chronicle of Ahimaaz.

were a number of Roman proselytes to Judaism, a trend that could only increase as the paganism of the Roman world waned. Church leaders campaigned vigorously against what they called 'the Jewish temptation'.

From the beginning of the 4th century a series of Church Councils adopted measures designed to separate Christianity more sharply from Judaism. The weekly Sabbath day (a Jewish custom unknown in the pagan world) was shifted for Christians from Saturday to Sunday. The date of Easter would no longer be tied to that of the Passover. Intermarriage was forbidden; so was conversion to Judaism, and even sitting down to table with Jews. Some of the Church's anti-Jewish pronouncements found their way into the legal codes of the Byzantine emperors.

Empire disintegrated under the blows of invading barbarian hordes – such as the Germanic tribes of the Goths and the Vandals, and the Huns who had come surging out of Central Asia. The Eastern Empire was to last almost a thousand years longer, until the Ottoman Turks took Constantinople in 1453. It became known as the Byzantine Empire, from the original name of its capital. Its territory expanded and contracted from time to time, but the Byzantine heart-land remained the area now covered by Greece, Bulgaria and Turkey.

Byzantine Empire lost Syria, Egypt, North Africa and Sicily to the conquering Arab armies. The majority of the Jewish people was now under Moslem rule. Official attitudes stiffened against the Jewish communities left within the confines of the shrunken empire. Thus an imperial Council in 692 prohibited mixed bathing of Jews and Christians and the employment of Jewish physicians by Christians. Decrees ordering forced baptism were issued by the emperors Leo III in 721, Basil I in 873, and Romanus I in 943, but they were not seriously enforced in practice.

Christian Spain

The Christian Visigoth kingdom of Spain lasted from the 5th century to the Moorish (Moslem Arab and Berber) invasion of AD 711. The Moslems occupied the whole Iberian Peninsula (Spain and Portugal) except for a small Christian enclave in the north-east corner of the country. The next eight centuries witnessed a fluctuating struggle between the Crescent and the Cross for the mastery of Spain. Gradually the Christian kingdom led by Castile expanded southward, and Moslem-held territory shrank. In 1492 Granada, the last Moorish foothold in Spain, surrendered to the forces of Ferdinand and Isabella, and the Christian 'Reconquista' was completed.

In the course of the 'Reconquista' the majority of Jews in Spain passed from Moslem to Christian rule, where they came under the direct protection of the Catholic kings, on the model of the rest of mediaeval Europe.

Jewish life in Christian Spain flourished until the 14th century, continuing the Golden Age that had started in Moslem Spain. The Jews then came under increasing pressure; the community did not recover from the disastrous persecutions of 1391. Many Jews were killed, others fled, and there were large-scale conversions, bringing into existence a substantial community of 'Conversos', also called New Christians and Marranos. The final blow came with the expulsion decree of 1492, immediately after the fall of Granada.

With the Expulsion, twelve centuries of Jewish life in Spain came to an end. That experience, under Roman, Visigoth, Moslem and Catholic regimes, cannot be reduced to one single pattern. Interludes of freedom and glittering achievement alternated with repression and tragedy, and the double life of the Marranos formed a strange thread in the story. (See page 134.)

Under Visigoth Rule

As early as the 3rd century AD there was a substantial Jewish community in what was then the Spanish province of the Roman Empire. The Jews were mostly located in the south

Below *A Jewish tombstone of the girl Meliosa from Tortosa in northern Spain, inscribed in Hebrew, Latin and Greek. Its date is probably between the 4th and 6th centuries AD.*

in the Cordoba area. They were traders, craftsmen and tillers of the soil, cultivating their own vineyards and olive groves. As Roman citizens, they were free of legal restrictions.

With the break-up of the Western Roman Empire in the 5th century, Spain became a kingdom ruled by the Visigoths, one of the Germanic tribes that had dismembered the empire. The Visigoth kings were at first sympathetic to their Jewish subjects, and treated them on the same footing as the other former Roman citizens of the country. But the official attitude changed for the worse towards the end of the 6th century, and the Byzantine measures regarding the Jews were applied under pressure from the Church. From time to time a fanatical ruler would present the Jews with a blunt choice between conversion and exile. When that happened thousands of them left Spain to take refuge elsewhere. A number of others went through a formal rite of baptism, while remaining Jews in private.

At the beginning of the 8th century the Visigoth rulers were already fearful of the wave of Arab conquest that had swallowed up North Africa. The Jews were suspect as potential collaborators with the Moslem enemy.

Those Jews who did not manage to escape were declared slaves and handed over to Christian masters. Their property was confiscated and their children from the age of seven were taken away to be brought up as Christians. It is hardly surprising that the Moorish invasion in 711 should have been welcomed by the Jews.

A Synagogue Wall from Toledo

See below

This is part of the eastern wall of the Toledo synagogue built in 1357 by Don Samuel ha-Levi Abulafia. The wall decorations contain foliate designs and biblical quotations in stylized Hebrew lettering. The inscriptions seen in the picture are from the Psalms. After the Expulsion of 1492, the synagogue became a church named El Transito. In the 19th century the building was renovated and declared a national monument. In 1964 it was turned into a historical museum for the Jews of Spain.

Before the persecutions of 1391 the Toledo community was one of the largest and most flourishing in Spain, with a number of fine synagogues and

a reputation for Jewish scholarship. The Abulafias were one of the city's leading families. Don Samuel's house was later occupied for a while by the painter El Greco.

The Reconquista and the Jews

See map overleaf

For nearly eight centuries after the Moorish invasion of AD 711, Spain remained a battlefield between the opposing forces of the Cross and the Crescent. The Christian reconquest of the country (known in the history books by the Spanish name 'Reconquista') started in the north with the establishment of the kingdoms of Castile, Navarre and Aragon. Slowly the area under Christian control expanded southward, until in 1085 a Castilian army scored a resounding victory with the capture of Toledo, the former Visigoth capital. A Moslem counter-offensive halted the Christian advance, but it was resumed a half-century later.

In the early phase of the Reconquista, the Christian rulers in northern Spain reverted to the anti-Jewish laws of the late Visigoth kingdom. But as more of the country

came under their control, they found the Jews a valuable asset. They helped to revive trade in the newly-occupied territories, took over abandoned Moslem estates and served as a source of tax revenue and loans. No hindrance was imposed on Jewish worship and communal autonomy. As each town was regained, its Jewish quarter was left unharmed, and was given better treatment than the local Moslems received. An influx of Jews from Moslem Spain and elsewhere was officially encouraged. Members of wealthy and aristocratic Jewish families were appointed to offices at the Christian courts. Prominent rabbis enjoyed wide respect and influence even outside the Jewish fold,

such as Moses ben-Nachman (Nachmanides) of Catalonia (1194–1270), known from his initials as Ramban; Solomon ben-Abraham Adret of Barcelona in Aragon (1235–1310) known from his initials as Rashba; and the Abulafia family in Toledo. Jewish intellectual and cultural life continued to flourish. To this period belonged the greatest of mediaeval Jewish poets, Judah ha-Levi (1074–1141); also the wandering scholar and poet Abraham ibn-Ezra (1092–1167). It is mistaken to regard the Golden Age of Jewish civilization in Spain as related only to the Moorish regime, it extended also to Christian Spain.

The Jewish position deteriorates *See right*

From the 13th century onwards the situation of the Jews in Spain deteriorated, and the climate of bigotry and persecution in France and Germany permeated south of the Pyrenees in the wake of the Crusades. In 1391 there was a bloody outbreak of mob violence against the Jewish quarter in Seville. It sparked off a wave of massacres that spread across Castile and into neighbouring Navarre and Aragon. Measures taken by the authorities to check the disturbances were belated and ineffective. Tens of thousands of Jews were murdered; Jewish quarters were

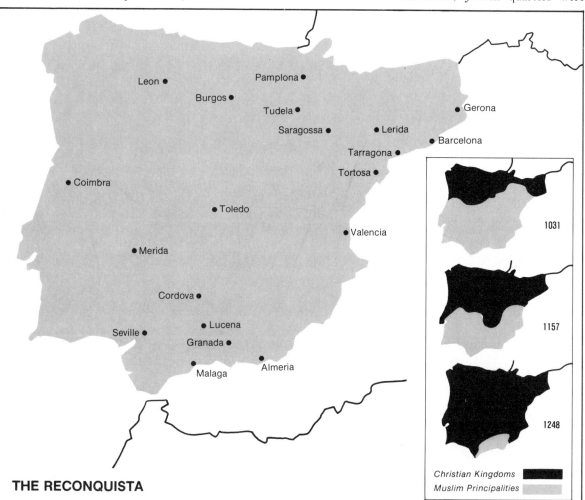

THE RECONQUISTA

Christian Kingdoms
Muslim Principalities

The fanatical Dominican friar Vicente Ferrer (1350–1419) bursting into a synagogue in Toledo.

pillaged, and synagogues destroyed. There were wholesale baptisms, including in some cases entire small congregations. The face of Spanish Jewry had been brutally altered in that one year, and a large community of 'Conversos', or 'New Christians', had come into existence.

At the beginning of the 15th century, Friar Vicente Ferrer was the arch-enemy of the Spanish Jews. In 1411, with royal backing, he embarked on a crusade from synagogue to synagogue, first in Castile and then elsewhere in the country. Everywhere he denounced Judaism and demanded conversion. He met with some success, especially in small country communities, since Spanish Jewry was still weakened by the violent outbreaks of 1391.

The Jewish role in navigation

See map overleaf

Jewish scholars introduced into Christian Spain the fruits of Arab-Jewish co-operation in Moorish Spain in philosophy, medicine, and science. This contribution was of special importance in the fields of cartography and astronomy, at a time when Spanish and Portuguese navigators were setting out on epoch-making voyages of exploration that would lead to the discovery of America and the opening of the sea-route to India round Africa.

The world map was executed in 1375–7 by the Majorcan Jewish cartographer Abraham Cresques and his son Judah for Pedro IV, King of Aragon.

The map was regarded as so important that in 1381 a copy was sent as a gift to Charles VI of France. Pedro IV granted father and son royal protection, generous revenues and exemption from wearing the Jewish badge. After Abraham's death in 1387, Judah continued to serve as the royal cartographer in Aragon. In the massacres in Spain in 1391, he converted to Christianity and changed his name. He was later employed as map-maker by the famous Portuguese sea explorer, Prince Henry the Navigator.

One of the greatest astronomers of the period was Abraham ben-Samuel Zacuto (1452–c.1515) of Salamanca. He taught astrology and astronomy at the University of Salamanca, and wrote a major astronomical textbook (1473–8). The work was apparently written in Hebrew, but survived only in Spanish translation. He invented an accurate copper astrolabe, and produced greatly improved astronomical tables and maritime charts, which were used by Christopher Columbus to cross the Atlantic and by Vasco da Gama to reach India round Africa.

The Disputations

In mediaeval Europe of the 13th to 15th centuries the Church authorities from time to time arranged public Christian-Jewish 'disputations' in order to demonstrate the validity of Christianity as opposed to the 'errors' of Judaism. As a rule, the Church spokesman was a Jewish apostate familiar with Jewish religious writings.

In Spain there were two notable Disputations, one in Barcelona, Aragon in 1263, and the other at Tortosa, Catalonia, in 1413–14.

The Barcelona Disputation took place in the palace in the presence of the king, James I, and his court, as well as leaders of the Dominican and Franciscan Orders. The side of the church was represented by a French-

A detail from the Catalan Nautical Atlas *by Abraham and Judah Cresques.*

born Jewish convert to Christianity. He had taken the name of Pablo Christiani, joined the Dominican Order and was sent to Aragon to proselytize the Jews. The defender of the Jewish side was the leading Jewish scholar of his time, Rabbi Moses ben-Nachman, usually known as Nachmanides. Christiani undertook to prove from the Talmud itself that the Messiah foretold by the Prophets had already come, in the person of Jesus.

Having obtained the right to speak freely, without fear of punishment, Nachmanides made a remarkably frank reply. The Prophets had foretold that the coming of the Messiah would usher in an era of universal peace, yet the Christian world had

Nachmanides in a Disputation before James I, king of Aragon.

never ceased to engage in warfare and extol martial virtues. How difficult it would be for the king and his knights if war was no longer permitted! Clearly, therefore, the messianic age had not yet come. As for the dogma of the divinity of Christ, the Son of God born of a woman and killed by man, reason could not agree to it, nature opposed it, and the Prophets never said such a thing. Such beliefs could not convince any Jew.

The king had great esteem for Nachmanides, and had on occasion consulted him on matters concerning the Jewish community. At the end of the Disputation the king commended him on the eloquence of his argu-ments and made him a gift of 300 dinars in appreciation. When the angry Dominicans had him sum-moned to trial for attacks on Chris-tianity, Nachmanides invoked the king's promise that he could speak openly without retribution, and was saved by royal intervention. The Dominicans then obtained a letter from Pope Clement IV demanding that the king punish the blasphemous Jew. Realizing he was now in grave danger, Nachmanides escaped from Spain and settled in the Land of Israel.

The Tortosa Disputation lasted for nearly two years and took up sixty-nine sessions. Again, the Church side was represented by an apostate, the former Talmudic scholar Solomon ha-Levi, who had adopted the name of Pablo de Santa Maria, taken Holy Orders and become Bishop of Burgos. The proceedings were con-ducted in Latin. Only one of the twenty-two-member Jewish dele-gation of rabbis and scholars was familiar with Latin, and he therefore served as the main spokesman. Among the issues debated were the nature of the messianic prophecies and the alleged immoral and anti-Christian elements in the Talmud. This time, without a royal umpire, the verdict was in favour of the Christian side.

The Marranos

During the 15th century the attention of the Church and the public in Spain was focused less on the Jews than on the Conversos or New Christians. While the Jews were regarded as infidels, adherents of another religion, those of the Conversos whose acceptance of Christianity was less than whole-hearted were regarded as heretics, which was much worse in the eyes of the Church. After the mass conversion of 1391, a small number of the New Christians joined the ranks of the Jew-baiters with self-justifying ardour. The majority of the Conversos outwardly adhered to Catholicism but secretly continued to practise the Jewish faith. It was the Old Christians who scornfully called the New Christians 'Marranos' (swine).

For several generations the Marranos prospered. A number of them became affluent, rose to prominent positions in public service, the professions and academic life and intermarried with established Spanish families. There are few old families in modern Spain or Latin America today that do not have a Marrano ancestor. But the very success of the Marranos inevitably provoked a backlash of envy and dislike.

Queen Isabella, an extremely devout Catholic, was persuaded that heresy had to be stamped out among the New Christians. For this purpose, the Inquisition was introduced and the Queen's own confessor, the fanatical Tomas de Torquemada, was appointed Inquisitor-General. As an instrument for dealing with heretics the Inquisition had already existed in Western Europe for 250 years, under

A Marrano family secretly observing the Sabbath in a cellar.

the direct control of the Popes. The newly-launched Spanish Inquisition operated as an independent agency, with a ferocity unequalled elsewhere. Good Christians were required to inform on Marrano neighbours who showed the slightest sign of a Jewish 'taint', such as giving biblical names to their children, washing their hands before meals or prayers, wearing clean garments on Saturdays or the dates of Jewish festivals, and eating unleavened bread during the Passover period.

The Spanish Inquisition started in 1478, and it is estimated that during the following seven years about 700 Marranos were burnt alive at the stake, and over 5,000 more punished after they had confessed under torture and recanted the 'sin' of clinging in private to the faith of their ancestors.

The Inquisition continued for centuries, and extended to the Spanish colonies in the New World. Many Marranos fled, reverted to Judaism and joined Sephardic (Spanish) communities that had grown up in other countries; others, probably the majority, eventually accepted Christianity and lost any Jewish identification. In Belmonte, Portugal, there is still a small Christian group that retains some crypto-Jewish customs of Marrano origin. A few families came to Israel from the island of Majorca, claiming to be Jews of Marrano descent, but they went back again.

A modern secular mind is repelled by the belief that souls should be saved by tearing bodies to pieces on the rack or burning them alive. Yet mediaeval men would have found it equally hard to grasp that in 20th-century totalitarian states racial or political purity should be sought by means of gas-chambers and Gulag archipelagoes.

The Expulsion

In 1468 Isabella, heir to the throne of Castile, was married to Ferdinand, the crown prince of Aragon. They became co-rulers of Castile in 1474 and of a joint kingdom when Castile and Aragon were joined five years later. At first the royal pair showed no special hostility towards their Jewish subjects. In fact, professing Jews held important offices at the court. One of them, Don Abraham Seneor, was the Chief Rabbi of Castile and at the same time the tax commissioner for the whole of the joint kingdom. Another, Don Isaac Abrabanel, was a member of an illustrious Jewish family and a leading biblical commentator. Born in Lisbon, he had been the treasurer to the king of Portugal until 1484, when he moved to Castile and took service with Ferdinand and Isabella. He acted as tax farmer under Abraham Seneor for a good part of Castile, and as the promoter of huge loans for the Crown, to finance the campaign against the remaining Moslem state of Granada in the south.

The Expulsion edict signed by Ferdinand and Isabella.

To the head of the Spanish Inquisition, Torquemada, and to his associates, it was intolerable that they should be busy sniffing out surviving traces of Judaism among the Marranos while Jews could go on practising their religion openly. An historic opportunity to drive home that point came with the surrender of Moslem Granada in 1492, thereby bringing the whole of Spain under Christian rule. Ferdinand and Isabella were prevailed upon to celebrate the occasion with a decree expelling all Jews from Spain. The decree was signed in the magnificent Moorish palace of the Alhambra in Granada on 31 March 1492, and was to be carried out within four months. On the return of the king and queen to Toledo, Abraham Seneor and Isaac Abrabanel gained an audience with them and pleaded in vain for the decree to be annulled. Their appeal was directed less to compassion than to greed; Abrabanel offered to arrange for the cancellation of the royal loans he had raised, and to place further sums at the disposal of the treasury. It is related that Torquemada burst into the chamber with his eyes blazing, flung down a crucifix and cried out, 'Judas sold his Master for thirty pieces of silver; you would sell Him again.'

During the next few months over 100,000 Jews streamed out of Spain, leaving behind nearly all their property and possessions. On 31 July, exactly four months after the signing of the decree, the last person professing to be a Jew left Spanish soil.

The largest contingent of the *emigrés* crossed the border into Portugal, where the Jews had on the whole led a more sheltered existence. This haven was theirs for only another five years. The young Portuguese king, Manoel the Fortunate, wanted to keep the Jews in his realm. At the same time, he wanted to marry the daughter of Ferdinand and Isabella, and the match was made conditional on his ridding Portugal of infidels, whether Jewish or Moslem. He too signed an expulsion order, then did everything possible to thwart it by forcing Christianity on his Jewish subjects. First the children were seized and bap-

Abraham Seneor and Isaac Abrabanel appearing before the Spanish rulers Ferdinand and Isabella in 1492. The inquisitor Torquemada is on the left.

tized. Then, before the parents could embark, they were declared royal slaves and put willy-nilly through a hurried token baptism.

These Portuguese New Christians remained Jews in all but name for nearly fifty years, until the Inquisition was permitted into Portugal as well. Some of the Marranos then left the country; the rest were absorbed into the Portuguese people.

Most of the Jewish refugees from Spain and Portugal scattered through the Moslem lands in North Africa, the Balkans and the Near East,

including Palestine. Other groups settled in Italy and France. In these countries of refuge, whether Moslem or Christian, they were drawn into the Sephardic (Spanish) congregations established by earlier emigrés. In the next two centuries or so these communities were augmented by Marranos who escaped from the continuing harassment of the Inquisition and reverted to Judaism.

Organized Jewish life had come to an end in the Iberian Peninsula, but a widespread Sephardi Diaspora had come into existence elsewhere.

slowly through the Provence region of southern France, noting the centres of Jewish scholarship that had developed in the communities of Narbonne, Montpellier, Arles, Avignon, and elsewhere. He took ship to Genoa and travelled down Italy from Pisa to Rome, where among other matters he gave a fine tourist-guide description of the antiquities.

Sailing from southern Italy, he went through Corfu and Greece to Constantinople, where he stayed for a while, studying life there in some depth. He continued by boat through the Aegean Sea to Rhodes and Cyprus. Landing at Antioch in Syria, he went to Aleppo, Damascus and Baghdad, where he described the Caliph's court and wrote down the extraordinary story of the false messiah, David Alroy. In Palestine, then under Crusader rule, he visited all the main towns and holy places. He returned to Spain via Egypt, Sicily and France.

The information in his book about Persia, India, Ceylon and China obviously relies on travellers' tales from other sources, and is coloured by fancy. Where Benjamin bases himself on his own observations he is sober, clear and factual. Of particular interest is his account of specialized Jewish crafts in certain locations, like the cloth-dyers of Brindisi in southern Italy, the silk-weavers in Greece, the tanners in Constantinople and the glass-workers of Aleppo and Tyre. However, his stories about the fearsome Jewish brigand tribes of central Arabia and the Yemen must be treated with reserve, as it is unlikely that he penetrated the Arabian Peninsula.

Since it is the most important and detailed account of the Mediterranean and Middle East region at that period, Benjamin's book has been translated into nearly all European languages and is a valuable source for students of Jewish and general mediaeval history.

Benjamin of Tudela

See colour pages 178 and 179

Benjamin ben-Judah, from the town of Tudela in northern Spain, was the great 12th-century roving reporter of Jewish life in the Mediterranean – Near East region. His journeys may well have taken up to eight years (the exact duration is uncertain) and ended about 1173. He must have kept detailed journals from which he composed his *Book of Travels* (*Sefer ha-Massa'ot*). It first appeared in Constantinople in 1543, and from a somewhat different manuscript in Ferrara, Italy, in 1556.

Nothing is known about Benjamin's personal background, not even his occupation or the reason for the lengthy travels he undertook. From evidence in his book, it is surmised that he may have been a merchant, possibly in precious stones. Although he depicted conditions and places of general interest in the countries he visited, his primary concern was with their Jewish communities. He investigated and described them in detail – their size, their occupations, their way of life, their scholars and communal leaders and the way they were treated.

From Spain, Benjamin travelled

Ashkenaz

Ashkenaz is a Hebrew word commonly used for Germany. The Jews who settled in the Rhineland and northern France spread across France and Germany, and later migrated into Eastern Europe, were known as Ashkenazim.

The history of the Ashkenazi Jews started with the Jewish traders who followed the Roman legions into Gaul, and settled in the new towns that grew out of the military camps along the Rhine valley. In AD 800 Charlemagne founded the Carolingian Empire that covered Western and Central Europe and lasted almost two centuries. Jews were encouraged to come into the empire and its successor states, in order to derive advantage from them as traders. In that period the Jews participated in the international commerce between Europe, the Mediterranean and the East. Living in both the Christian and Moslem worlds, Jewish merchants could act as a bridge between them.

In 1000 there were a number of established Jewish communities along the river valleys that formed the main trade routes: at Cologne, Mainz, Worms and Speyer in the Rhine Basin, at Augsburg and Regensburg on the Danube, at Prague in the east, at Paris and Troyes on the Seine, and at Avignon, Arles, Narbonne and other centres in Provence round the lower course of the Rhone. After 1066 French Jews reached England with William the Conqueror.

Up to the end of the 11th century, Jewish life in the Ashkenaz region was relatively unharassed, except for spasmodic local incidents. Reactionary churchmen continued to press for enforcement of the anti-Jewish laws enacted in the Byzantine empire and endorsed by Church Councils. But rulers found it expedient to ignore this ecclesiastical pressure. There does not seem to have been widespread hostility to Jews among the general populace; in fact, some prelates complained bitterly about this co-existence between Jew and Gentile. One of the most vocal of these was Agobard, the Archbishop of Lyons (814–40), whose anti-semitic pamphlets castigated the Jews as 'sons of darkness'. Matters had reached a stage, he wrote, 'where ignorant Christians claim that the Jews preach better than our priests . . . some Christians even celebrate the Sabbath with the Jews and violate the holy repose of Sunday . . . Men of the people, peasants, allow themselves to be plunged into such a sea of errors that they regard the Jews as the only people of God, and consider that they combine the observance of a pure religion and a truer faith than ours.'

Agobard and his equally virulent successor Bishop Amulo failed to convince the emperors to repress the Jews. Moreover, there still lingered in the Church the less fanatical school of thought enunciated in the 7th century by the revered Pope Gregory I, and before that by the most learned of the early Church Fathers, St Augustine. Yet the attacks of men like Agobard sank into the popular mind, and would bear evil fruit in the Middle Ages.

During this period Jewish scholarship flourished in the area.

Ecclesia and Synagoga

These two graceful effigies of queens appear at the side entrance of Strasbourg Cathedral in Alsace, completed in 1230. One represents Ecclesia (the Church), a crown on her head. The other, Synagoga, is blindfolded, dejected of mien, without a crown and holding a broken staff.

Such figures, denoting the triumph of Christianity and the defeat of Judaism, were frequently

The First Crusade. In the massacres of 1096, the communities of Mainz, Speyer, Worms, Cologne and others were destroyed.

used on the exterior of mediaeval cathedrals. Another well-preserved example is on the 13th-century cathedral at Bamberg, Germany. They are also found sometimes in a mutilated form on the cathedrals of Rheims, Paris and Bordeaux in France, and Lincoln, Salisbury, Winchester and Rochester in England. The same images occur in many mediaeval illuminated manuscripts.

Important academies developed in some of the cities, while renowned scholars like Rabbi Gershom of Mainz and Rabbi Shlomo ben-Isaac of Troyes (Rashi) had an influence throughout the European region and beyond it. Ashkenaz had become a new and major centre of Jewish learning.

The era of relative tolerance came to an end for the Jews of Europe at the end of the 11th century. From then on they were plunged into an inferno of mediaeval persecution. The turning-point was the First Crusade (1095–9). An emotional reaction had been provoked in Europe by stories from returning pilgrims that the Holy Land and the sites in it sacred to Christianity were being defiled by the Moslem Arabs, who had taken the country four centuries earlier from Christian Byzantium. On 26 November 1095, in a sermon to the Church Council in Clermont, France, Pope Urban II called on Christendom to recover the Holy Land from the infidel. The princes and knights who responded to this call were called Crusaders, from the ceremony of 'taking the cross'.

The movement quickly spread through Europe. It was fuelled by

(continued on page 141)

The Jews in England: 11th –12th centuries AD

The mass suicide of the York Jews in the royal castle, known as Clifford's Tower, took place on 16 March 1190. It was the worst incident in the outbreak of anti-Jewish disorders in a number of English towns that spring. The background was the religious fervour aroused by the Third Crusade, of which Richard I (the Lionheart) of England was a leading figure.

In September of the previous year Richard had been crowned in Westminster Hall, London. The excited crowd outside ran amok, killed a number of Jews and looted their homes. Order was quickly restored, but after the departure of Richard and his troops for the Holy Land, the disturbances flared up again in the provincial centres.

In York the Jews took refuge in the castle. They were led by the head of the community, Josce, and their rabbi, Yomtov ben-Isaac, a well-known scholar and liturgical poet who had come from France to York a decade earlier. The castle was cut off and besieged by the mob. When the situation of the Jews had become hopeless, and they suspected that the warden was about to hand them over, they decided to take their own lives. Each man killed the members of his family and then himself. Finally the rabbi ended Josce's life and took his own.

When Richard fell captive to the Saracen foe, his ransom money was to a large extent exacted from the English Jews. On his return to England, the king was angry at the anti-Jewish attacks that had occurred in his absence. As elsewhere in Western Europe, the Jews belonged to the king and were under his direct protection. Moreover their money-lending transactions (the only occupation still permitted to them) provided substantial tax revenues for the Royal Exchequer. During the disturbances many of those who had received Jewish loans had simply burnt the bonds and refused to pay. In order to preserve for the future the royal stake

Clifford's tower in York.

in such dealings, Richard instituted a system whereby an official registry of Jewish loans was kept in each one of the larger English towns. In Whitehall an 'Exchequer of the Jews' was established to oversee this process in twenty-six different towns and collect the king's share of the interest. Richard also created the office of Jewish Archpresbyter, held by a succession of leading Jews. The Archpresbyter served as liaison between the palace and the Jewish community in England.

The Jews were latecomers to England, arriving shortly after 1066 from France with the Norman Conquest and provided financial services to William the Conqueror and his barons. They retained links with French Jewry, and for a generation or two continued to speak French among themselves. By the middle of the 12th century there were about 4,000 Jews in England. The largest community was in London, which at that time had the only consecrated Jewish burial-ground in the country. Smaller communities existed in several provincial towns, including Lincoln, Winchester, York, Oxford, Norwich and Bristol. A few of the Jews prospered. One of them, Aaron of Lincoln (1125–86) became very wealthy, and was considered one of the richest men in England. When he died, his estate was confiscated by the Royal Treasury, and a special department, called the Exchequer of Aaron, was set up to collect his outstanding loans. The huge loans owing to him by the king were simply cancelled. All the bullion and other treasure seized from Aaron's estate was despatched by ship to France to finance a military campaign there, but the ship sank in a storm in the English channel.

mixed motives: religious zeal, greed for land and booty, the opening up of lucrative trade routes and the lure of adventure. For the Jewish community that lay in its path (especially in the Rhineland), the Crusade was a bloody disaster. Undisciplined bands of peasants fell upon the defenceless Jewish communities, murdering and looting, as did the camp followers who accompanied or preceded the main body of the Crusaders. There were smaller contingents of knights who also saw the Jews as fair game. Many of the Jewish communities were wiped out before the first Crusader had left Europe. The climax came in the Holy Land in July 1099, when the Crusader army led by Godfrey of Bouillon captured Jerusalem and slaughtered all the Moslem and Jewish inhabitants of the city.

In the next two centuries there were eight more Crusades (not including the tragic Children's Crusade). Their object was to support the Latin kingdom of Jerusalem and the adjacent Crusader principalities, that were battling to survive against the Moslem counter-offensive. The final Crusade was not long before the fall in 1291 of Acre, the last Crusader stronghold in Palestine.

The brutal treatment of the Jews in the mediaeval period was not caused only by the religious bigotry worked up by the Crusades, but the anti-Jewish excesses must also be seen in the context of the general conditions. Western Europe was still a barbarous and insecure region. The nobility was a military caste, prizing above all the skills and the code of honour of the fighting man. The bulk of the population lived in ignorance, squalor and superstition. All calamities – whether pestilence, famine or the outbreaks of fire that ravaged the towns – were attributed to malignant forces. The region was torn by religious

Trade between a Jew, wearing the pointed hat, and a Christian peasant. From the Dresden Sachsenspiegel, Germany, 1220.

wars that devastated whole countries. The Jew, the only non-Christian minority in a Christian world, was the natural scapegoat for the ills and tensions of mediaeval society. He stood outside the feudal structure of that society, composed as it was of the land-owning aristocracy, the Church, the peasants, and the burgeoning cities.

The vulnerability of the Jews increased as their economic base shrank. They had long been cut off from the soil and were concentrated in the towns. As urban traders and artisans, they were now largely squeezed out with the rise of tightly-organized merchant and craft guilds from which Jews were excluded. In international trade, the Crusades opened up lucrative business opportunities for such powerful Christian interests as the Italian port-republics of Venice, Genoa and Amalfi.

The one occupation left open to Jews, because it was forbidden to Christians, was money-lending. It was despised, unpopular, degrading and often hazardous. But for some while it was essential. By the mediaeval period, Church doctrine had crystallized against 'usury', which meant the lending of money at any interest, large or small. The Third Lateran Council, which met in Rome in 1179, formally banned money-lending for Christians and ruled that anyone violating the ban would be denied a Christian burial.

Jewish doctrine on the subject was derived from the *Book of Deuteronomy*, which laid down that: 'To a foreigner you may lend upon interest, but to your brother you shall not lend upon interest.' *Deut. 23:20*. This was interpreted to mean that a Jew was permitted to make a loan to a non-Jew and charge interest on it. For the Jews in mediaeval Europe that rabbinical ruling became the key to sheer survival. As they were pushed out of regular trading, their capital was diverted into what was in effect the earliest banking and financial services for Christian Europe. Everyone needed money: the kings and barons for their perpetual wars, the landowners to tide them over poor harvests, the Church and the monastic orders to build their splendid churches and abbeys, the city merchants to finance their business ventures, the squires to buy their way out of military service (by the custom known as 'scutage'), and the artisans to purchase the tools of their trade. The Jew was the source of loan capital for all these purposes. Interest rates were very high, but so were the risks. When the Jewish money-lender was murdered or driven out, the loan went to the king.

The king had a double financial interest in his Jewish subjects. They raised money directly for his needs, and they also paid him taxes on the loans they made to others. The Jews were a valuable asset to the rulers, and their legal status became that of *servi camerae regis* (Latin for 'servants of the king's chamber').

The principle was clearly stated in 12th-century England in the *Laws of Edward the Confessor*. The relevant provision reads: 'All Jews, wherever in the realm they are, must be under the king's liege protection and guardianship, nor can any of them put himself under

(continued on page 144)

The citizens of Tournai burying their dead during the Black Death. From a Belgian manuscript, 14th century.

The Black Death

The Black Death was an epidemic of bubonic plague that started in Constantinople in 1344 and spread all over Europe and Asia, decimating the population. It may have been carried by returning Crusaders and pilgrims to Western Europe, where it raged for the two years, 1348–50. By the time it burnt itself out an estimated one-third of the inhabitants of the region had died a horrible death.

In 1894 medical science established that the source of the disease lay in bacteria transmitted by the fleas carried by rats. Five centuries earlier, in mediaeval Europe, no rational explanation was available. A person would mysteriously start to shake with fever and then rant in delirium; suppurating sores would break out from the lymph glands; the blood would turn blackish (hence the name Black Death); and within a few days the person would be dead.

The Church declared the plague a scourge of God, and called on sinners to repent while there was yet time. The populace sought the cause in some malignant human design. The

story spread like wildfire that the Jews had poisoned the wells. Some said the Jews had plotted with the Moslem enemy to destroy Christianity. Some credence was added to this story by the fact that the Jews seemed to have greater resistance to the ravages of the plague. It was useless to point out that they lived in segregated quarters and maintained a higher standard of hygiene than their neighbours.

Throughout the Ashkenaz region there were spontaneous outbreaks of violence. The mobs overran Jewish quarters, murdering the inhabitants and destroying their homes. A special bull issued by Pope Clement VI discounted the charge and called for the attacks on the Jews to cease, but in the prevailing atmosphere it had little effect.

The frenzied attacks were also fed by a material factor. Loans obtained from Jewish money-lenders were usually wiped out when they were killed. In Germany alone the disturbances occurred in some 350 localities, 60 of the larger Jewish communities and 150 of the smaller ones were completely liquidated. It was by far the worst series of massacres suffered by the Jews in mediaeval Europe.

Jews being burned at the stake. A woodcut from Schedel's Weltchronik, *1495.*

the protection of any powerful person without the king's license, because the Jews themselves and all their chattels are the king's. If, therefore, anyone detain them or their money, the king may claim them, if he so desire and if he is able, as his own.' That status cut both ways. The Jews were given royal protection where their royal master was able and willing to extend it; but they were also at the mercy of royal greed. There were kings who ruined 'their' Jews by exorbitant taxes and levies, or imprisoned and expelled them in order to confiscate their assets and wipe out their debts to them.

In the later mediaeval period the Jews lost their exclusive function even as money-lenders. Christian rivals moved into this field by adopting various legal devices and fictions to get round the anti-usury laws. Thus, the capital amount of the loan might be inflated in the bond, or interest disguised as a penalty for non-payment on due date. In particular, there were the thriving groups of French money-lenders known as 'Lombards' or 'Cahorsins' – the forerunners of later banking-houses.

The Middle Ages left embedded in the European mind an image of the Jew as a rapacious usurer. It was a Shylock-image without the redeeming touches of humanity and pathos Shakespeare gave to his stage character.

In general, Jewish life in mediaeval Europe from the 12th to the 15th centuries was a picture of unspeakable persecution. Tens of thousands of Jews were massacred, tortured, burnt alive at the stake or driven to suicide. In place after place the fury of religious fanaticism and mob violence was unleashed on them. They were accused of ritual murder, of drinking Christian blood, of venting their spleen on the consecrated Host, of poisoning the wells. They were forced to wear badges as a visual symbol of their inferior status. One country or city after another expelled them, after robbing them of their possessions.

Nevertheless some Jewish life survived in the Ashkenaz region after centuries of this ordeal because all the Jews in it were not under attack at one and the same time. When fleeing from one place they could generally find refuge elsewhere. Sometimes those who had expelled them realized how useful they were and tried to lure them back. In a number of cases rulers, nobles, bishops or city authorities sheltered them from mob violence. What was remarkable was not that Jews survived, but that they emerged with their belief in God intact and their spirit unbroken. At any time they could have ended their sufferings by accepting baptism, and coming under the protective umbrella of the Church. Yet few took this escape route. Many found the strength to endure by means of a social and spiritual withdrawal and an intensified attachment to their own faith. From this inner source they gained a stoical acceptance of suffering and death. It was an attitude summed up in the phrase *Kiddush ha-Shem* – 'Sanctification of the Name' (of God).

The concept of Kiddush ha-Shem goes back to ancient times. In general, it stands for conduct in a Jew that demonstrates his staunch adherence to his ancestral religion and values. The opposing concept is *Chilul ha-Shem* ('Desecration of the Name') – that is, unworthy or impious conduct. In mediaeval Europe Kiddush ha-Shem acquired a special and poignant dimension, it denoted martyrdom in the name of God. Death under these circumstances, even death by one's own hand, was touched by holiness. It could be faced with a calm, sometimes with an ecstasy, that baffled the tormentors and executioners of the mediaeval Jews.

In the 16th century a movement of religious dissent sprang up in Germany that became known as the Reformation. It would permanently divide the Christians of the Western world into two camps, Catholics and Protestants. The Jewish communities in Western Europe, shrunken and impoverished by the mediaeval persecutions and expulsions, were at first hopeful that the Reformation would usher in for them a new era of tolerance. Its leader, Martin Luther (1483–1546), and other important figures in it appeared sympathetic. They took a renewed interest in the Old Testament and turned to the rabbis to teach them Hebrew. Luther himself translated the Old Testament into German. Some Protestant groups even started leaning towards Jewish practices, like the Anabaptists in Moravia and other Sabbatarian sects.

The title page of Martin Luther's pamphlet Concerning the Jews and their Lies, *Wittenburg, 1543.*

Why should the Jews convert, Luther asked, when the Christians treated them like dogs? His great hope was that they would find it easier to embrace Christianity in its Protestant form. When that failed to happen, he was bitterly disappointed, and in his last years turned violently anti-Jewish. In his treatise *Of the Jews and their Lies* (1543), he repeated the well-worn calumnies of the blood-libel and the poisoning of wells, and advocated that the synagogues and schools of the Jews be burnt down, their sacred books confiscated, their assets taken from them and their livelihood as money-lenders forbidden. As a result of this incitement two German Protestant states, Saxony and Hesse, did in fact expel the Jews.

A more humane Protestant attitude to the Jews found an eloquent spokesman in a respected German Christian scholar, Johannes Reuchlin. He mastered Hebrew, and published the first Christian textbook on the Hebrew language in 1506. Reuchlin also studied the Kabbalah (Jewish mysticism) and the biblical commentaries of Rashi and other Jewish scholars. When the emperor Maximilian set up an ecclesiastical commission in 1510 to study whether the Talmud should be destroyed, Reuchlin was the only Christian academic who had the courage to appear before it and defend the Jews. He denounced the charges against them and their sacred writings as wholly false. For a while Reuchlin himself came under attack as a 'Jew-lover', and a pro-Jewish pamphlet he had written was condemned.

While there were these conflicting trends among Protestants, the Jews on the whole were no better off as a result of the Reformation. In some respects they suffered more. Thrown onto the defensive, the Catholic Church regarded the Jews as sympathetic to the Reform-

Jews extracting blood from Simon of Trent, the subject of the Italian blood libel of 1475. A German woodcut, 15th century.

ation. The Counter-Reformation swept away the humanist attitude towards the Jews shown by some of the Renaissance Popes, and revived all the harsh anti-Jewish ordinances of the mediaeval period.

It was only in the 17th century that the Jews began to enjoy tolerance in two Protestant countries, Holland and England. Both of them were mercantile and seafaring powers with rising prosperity and the beginnings of overseas empires. In them, the Jews driven out of Spain and elsewhere could find new homes and opportunities.

The Blood-Libel

In the evil image of the Jew shaped by mediaeval Europe, one ingredient was the grotesque 'blood-libel' – the charge that Jews killed Christians to use their flesh or blood for ritual purposes.

That myth occurs in the anti-semitic writings of Apion, an Alexandrian Greek of the 1st century AD. According to him, the Jews would annually kidnap a Greek, fatten him in the Jerusalem Temple, then sacrifice him and eat his flesh. But it was not only the adherents of Judaism who faced such an allegation. Ironically, the early Christian sect suffered from it too. The 2nd-century Church Father, Tertullian, wrote that, 'We [the Christians] are said to be the most criminal of men on the score of our sacramental baby-killing and the baby-eating that goes with it...' He complained that the Roman authorities arrested and tortured Christians to wring out of them 'confessions' concerning the number of babies they had tasted.

The first blood-libel case in the Middle Ages was at Norwich, England, in the year 1144. The body of a skinner's apprentice called William was found in a wood on Easter Saturday. A rumour spread that the youth had been taken into a Jewish home during the Passover and had been crucified in mock imitation of the death of Jesus. The Jews in the town took refuge in the castle from an angry mob and were protected by the sheriff. The body of the 'boy martyr' was buried in Norwich Cathedral and miracles were attributed to it.

A Jewish apostate named Brother Theobald later offered 'evidence' of the alleged ritual murder. He claimed that an assembly of Jewish leaders met each year at Narbonne in France and decided on the next place for a human sacrifice. This story contained two sinister elements that would figure prominently in later anti-semitic literature, with tragic consequences for the Jews. One was the claim that Jews were required by their religion to kill Christian boys at Passover; the other was that an international assembly of Jews met secretly to plot the overthrow of the Christian world – a foretaste of the notorious *Protocols of the Elders of Zion*.

There were another seven blood-libel cases in English towns before the expulsion of the Jews from England in 1290. The most famous of these

occurred at Lincoln in 1255. The body of an eight-year-old boy was found in the cesspool of a house in the Jewish quarter. The owner of the house, a Jew named Copin, was arrested and tortured until he 'confessed' that the child had been murdered for Passover ritual purposes. King Henry III sentenced him to death, and he was publicly hanged. Ninety other members of the Lincoln community were rounded up and thrown into the Tower of London, and eighteen of them were executed.

In the 12th and 13th centuries scores of blood-libel cases erupted all over Western Europe, generally at the time of the Jewish Passover and the Christian Easter. While the emphasis was on the crucifixion theme, the stories developed a further feature, namely, a ritual drinking of the victim's blood – hence the term 'blood-libel'. In Eastern Europe, where the blood-libel spread in the late Middle Ages, it acquired yet another twist – that Christian blood was used in the baking of matzot, the unleavened bread eaten during the Passover.

Enlightened Christian leaders tried to counteract the charges. One of them was the Holy Roman Emperor, Frederick II (reigned 1220–50). In 1235, thirty-four Jews in the small German town of Fulda in Hesse were burnt to death on a blood-libel charge. The emperor sought the opinion of Church leaders whether there was any basis to such charges, and received inconclusive answers. He then convened a synod of learned Jewish converts to Christianity who, he presumed, would know the true facts. They advised him that 'there is not to be found, either in the Old or the New Testament, evidence that the Jews are desirous of human blood. On the contrary, they avoid contamination with any kind of blood.' The emperor published their finding that blood libel charges were 'cruel and unnatural'.

A few years later, in 1247, Pope Innocent IV also condemned the blood-libel. But neither emperor nor Pope could eradicate a belief that would remain rooted in popular myth-

ology right up to the 20th century. In some areas local Church authorities were themselves responsible for perpetuating the myth. For instance, in 1475 the whole of the small Jewish community in Trent, northern Italy, was put to death on the allegation that it had murdered a boy, called Simon, for religious purposes. The relics of this 'boy martyr' were preserved in the cathedral, where there was an annual ceremony in his memory, and in 1582 he was officially beatified. Only in 1965 did the Church reopen the case and annul the beatification.

In the 18th century the blood-libel had become so prevalent in Poland that the Council of the Four Lands, the representative body of Polish Jewry, sent an emissary to Rome with a request that the Holy See investigate the whole subject. The task was entrusted to Cardinal Ganganelli, later Pope Clement XIV. In 1759 he produced a lengthy report calling the charges a calumny against Judaism and asking that measures be taken to protect the Jews of Poland.

In spite of such authoritative declarations, there were a number of blood-libel cases from the 18th to the 20th century, mainly in Czarist Russia, but also in Germany and in the Ottoman empire. Two of these cases in particular attracted worldwide attention. One was the Damascus libel case of 1840; it drew the personal intervention of the most influential Jewish leaders in the West, Sir Moses Montefiore of England and Adolphe Cremieux of France. Another was the Beilis case in Kiev, Ukraine, in 1911. The 'evidence' was deliberately fabricated by the Russian authorities as part of their effort to divert popular discontent into anti-Jewish channels. The case roused a storm of protest inside and outside Russia. Beilis was acquitted for lack of proof.

The blood-libel charge featured prominently in the Nazi propaganda drive against the Jews. Dr Goebbels discovered that in the 20th century, 800 years after the Norwich case, the malevolent story that Jews were ritual murderers of Christians could still be used as a potent weapon against them.

Ein grawsamlich geschicht Geschehen zu passaw Von den Juden als hernach volgt

Nach christi gepurt. M.CCCC.LXX

The Desecration of the Host

This German broadsheet, printed about 1480, depicts in twelve scenes the alleged desecration of the Host by Jews in the town of Passau, Bavaria, in 1478.

According to the account, a Christian steals consecrated wafers from a church and sells them for one gulden to local Jews, identified in the pictures by the circular badges on their clothes. The Jews take the wafers to the synagogue and stab one of them, drawing blood. Some of the wafers are sent to the communities of Prague and Salzburg and the Jews try to burn the rest in an oven. Angels and doves fly out of the oven, while the face of a child appears on the wafers. The Jews who take part in this act of desecration are tortured and two of them beheaded. The rest of the Jews are hanged. The synagogue is converted into a church.

Charges of desecrating the Host, like the blood-libel charges, were widespread in mediaeval Europe and added to the picture of the Jew as a sinister enemy of the Christian faith.

In 1215 the Fourth Lateran Council officially endorsed the Doctrine of Transubstantiation, whereby the wine and the bread wafers (called the Host) used in the sacrament of the Eucharist during Mass are miraculously transformed into the actual substance of Christ's body. The story gained credence that Jews obtained consecrated wafers, pierced them to make them bleed, thereby re-enacting for their own satisfaction the Passion of Christ. In many places this alleged act of desecration resulted in Jews being persecuted and put to death, as was the case in Passau.

148

A prophet, depicted as a contemporary Jew, wearing a badge in the shape of the Tablets of the Law. From an English manuscript of 1275.

'The Badge of Shame'

Jews were first obliged to wear a distinctive item of apparel in the Islamic countries. This rule applied to all non-Moslem communities, Christians as well as Jews. Yellow was often used for Jews and blue for Christians. The same practice was enforced for the Jews in Christian Europe during the Middle Ages.

A distinctive mark for Jews was made compulsory for the whole Christian world by the Fourth Lateran Council in 1215. The specific reason given by the Council was that Christians might inadvertently fall into grievous sin by having sexual intercourse with Jews. The Council's decree did not specify what kind of mark should be used. It took different forms in different countries. In Germany, in the 13th and 14th centuries, Jews were depicted wearing yellow, pointed, 'Jewish hats'. In the 15th century a yellow patch sewn onto the outer garment became the rule. By the laws of England, the badge was a patch of yellow cloth in the form of the tablets of the Law, worn on the left side of the breast. In France a round disk was worn on the breast and sometimes also on the back. It was yellow in some localities, and in others half red and half white. The royal treasury in France gained revenue from these badges, since the Jews had to buy them from the tax collectors. In Spain the Jewish badge was a circular red patch. In Italy the round badge was usually yellow, but red in the Venetian republic. The distinguishing mark laid down in the Papal dominions was a yellow hat for Jews and a yellow kerchief for Jewesses.

The so-called 'badge of shame' for Jews gradually fell out of use between the 16th century and the beginning of the Emancipation in the 18th century. It was not formally abolished until the French Revolution, first in France and then in other European countries occupied by the French armies.

The Jewish badge in the form of a yellow six-pointed star, the Shield of David, was revived by the Nazis in the Second World War throughout Nazi-occupied Europe.

The Expulsions

See illustration overleaf

From the 12th to the 15th centuries the Jews were expelled at one time or another from most of the countries of Western Europe. The causes were partly religious bigotry, partly the avarice of rulers eager to replenish their treasuries by the seizing of Jewish property.

At first the Jews were banished from a number of individual towns. In this way the rising guilds of Christian merchants and craftsmen were able to rid themselves of Jewish competitors. Since these were local measures, the Jewish communities concerned were able to move elsewhere in the area though stripped of their possessions. In most cases, some of them came back after an interval, and their organized communities slowly revived.

The first national expulsion order

The expulsion of the Jews from France in 1182. A miniature from Grandes
Chroniques de France, *1321.*

was that signed by King Philip
Augustus of France in 1182. It was
only partially implemented, because
powerful and independent barons
ignored it in their own domains.
Sixteen years later it was repealed,
and the Jews were invited back.

The Jews of England were expelled
in 1290. On mounting the throne in
1272, Edward the Confessor found
that the situation of the Jews in the
kingdom had gravely deteriorated.
They had been impoverished by the
crushing exactions of previous rulers,
and their occupation of money-
lending was no longer an important
source of revenue for the crown.
Popular feeling had been inflamed
against them by charges of blood-
libel and desecration of the Host,
culminating in the classic case of
Hugh of Lincoln in 1255. The Jews
had been banished on local initiative
from a number of provincial towns,
such as Newcastle, Leicester, Derby
and Windsor. There were increasing
incidents of mob attacks on Jewish
quarters. King Edward felt that the
problem of the Jews could be settled,
together with the religious problem of

usury, if they were permitted to enter
other occupations such as trade,
handicrafts and the leasing of farms.
He instituted an economic programme to this effect, but it proved
ineffectual. The king thereupon decided to get rid of the Jews altogether,
and signed the expulsion order of
1290. About 5,000 Jews were shipped
out of England, after being stripped
of their property. They made their
way as refugees to France and Germany. There would not be another
person professing to be a Jew in
England for 400 years – until the time
of Oliver Cromwell.

In the 14th century there were
fresh expulsion orders in France. The
one in 1306 was actuated by purely
mercenary motives: the desire of
King Philip the Fair to take over the
property and outstanding loans of the
Jews. The order was reversed nine
years later by Louis X, and the Jews
were allowed to return, initially for a
period of twelve years. Another expulsion order was signed in 1322, and
repealed only in 1359. In 1394, the
Jews were again banned from France,
by the deranged Charles VI. Most of

them found refuge in Italy, Spain and
the kingdom of Provence.

In Germany, where the worst
persecutions and massacres of the
Jews took place in the mediaeval
period, there was no general expulsion order against them. The authority of the Holy Roman Emperor
had waned, and political power was
distributed among a great number of
small autonomous units: principalities and duchies, bishoprics and
certain towns. This fragmentation
meant that the Jews could no longer
rely on the protection of the emperor,
to whom they in theory belonged. On
the positive side, they could not be the
victims of a single decree banishing
them from the whole of Germany, as
had happened in England and
France, and later in Spain and
Portugal.

Though sadly depleted by persecution and constantly uprooted in one
locality or another, the Jewish community of Germany had a continuous
existence on German soil. At the end
of the mediaeval period, local communities of any size were left only in
two German cities, Worms and
Frankfurt.

The last and most permanent of the
general expulsions in the Middle
Ages was that from Spain in 1492. In
Portugal in 1497, though Manoel II
ordered the Jews expelled, he changed his mind and had them converted. In both cases a community of
Marranos remained behind. Many of
them would also leave to escape the
pressure of the Inquisition, revert to
Judaism and join the Sephardic
congregations in other lands.

Renaissance Italy

Italy, like Germany, did not become a single united country until the late 19th century. From the 10th to the 13th century the northern part of the Italian peninsula was part of the Holy Roman Empire, and nominally under the rule of the German emperor. But his authority was weak south of the Alps and was contested by the popes. In effect, Italy was a mosaic of small and virtually independent political units. In the south there were two feudal kingdoms, those of Naples and Sicily. Apart from being the spiritual head of the Church, the Pope was also a temporal ruler over the Papal States in the centre of the country, including Rome.

Among nearly a score of other separate entities in Italy were half-a-dozen duchies, like Milan and Savoy, and a number of rising city-states. Some of these cities were ruled by hereditary dynasties, others were republics. The most prominent of the latter were Venice, Genoa and Florence. Indeed, the merchant port-cities of Venice and Genoa developed into Mediterranean powers in their own right, with colonial possessions, fleets and ambassadors.

These duchies and cities had chronic feuds with each other that spilt

Italian Jews and Renaissance culture

During the Renaissance, Italian Jews were drawn into the mainstream of general and artistic intellectual life, while continuing to contribute to Jewish scholarship. As elsewhere, they were noted for their medical skill, and many Jewish physicians served at the courts of the Popes and at the courts of local rulers. They were writers, poets and translators. The latter vocation was especially important since erudite Jews in Sicily and southern Italy were familiar with Arabic literature and could translate philosophical and scientific works from that language into Italian and Latin, the European language of scholarship. Like the Spanish Jews, therefore, they helped to introduce ancient Greek writings, especially those of Aristotle, into mediaeval Europe through the works of Arab scholars.

Faraj ben-Solomon (bottom drawing) *translating the Arabic medical encyclopaedia* Al Harvi *into the Latin* Liber coninens, *and presenting it to the King of Naples. From a 13th-century Sicilian manuscript.*

The opening page of Madrigaletti by Salomon de Rossi (1570–1629), the greatest Jewish composer of his time, who introduced many innovations into Jewish liturgical music.

over into recurrent local wars. The fighting was conducted by hired mercenaries called *condottiere*, and did not seriously disrupt normal life and business.

In such a fragmented Italy, policy towards the Jews was not uniform. They were better off in some places and times, and worse off in others. But on the whole the attitude towards them by Popes, nobles and city authorities was more enlightened and tolerant than that which prevailed in the Ashkenaz region. Anti-Jewish attacks were sporadic and localized, without the scale and ferocity of the persecutions in Germany. Until the late Middle Ages the Jews were able to find their own distinctive place in both the economic and cultural life of mediaeval Italy. They were mainly concentrated in the southern parts of the country and the island of Sicily.

These communities were well-established and flourishing from the 9th century, and evolved their own considerable centres of Jewish learning. In the centre and north of the country the largest and oldest community was that in Rome, dating back to at least the 2nd century BC. Other organized communities developed in Florence, Mantua, Ferrara, Venice, Padua and Ancona. The northern communities were augmented from the 14th century by an influx of refugees from Germany.

Economic activity was less restricted for the Jews in Italy than in

Jews were active in the performing arts – in music, dance and the theatre, where they appeared as playwrights, actors and directors.

Some of the leading Renaissance Christian intellectuals developed an interest in Hebrew, Jewish learning and the Kabbalah, and received tuition from rabbis.

Franco-Germany. There was a relatively small and well-to-do class of money-lenders, but the Jews were by no means confined to that occupation. Nor were Gentile interests dependent for loans just on the Jews, since a class of Italian Christian money-lenders and bankers arose in the mediaeval period. (That was the basis for the fortune of the celebrated Medici family in Florence.) The growing prosperity of the Italian states and cities derived mainly from commerce. The Italian merchants served as the middlemen in the trade route between Europe and the East through the Mediterranean, and the Italian ports flourished from the *entrepôt* trade that was stimulated by the Crusades. In the general conditions of prosperity and economic growth, there was no strong incentive to oust Jewish traders or skilled craftsmen. A notable example was the spinning and weaving of silk in southern Italy, an industry that was mainly Jewish. Inevitably some Christian guilds did try to restrict Jewish competitors.

The Christian Hebraist, Giovanni Pico della Mirandola and his Jewish teacher (the bearded figure). A detail from a fresco by Cosimo Rosselli, Florence, 15th century.

Servi camarae regis. *The Jews of Rome receive a charter of privileges from Emperor Heinrich VII in 1312. From* Codex Baldvini, *the Rhine, early 14th century.*

In the 14th century there started in Italy that epoch of cultural flowering known as the Renaissance (the French word for rebirth). It was marked by intellectual freedom, brilliant innovations in literature, art and architecture, and a liberation from the dead hand of feudal Europe. It had a permanent impact on Western civilization as we know it. For the Italian Jews the Renaissance brought about one of the periods of cultural synthesis between traditional Jewish scholarship and a surrounding culture of a high level. That had happened in ancient Alexandria and in the Golden Age in Spain.

At the end of the 15th century the Jewish community in southern Italy fell victim to the expulsion of the Jews from Spain. After periods of Moslem Arab and then Norman rule, the kingdom of Sicily had become a dependency of the Spanish kingdom of Aragon. The expulsion order signed by Ferdinand and Isabella in 1492, therefore, applied to the Jews on the island as well. The total community, numbering nearly 40,000 souls, was expelled, and their homes and businesses confiscated. Most of them moved into the neighbouring kingdom of Naples, while others found refuge in North Africa and the

Servi camerae regis

From the 10th century to the latter part of the 13th century, Italy belonged to the Holy Roman Empire, and the Italian Jews, like the German Jews, had the legal status of *servi camerae regis*, that is, they were 'servants of the royal chamber' and nominally under the protection of the German emperor. In practice his rule was distant and ineffectual. It was said that his realm was neither Holy nor Roman nor an Empire.

Ottoman empire, chiefly in Constantinople and Salonika. The expulsion decree also applied to the smaller Jewish community on the island of Sardinia, another Spanish possession.

In addition to Sicilian Jews, thousands of Spanish Jews and Marranos found refuge in the kingdom of Naples; a few years later that kingdom also came under Spanish rule. In 1515 the majority of its Jews were expelled, leaving 200 affluent families who were allowed to remain on payment of a large annual subsidy to the crown. In 1541 what remained of the community was finally banished. There would be no Jewish life in Naples for the next three centuries, until it was revived on a small scale by Baron Karl von Rothschild, a member of the banking family.

In the middle of the 16th century the mild air breathed by the Jews in Renaissance Italy gave way to the bleak winds of the Counter-Reformation. A warning blast came with the edict in 1553, and the public burning of copies of the Talmud and other Jewish religious works in a square in Rome. The last case of this kind had been in France three centuries earlier. This time, as before, the 'evidence' for the condemnation of the Talmud was provided by a Jewish apostate. The occurrence was instigated by the powerful and fanatical Cardinal Caraffa. Two years later he was elected Pope, and took the name of Paul IV. He promptly issued a papal bull launching a programme of anti-Jewish measures that had previously been enforced in other countries. The ghetto institution, existing until then only in Venice, now became general in Italian cities. The Jewish badge was introduced; the Jewish merchants were to be confined to dealing in rags and second-hand clothing; Jewish physicians would not be permitted to treat Christian patients.

These and other harsh provisions were only partially implemented by the rulers of many of the Italian petty states, some of whom resisted papal pressure. But in general the era of tolerance had ended for the Italian Jews, and the benevolence towards them of the Renaissance popes was replaced by hostility from the Holy See.

In the Renaissance period the Italian Jewish communities were augmented in size and their culture and economic activities enriched by the immigration of Spanish Jews. This movement started with the anti-Jewish riots in Spain in 1391. It became a large-scale influx with the expulsions from Spain in 1492 and the exodus from Portugal in 1497. Where they settled in sufficient numbers in any locality, they set up their own Sephardic congregations.

With the establishment of the Inquisition in Spain and Portugal at the end of the 15th century, there was also a steady stream of Marrano refugees from those two countries. Those of them who had been secret Jews reverted openly to Judaism in Italy. Others retained the Christian faith, and formed distinctive Marrano communities. In the earlier part of the 16th century the Marranos were well received, and even encouraged to settle, by local rulers eager to utilize their trading and financial skills. But their position remained insecure. The normal

(continued on page 159)

The Ghetto

In 1509 a group of Jewish immigrants from Germany sought permission to live in Venice, which had been closed to Jews for a number of years. They were allotted a small island among the city's canals, and were obliged to live there enclosed by a high wall. The island was less than two acres in extent, and reached by three bridges. The quarter was known as Ghetto Nuovo, Italian for the New (iron) Foundry, built there for the making of cannon. Later, an adjacent area, the 'Ghetto Vecchio' (Old Foundry) was added to accommodate a group of Turkish Jews.

From then on, the word 'ghetto' was adopted for all the urban quarters where Jews were segregated. In contemporary usage the term has been extended to cover an urban district inhabited by any ethnic minority group – for instance, Negro Harlem or Spanish (that is, Puerto Rican) Harlem in New York.

From the beginning of the Diaspora it was customary for Jews to cluster in separate quarters in the towns in which they lived. They did so for mutual protection against attack, and in order to maintain organized communal life around their synagogues. In mediaeval Europe such quarters were called Jewry in England, Juiverie in France, Judengasse in Germany, Juidecca in Italy and Juderia in Spain (except where the Arabic word Aljama survived from Moorish Spain). The same system prevailed in the Islamic countries. In Morocco it was known as the Mellah, and elsewhere by various Arabic equivalents of the term 'Jewish Quarter'.

What was new about the Venetian ghetto was that the segregation had been made compulsory. That symbolized a hardening anti-Jewish attitude in Italy from the beginning of the 16th century. In 1555 the precedent of Venice was followed in Rome. By papal order the ancient Jewish com-

Campo del Ghetto Nuovo – a view of the New Ghetto in Venice – a contemporary photograph.

munity was concentrated in a swampy area on the left bank of the river Tiber, and a wall built around it to isolate it from the rest of the city. It remained the most rigid and restricted of all Italian ghettoes.

In the latter half of the 16th century the rulers of other Italian states followed suit, under pressure from the Church. The institution of the ghetto was one aspect of a general anti-Jewish drive also marked by the forced wearing of Jewish badges, restrictions on Jewish occupations and the enforced attendance of Jews at church sermons that aimed to convert them.

The compulsory ghetto also spread to German cities and states. As the

Piazzetta del Pancotto (Bread Square) in the Rome Ghetto, 1886.

Jews had by then already been expelled from England, Spain and Portugal, and to a large extent from France, the ghetto institution was not relevant to those countries.

Since the ghettoes were not increased in area as the Jewish communities expanded, they became overcrowded and unhealthy, with the houses rendered unsafe by the additional storeys added to them. As a general rule the gates were locked at night and were in the charge of Christian gatekeepers. It was only at the end of the 18th century, shortly after the French Revolution, that European ghettoes were abolished. Wherever the French Revolutionary armies advanced, notably in Italy, they

knocked down the ghetto gates and gave their occupants freedom. After the defeat of Napoleon the ghetto was reinstated in Rome by the Pope. The restriction was lifted only in 1870 when the recently-unified kingdom of Italy annexed the Papal States, and the ghetto was demolished in 1885.

The name and concept of the Jewish ghetto acquired a new and tragic dimension during the Nazi Holocaust. The Jews in Nazi-occupied Europe were rounded up and herded together in ghettoes enclosed by walls. From there they were ultimately transported to the death camps. In some cases, like that of the Warsaw ghetto, Jews organized a brave but hopeless resistance.

157

The Soncino printing family

The Soncinos were a famous family of Hebrew printers in the 15th–16th centuries. They took their family name from the small town of Soncino in Lombardy, northern Italy, where they came to settle from Germany in 1454. Their printer's mark was probably taken from the municipal crest of the town. The printing activities of the family covered six generations, and spread to a number of Italian cities, as well as to Salonika, Constantinople and Cairo. They published more than 130 Hebrew books and about the same number in Italian and Latin. The most important Hebrew work was a complete Bible with over 400 illustrations.

For some years at the end of the 15th century theirs was the only Hebrew press in the world. In the early 16th century their main rival was the Christian printer Daniel Bomberg in Venice, who specialized in high-quality Hebrew books. He was the first to produce a complete printed edition of the Talmud.

Printing from movable type was adopted by Jews within a generation after it began with Johann Gutenberg in Mainz, Germany, in the year 1454. At first Hebrew printing encountered some rabbinic reservations, since the scribes who copied the Torah and other religious documents by hand were regarded as being engaged in a sacred task. The rapid proliferation of printed Hebrew books had a revolutionary impact on the religious and cultural life of Jewish communities everywhere. Copies of the Bible, the Talmud, prayer books, grammars and dictionaries were now for the first time plentiful and relatively cheap. Printing was accepted as a means to realize the prediction of the prophet Isaiah that 'the earth shall be full of the knowledge of the Lord' (*Isa. 11:9*).

The printer's mark used by Gershon Soncino between 1533 and 1552, in Rimini, Salonika and Constantinople.

The Norsa family

The Norsas (or Nurzis) were a wealthy and distinguished family of bankers and rabbinical scholars who settled in Mantua in the 15th century. At that time the Gonzaga dynasty that ruled the duchy of Mantua encouraged Jewish bankers and merchants to settle in their domain. The community prospered and became a centre of Jewish music and theatre. In the 16th century it suffered attack and persecution in the hostile atmosphere of the Counter-Reformation. The Norsa family home was seized and demolished by order of the Duke, and the Church of Santa Maria built on the site, to commemorate the victory of Mantua over a French army.

Four members of the Norsa family wearing Jewish badges, a detail from an anonymous oil-painting Madonna della Vittoria, *Mantua, 15th century.*

local resentments against competitive immigrants was compounded in their case by their Jewish descent and by the pressure exerted on Italy by the Spanish Inquisition. In the atmosphere of the Counter-Reformation that pressure was reinforced by the papal authorities in Italy. Marranos who had remained Christians were thus also caught up in the reactionary drive against the Jews.

A glaring example was Ancona, a port under papal rule on the east coast of Italy. A group of Portuguese Marranos was invited by the Pope to settle there, in order to develop its port and the trade with the Ottoman empire. They were given a guarantee of immunity from the attentions of the Inquisition. Pope Paul IV rescinded that immunity. Twenty-five of the town's Marranos, including one woman, were burnt at the stake as heretics, and a similar number were condemned to be galley-slaves. The Jewish leaders of Constantinople and Salonika tried to organize a punitive boycott of Ancona.

A flourishing Marrano community grew up in Ferrara under the protection of its rulers. In 1581 the Duke of Ferrara yielded to the pressure of the Pope. Many of the Marranos were imprisoned, and three of them were taken to Rome where they died at the stake. Some of the stronger and more independent Italian rulers resisted the Church and prevented the Inquisition from molesting their Marrano communities. That happened in Venice, and the Grand Duchy of Tuscany, whose ruler granted a special charter in 1593 to the Marranos willing to settle in Leghorn. A similar charter was granted to the Marranos by the Duke of Savoy in 1572. His object was to use them for the development of Nice as a major Mediterranean port. But he came under the combined pressure of the Holy See and the king of Spain, and in the following year he cancelled the charter and signed a decree expelling the Marranos.

From the 16th century onwards Italy was a cockpit for the imperial rivalries of Spain, France and Austria. Compared to their position during the Renaissance period, the Italian Jews sank into obscurity. They remained confined to their ghettoes until they were liberated by the invading French forces after the French Revolution of 1789.

17th-century Amsterdam

The Jewish community in Amsterdam in the 17th century provided one of the shining pages in the Diaspora story. Its context was the rapid rise at that time of the small Dutch nation.

In 1578 the seven northern provinces of the Low Countries, all of whom had become Calvinist Protestant, banded together in a union and shortly after declared their independence of Spanish rule. That independence was not finally recognized until 1648, by the Peace of Westphalia that ended the Thirty Years War. By then the wealth and power of the United Provinces (Holland) was expanding at a rate that turned it into a major European power. Dutch ships sailed the seven seas; Dutch merchants dealt with every continent; and Dutch trading posts in the New World and the Far East were turning into colonial possessions, the nucleus of a sprawling empire. The emergence of a prosperous middle-class was accompanied by a cultural golden age in

The Marranos in Holland

A Hebrew historical work, *She'erit Israel* (*The Remnant of Israel*), published in Amsterdam in 1741, gives an interesting account of the arrival of the first group of Marranos in Holland. The story is illustrated by this series of five pictures. The accompanying captions are based on *She'erit Israel* and other sources.

A Safe Refuge. In 1604 two ships arrived from Spain carrying – apart from valuable merchandise – ten Marranos with their wives and children. After enduring violent storms,

(continued on page 165)

they landed at Emden in Friesland.

A Hebrew store sign. They found a place to stay in Emden and went out to view the town. They saw a Hebrew sign: 'The world is founded on truth and peace' and nearby a man carrying a goose. They were delighted to find Jews there.

Secret consultation. The next day, two of them went to the home of Rabbi Moses Uri Halevi and his son Rabbi Aaron and, in strict privacy, revealed they were of Jewish origin and that all the males wished to be circumcised. Then they went on to

Amsterdam, and soon Rabbi Moses and Rabbi Aaron came and circumcised them. There was great rejoicing and the rabbis arranged a special room in their home to serve as a synagogue and they prayed there in fear and trepidation.

Permission is granted. Shortly afterwards, they were reported to the city councillors and Rabbi Moses and Rabbi Aaron were imprisoned. The judge asked whether they had permission to make a new faith. Rabbi Moses answered: 'We have an old faith – the faith of our ancestors. May God be praised for freeing your land

from the yoke of Spain. As a result of that, these people have come here and they will advance the commerce of the country. Moreover, their brothers in Spain will also come, and the city will benefit.' And the judges gave them every freedom.

More Marranos Return to Judaism. Immediately they wrote letters to all their relatives and loved ones about the rights and liberties they had received in Amsterdam. Within a short while many more Marrano families had gathered and over 2,500 males were circumcised.

The central square of the Jewish quarter in Amsterdam with the Great Portuguese Synagogue on the left, and the Great Ashkenazi Synagogue on the right. An engraving by Adolf van der Laan, c.1710.

The Great Portuguese Synagogue *See above*

The Great Portuguese Synagogue in Amsterdam was dedicated in 1675. The splendid building is in an elegant but restrained style that has been described as Protestant Baroque. In the 17th century it was a visible symbol of the wealth, piety and good taste of the Sephardi community in the city. The synagogue still stands today as originally built. Its high barrel-vaulted ceiling is supported by a double row of massive Ionic columns. It is lit by the glow of hundreds of candles in four great central candelabra and a number of smaller ones.

The 'bimah' and warden's pew are carved from Jacaranda wood originally imported from Brazil. The edifice includes offices, schoolrooms and a fine library.

The synagogue became a prototype for Sephardi houses of worship built elsewhere in Western Europe. One example is the Bevis Marks synagogue in London, completed in 1701 for the Spanish and Portuguese congregation. Its Quaker architect adapted the plan from the Amsterdam one.

Jewish occupations in Amsterdam *See right*

The prosperity of the Amsterdam Jewish community – like that of Holland as a whole – was based mainly on international commerce. Jewish merchants were involved in the lucrative trade with the Ottoman Empire, Italy and Spain, the Far East, via the sea-route round the Cape of Good Hope opened by the Portuguese navigators; and the colonies in the New World, where some of the Dutch Jews began to settle. Jews were substantial shareholders in the two great chartered corporations, the Dutch East India Company and the

As was the case elsewhere in the Diaspora, Jews were outstanding in the medical profession. Eminent Marrano physicians from Spain and Portugal reached Amsterdam as refugees. One of them was Joseph Bueno (who died in 1641), who was also a distinguished Hebrew-Spanish scholar, translator and poet. In 1625 he was called in to attend the Prince of Orange on his death-bed. He was a close friend of Rembrandt and was the model for Rembrandt's painting *The Jewish Doctor*. The most renowned Jewish physician of the time was Abraham Zacuto (1575–1642) who was born in Lisbon into an illustrious Marrano family. At the age of fifty he moved to Amsterdam, openly returned to Judaism, had himself circumcised and shed his Portuguese name – Manuel Alvares de Tavara. In addition to his huge clinical practice, he wrote a number of influential medical treatises that were collected and published in two volumes after his death.

Amsterdam was a major centre for both general and Hebrew printing and book publishing. The first Hebrew press in the country was set up in 1626 by the noted Sephardi rabbi, Manasseh Ben-Israel. He adapted to Hebrew printing the Dutch style of type, format, composition and decoration. The Amsterdam model became dominant for Hebrew printing all over Europe. The most successful of the Amsterdam Sephardi printers and publishers was Joseph Athias (died 1698), succeeded by his son. The best-known Athias publication was the 1661 Hebrew Bible. Athias said he printed more than a million Bibles in English for export to England and Scotland.

Diamond polishing. An engraving from Luiken's Het Menselyk Bedryf.

Dutch West India Company, that were laying the foundations for Holland's overseas empire.

Jewish bankers and stockbrokers played an active part in Amsterdam financial circles and were prominent in the Stock Exchange. In 1688, when William III of Orange sailed from Holland to gain the throne of England for his English wife Mary and himself, the expedition was financed to the extent of two million gulden by the richest Dutch-Jewish banker of the 17th century, Isaac (Lopes) Suasso.

In addition to commerce and finance, the Dutch Jews helped to develop the tobacco, silk, diamond, printing and optics industries. Diamond-cutting and polishing became a very Jewish craft.

MEDICUS. ÆTATIS SUÆ. LVIIII. Anno 1634.

DOCTOR ZACUTUS LUSITANUS

Zacuti faciem prochve est sculpere, mentem
Quod memoret Coelum? quod vel Agalma ferat?
Quod nequeunt oculi monstret doctrina Zacuti,
Et memorandi acies prædicet ingenium.

Nicolaus Fontanus MED.

S. Saveri fe

The physician Abraham Zacuto (Zacutus Lusitanus). An etching by S. Savari, 1634, Amsterdam.

literature, architecture, and above all, art. It was the period of Rembrandt, Franz Hals, Vermeer and the new landscape school of Ruysdael and others. Amsterdam replaced Catholic Antwerp as the major port and commercial centre in the North Sea region. The city was marked by a high intellectual and cultural level, solid bourgeois comfort and religious tolerance. Jewish life flourished in this atmosphere as it had not done in Europe for centuries.

The Amsterdam Jewish community began with a small group of Spanish and Portuguese Marranos who settled there about 1590. Marrano colonies already existed before then in a number of other European cities, among them Bordeaux, Hamburg, Antwerp, London. All these Marranos still outwardly professed the Catholic faith, but they openly reverted to Judaism in Amsterdam long before that became possible in other countries.

On throwing off the Spanish yoke, Holland had opened its gates to refugees from religious persecution elsewhere. These included Protestants from the Spanish Netherlands, and Huguenots, a Protestant minority suffering discrimination in France. This Dutch policy combined a humane attitude with shrewd commonsense, for the newcomers brought with them skills and business acumen that helped to build up the material wealth of Holland.

Some of the Marrano immigrant families in Amsterdam had been Christian for over a century, without breaking their ties with their Jewish past. Once they found themselves free of religious pressure in their new home, they changed their Spanish or Portuguese names to Hebrew ones, the males had themselves circumcised, and they sought instruction in religious observance and Hebrew. By 1620 there were three small Sephardi congregations in Amsterdam. (Although the word Sephardi means Spanish, the Sephardim in Holland were generally known as 'Portuguese'.) By a supreme touch of paradox, the Calvinist clergy and city fathers were, for a while suspicious of these newcomers with their strange rituals, thinking that they might really be a fifth column of Spanish Catholics pretending to be Jews while celebrating the Mass in secret. But they soon came to be accepted as genuine Jews and to be regarded with tolerance and respect.

The willingness of the Dutch to accept Jewish refugees was not limited to the Marranos. From 1620 there was a steady stream of Jews fleeing the persecution in Germany. After the Chmielnicki massacres in Poland in 1648, there was an influx of destitute Jewish immigrants from that country. The German and Polish Jews were Ashkenazi who did not merge with the Sephardi community but set up their own congregations. By the late 17th century the Ashkenazim were the majority of Amsterdam Jewry, though the upper class of wealth and culture remained Sephardi.

The Amsterdam Jews were fortunate in that they could participate freely in Dutch life. While maintaining their own traditions without any hindrance, the community supported fine Jewish schools and academies, and produced Hebrew scholars, teachers, writers and

(continued on page 167)

Rembrandt and Amsterdam Jews

The great Dutch painter Rembrandt van Ryn (1606–69) lived in Amsterdam next to the Jewish Quarter, and took a keen interest in its life. Two eminent members of the Sephardi congregation were his friends – the Rabbi Manasseh Ben-Israel and the physician Ephraim Bueno. He may also have known Spinoza, but that is uncertain.

Apart from Jewish portrait commissions, Rembrandt liked to make ink-and-chalk drawings of bearded old Jews in their long coats. Some of these may have served as models for figures in the artist's many paintings of Old Testament scenes. Perhaps the atmosphere and types in the Jewish community were a welcome change for him from the staid Dutch burghers whose individual and group portraits provided him with a living.

Above Ashkenazi Jews in the Synagogue, *an etching by Rembrandt, Holland, 1648.*

Left *Dr Ephraim Bueno, a detail from a painting by Rembrandt, Holland, 17th century.*

poets. Amsterdam provided rabbis, teachers and religious books for other Sephardi communities in Western Europe. It had particularly close relations with the Marrano communities in Hamburg and in London. In 1626 that remarkable rabbi, Manasseh Ben-Israel, founded a Hebrew printing press in the city. In 1672 a newspaper appeared in Ladino, the *Gazeta de Amsterdam*. It was the first Jewish newspaper in the world. In 1686–7 the Ashkenazi community followed suit with the *Dienstagish Kurant*, the first Yiddish newspaper to appear. Apart from Jewish culture, Jewish scholars and poets wrote extensively in the Spanish and Portuguese languages.

In later centuries the Amsterdam community remained one of the largest and most important in Europe, but it suffered economic decline. However, relations between Jew and Gentile remained good throughout. Unlike Jews in so many other lands in Diaspora history, the Dutch Jews never had to endure the swing of the pendulum from tolerance to repression.

167

A portrait of Baruch Spinoza, Holland.

Spinoza

The philosopher Baruch (Benedict) de Spinoza (1632–77) was by far the most important intellectual figure to emerge from the Amsterdam Jewish community. His father was a Portuguese Marrano who settled in Amsterdam, resumed the Jewish faith and became a prosperous and respected member of the Sephardi congregation. The young Baruch received a thorough Jewish education, including an excellent knowledge of Hebrew – in fact he compiled a new manual of Hebrew grammar.

The young Spinoza's studies ranged far beyond Jewish scholarship. He mastered the Dutch, Portuguese, Spanish and Latin languages, and was schooled in the scientific and philosophical works of Galileo, Kepler and Descartes. He became interested in the science of optics and took up the skilled profession of lens-making.

Spinoza's powerful and rational intellect focussed on the fundamental problems of religion and biblical interpretation – the most challenging but dangerous field of philosophical enquiry open to a man of his time. The core of the metaphysical and ethical system he evolved was the concept of a universal God, immanent in all creation. (He was later called 'a God-intoxicated man'.) Yet he regarded conventional religion, whether Jewish or Christian, as the product of men's minds; the Scriptures as a human document, not divine revelation; and the existence of an immortal soul apart from the body as an unproved thesis. He therefore helped to usher in the rationalist outlook of 18th-century Europe and the Higher Criticism of Bible scholarship in the 19th century. It is hardly surprising however, that his heterodox views should have provoked the anger and dismay of the Amsterdam rabbis. In 1656, at the age of twenty-four, he was formally excommunicated, and remained an outcast from the Jewish community for the rest of his life. He died in poverty at the age of forty-four. He had been consumptive from childhood, and this condition must have been aggravated by the fine dust from the lenses he ground and polished in order to eke out a modest livelihood.

In retrospect, the leaders of the Sephardi community have been criticized as narrow-minded and rigid for having banished their most gifted son. Yet with their Marrano background it was natural for them to stress the orthodox observance of Judaism, and to reject ideas that would undermine the traditions to which they had returned after so much suffering. Moreover, they must have been afraid to antagonize their Calvinist hosts. It must be remembered that the Jews were an immigrant group without full civic status, which they gained only at the beginning of the 19th century.

Spinoza retired to a village near Leiden and devoted himself to philosophical writings. He lived very simply, refused the offer of friends to give him an annuity and later rejected the chair of philosophy at the University at Heidelberg. His major works were *Philosophical Principles of Descartes* (1663), the *Treatise on Religious and Political Philosophy* (1670) and, above all, the *Ethics* (1677) which contains his doctrine of human happiness and freedom and his description of the right way of life.

His books remained neglected until interest in them was aroused by two great minds at the end of the 18th century, Lessing and Goethe. Since then Spinoza has been studied and admired by philosophers of every shade of thought.

The Return to England
See colour page 182

After the Jews were expelled from England in 1290, no English Jewish community came into existence for nearly 400 years. Before the end of the 16th century a small group of Spanish and Portuguese Marranos had settled in London, and some others were among the merchants of Bristol. Outwardly they were Catholics. One of them, Roderigo Lopes, was physician to Queen Elizabeth I, who had him hanged in 1594 on a charge of being connected with the plot of the hapless Earl of Essex.

The reappearance of open Jewish observance was brought about mainly by the Messianic zeal of one man, Manasseh Ben-Israel, a Sephardi scholar from Amsterdam. The historical context was the Puritan victory in the English Civil War and the appointment of Oliver Cromwell in 1653 as the Lord Protector of Britain.

Manasseh Ben-Israel (1604–67) came from a Portuguese Marrano family in Madeira. Soon after his birth, his father settled in Amsterdam, became openly Jewish, took the name of Joseph Ben-Israel and renamed his two sons Manasseh and Ephraim, after the sons of the Biblical Joseph. Manasseh was an accom-

Manasseh Ben-Israel, an etching by Rembrandt, Holland, 1636

plished scholar and linguist, writing theological works in Hebrew, Spanish and Latin. In 1650 he published *The Hope of Israel* in Latin and Spanish. In it he referred to the supposed discovery of the Lost Ten Tribes in South America. The advent of the millennium (he argued) and with it the redemption of the Jewish people would occur only when the Dispersion had reached all the corners of the earth. The only place left for the completion of this process was England. (Its name in French, 'Angleterre', could be taken to mean 'corner of the earth'.)

The Latin edition was dedicated to the English Parliament and an English translation aroused much interest. Manasseh followed this up by personal contacts and correspondence with a number of influential Englishmen, and then by a 'Humble Address' to the Lord Protector. Cromwell's response was sympathetic. The proposal appealed to him for both religious and economic reasons. Holland was England's chief trading rival. It was generally recognized that the Jews were making a significant contribution to Dutch commercial success, and Cromwell hoped to draw some of the Dutch Jews to England. He put the issue to the Council of State and invited Manasseh Ben-Israel to London to appear personally before the Council.

In London Manasseh encouraged some of the local Marranos to come out into the open as Jews. Together with six of them he signed a petition addressed to the Lord Protector, dated 24 March 1655. The petition boldly described its signatories as 'Hebrews at present residing in this city of London'. It made two requests: permission to conduct Jewish prayer meetings in private homes, and the right to acquire a burial ground outside the city.

Cromwell found the Council of State divided on the question of readmitting the Jews to England. He thereupon convened a Whitehall Conference in December 1655, made up of public figures, clergymen and lawyers. Manasseh Ben-Israel attended the conference at the head of a Jewish delegation. The constitutional experts advised that the expulsion decree of 1290 had been issued under royal prerogative; it did not have the status of a law, the repeal of which would require an act of parliament. However, strong reservations were expressed in the conference – partly from clerical quarters, partly from business interests that were loth to let in Jewish competitors. The opponents stirred up public agitation, and anti-Jewish pamphlets were widely distributed. When Cromwell found that the conference was likely to insist on onerous

conditions and restrictions on the return, he disbanded it.

It was assumed that Cromwell would now feel free to issue his own decree, by virtue of his powers as Lord Protector. But he refrained from doing so, no doubt because the subject had become too controversial. He did, however, give an affirmative reply to the petition of March 1655, thereby enabling the Marranos who were already residing in London to have services in their homes and a burial ground.

Manasseh Ben-Israel stayed on in London for a further year. During this time he published another book, *Vindication of the Jews*, refuting the anti-Jewish pamphlets in circulation. He returned to Amsterdam in the belief that his mission had failed. As a conciliatory gesture, Cromwell granted him an annuity of £100.

To this day the expulsion decree of Edward the Confessor has not been cancelled, nor has there been any formal enactment permitting Jews to return to England and live there; but the question was resolved in the pragmatic English fashion. After Cromwell had assented to the request in the petition of the Marranos, organized Jewish life in Britain was simply allowed to develop again of its own accord.

Important Events

Byzantium (from the 4th century AD)

306–33	Reign of Constantine the Great. Christianity becomes State religion.
313	Edict of Milan – first step towards establishing dominance of Christianity.
325	Church Council of Nicaea calls for 'seclusion and humiliation' of Jews.
330	Constantinople established as new capital.
395	Roman Empire split – separate Byzantine (Eastern) Empire.
361–3	Emperor Julian the Apostate sympathetic to Jews.
529	Code of Justinian – Jews allowed to practise their religion but subject to many disabilities.

Christian Spain

694	Jewish religion outlawed in Visigoth kingdom of Spain.
711	Moorish invasion
1085	Christian capture of Toledo marks turning-point in 'Reconquista'.
1165–73(?)	Travels of Benjamin of Tudela.
1263	Nachmanides appears in Barcelona Disputation.
1391	Outbreaks of mob violence against Spanish Jews.
1413–14	Tortosa Disputation.
1478	Start of Spanish Inquisition.
1492	Expulsion Decree of Ferdinand and Isabella.
1497	Forced baptism of Jews in Portugal.

Ashkenaz

c.800	Beginning of Jewish settlement in Franco-Germany.
1066	Jews reach England with William the Conqueror.
1096	First Crusade. Massacre of Rhineland Jews.
1144	Norwich blood-libel.
1190	Massacre of York Jews.
1236	Frederick II introduces *servi camerae* concept.
1242	Burning of Talmud in Paris.
1290	Jews expelled from England.
1306	First expulsion from France.
1348–50	Black Death massacres.
1394	Second expulsion from France.
1517	Martin Luther launches Reformation.

Renaissance Italy

1492	Expulsion of Jews from Sicily.
1516	Ghetto initiated in Venice.
1541	Expulsion of Jews from kingdom of Naples.
1553	Burning of Talmud.
1555	Pope Paul IV orders compulsory ghettos.
1797–99	French revolutionary army abolishes ghettos.

17th-century Amsterdam

1590	First Marrano group arrives.
1620	Jewish refugees from Germany.
1656	Spinoza excommunicated.

The Return to England

1655	Manasseh Ben-Israel heads delegation to London.
1656	Cromwell receives Jewish petition.

Chapter Thirteen

The Lands of Islam

The Covenant of Omar

The Prophet Mohammed fled from Mecca in AD 622, established himself at Medina, gained control of the Arabian peninsula and sent his armies marching northwards on their campaign of conquest. Though the local Jewish tribes had helped him in his earlier struggles, they later denied their support and refused to accept the new religion he had founded. It was then, in the first fervour of the new faith, that Mohammed turned against them, destroyed them, and thus eliminated Jewish life in most of Arabia.

As the victorious Arabs swept through the Near East and North Africa, it became impractical to put to the sword those segments of the conquered population that did not embrace Islam. Under the Caliph Omar and his successors a more rational policy evolved for regulating the status of non-Moslem communities. The position of the Jewish minority in the new areas under Moslem rule had much in common with that under Byzantine rule. One essential difference was that Islam was not impregnated like Christianity with a strong religious bias against Judaism and Jews. Ironically, another difference was that the status of the Christians under Islam was equated with that of the Jews. Both were 'peoples of the book' with a guaranteed but inferior status as *dhimmi* – that is, protected non-Moslems. As a rule they enjoyed religious freedom, communal autonomy, protection of life and property, exemption from military service and the right to administer justice in civil and family matters where only members of their own communities were involved. On the other hand, a number of restrictions were imposed on them in accordance with the injunction in the Koran that non-Moslems should be clearly separated from the faithful. They had to pay a special poll tax; they were not allowed to erect new places of worship; they could not have Moslem employees or slaves; they were not eligible for official posts; they were forbidden to accept Moslem converts, or to prevent the conversion of their own people to Islam; they could not build their homes higher than those of their Moslem neighbours; they were not permitted to ride on horses or mules; and they could not bear arms. They also had to wear distinctive items of dress, that could take the form of special hats, mantles, sashes

The Arab Empire
See illustration right

After Mohammed's death in AD 632, his first successor (Caliph) was his father-in-law and closest disciple Abu Bakr (Caliph 632–4), who brought the whole of the Arabian peninsula under Moslem rule.

Omar, the second Caliph (634–44) was the great Arab empire-builder. His generals conquered the whole Persian empire and wrested Palestine, Syria and Egypt from Byzantium.

In the ninety years of the Ummayad dynasty (661–730), with its capital in Damascus, the empire expanded dramatically. To the East it was extended as far as India. To the West it took North Africa from the Byzantine Empire and Spain from the Visigoth kingdom. By 750, when another dynasty of Arab Caliphs, the Abbasids, came into power, the Moslem Empire stretched in a great arc from Spain along North Africa and through the Near East to Central Asia.

In 762 the Abbasids established their capital at Baghdad on the Tigris river, in Mesopotamia. It remained the centre of the Moslem world for five centuries, until Abbasid rule was swept away in 1258 by the hordes of Mongol horsemen invading from the steppes of Asia.

The Caliph Omar takes Jerusalem
See colour pages 110 and 111

In AD 638 Jerusalem surrendered to a Moslem army, and Byzantine rule

Muslim horsemen riding to battle. From the Maqamat *of Al-Harini, Baghdad 1237.*

over the Holy Land came to an end. The Caliph Omar entered the city on foot, as a mark of respect. The Christian population was left unharmed and permitted to maintain their holy places and practise their religion. Omar annulled the Christian ban on Jews residing in Jerusalem, and allowed them to return to it for the first time in centuries. The ban was reimposed on Jews, and extended to Moslems as well, when the Crusader assault in 1099 regained the Holy City for Christianity.

Saadiah Gaon
See colour page 182

Saadiah ben-Joseph (882–942), the most illustrious Jewish scholar of his day, was the head of the Talmudic

or badges. As a rule the colour yellow was specified for Jews and blue for Christians.

These rights and disabilities concerning Christians and Jews were collated in the so-called Covenant of Omar, which remained the basic Islamic directive on the subject until modern times. As the name suggests, the Covenant is by tradition attributed to Omar, the second Caliph. He is remembered in Jewish history as a humane and friendly ruler. It is unlikely that Omar was the author of the long list of discriminations against non-Moslems set out in the Covenant. They were probably introduced at different times by various later Caliphs.

The Covenant of Omar was not uniformly carried out in practice. In some places restrictions were modified or ignored for economic reasons or through the personal influence on the rulers of Jewish financiers, advisers or physicians. On the other hand, there were fanatical regimes that trampled on the rights and protection promised to the Jews by the Covenant.

Under Moslem rule, far-reaching changes occurred in Jewish

academy of Sura in Babylonia. As such, he was one of the two Geonim (spiritual leaders) of the community, the other being the head of the academy of Pumbedita.

The official head of the Babylonian community was the hereditary ex-ilarch or *Resh Galuta* ('Prince of the Exile'), who lived in regal style and enjoyed a position of honour at the Caliph's court.

In 930 Saadiah Gaon attacked the incumbent exilarch, David ben-Zakkai, on the grounds that he failed to observe the Halachah (religious law) properly, exploited his office for personal gain and followed an ex-travagant life-style. The fierce con-troversy between the two went on for years and virtually tore the Baby-lonian community apart. Eventually, in 937, a reconciliation was brought about between the two, and given formal public expression in a cere-mony before the Caliph. In the picture the Exilarch is seated at the Caliph's left, as a mark of honour, and Saadiah Gaon, in white robes, is standing in front of the throne.

Even before the Moslem conquest in the 7th century the Babylonian community had become the leading centre of Jewish learning, and had produced the monumental Baby-lonian Talmud. After the conquest the community attained unques-tioned primacy among Diaspora Jewry. Apart from its scholarly pre-eminence, it was now situated at the centre of an Arab empire that ex-tended as far as Spain and included the bulk of the Jewish people. The Exilarch was regarded as the unoffi-cial king of all the Jews.

The Babylonian Talmud was ge-nerally accepted elsewhere as the basis for religious observance and daily life. The Responsa (rulings) of the Geonim were treated as binding in matters of faith (except by the Karaite sect after the 8th century). As the power of the Abbasid caliphate in Baghdad declined, in the 11th and 12th centuries, so did the dominance of the Babylonian centre in Jewish life. Other centres in the Arab Dias-pora rose to spiritual autonomy in Egypt, North Africa and Spain.

economic life. As in Christian lands, Jews were squeezed out of agriculture by onerous taxes and by the restrictions on using slave labour. There was a movement away from rural areas into the growing Arab cities. The overwhelming majority of Jews became townspeople, traders and artisans inhabiting crowded Jewish quarters. Such urban communities developed in a number of Arab cities. The most important was Baghdad in Iraq. Others were Basra, also in Iraq; Fostat (old Cairo) and Alexandria in Egypt; Kairouan and Fez in North Africa; Cordoba and Toledo in Moslem Spain. As merchants, Jews had the great advantage gained by their international ties with their fellow-Jews along the trade routes, both through the sprawling Arab empire and in Christian Europe.

On the social and cultural level, there was a steady adaptation to Arab life. Jews spoke Arabic as their daily tongue, wore Arab dress and Arabized their names. Jewish scholars started absorbing and then contributing to Arabic literature, philosophy and medicine. This intellectual co-operation reached its zenith in the Golden Age in Moorish Spain.

Moorish Spain

In AD 711 the Arab commander Tarik led his Moorish army from North Africa across the Straits of Gibraltar into Spain. (The name Gibraltar is derived from the Arabic Jebel-al-Tarik – the Mount of Tarik.) The Moors were a mixed force of Arabs and Berbers, the indigenous North African tribes that had been conquered by the Arabs and converted to Islam. Tarik swept through the Visigoth kingdom without serious resistance and occupied the whole of the Iberian peninsula up to the Pyrenees, except for a Christian enclave that held out in the rugged terrain of north-east Spain. The new Moslem regime evolved into an Ummayad Caliphate independent of Baghdad, with its capital in Cordoba.

Moorish Spain became the most cultured and enlightened country in Europe. Under its auspices Spanish Jewry rapidly revived. Its numbers were swelled by Conversos who reverted to Judaism, by exiles returning from North Africa, and by new settlers from other parts of the Moslem empire. Though they bore a heavy tax burden, the Jews shared in the rising level of prosperity and spread into a wide range of occupations. *See colour pages 250 and 251.*

Contact was resumed with the Geonim and academies in Babylonia, and local schools of learning started attracting scholars from else-where, notably that at Lucena, south of Cordoba, headed by the eminent scholar Isaac Alfasi. By the 10th century, a cultural renaissance was under way that would make Spain a major centre of Jewish scholarship, as the pre-eminence of Babylonian Jewry de-clined. During the next two centuries the Spanish Jews were to demonstrate a remarkable capacity to develop their own religious and spiritual heritage while at the same time taking a conspicuous part in the Arab life and culture of the country. This era was ushered in by the

174

(continued on page 176)

Hisdai ibn-Shaprut

See colour page 183

This mural, painted in the style of mediaeval Spanish illuminated manuscripts, shows scenes from the career of the Jewish leader Hisdai ibn-Shaprut (915–75) from Cordoba in Spain. He is shown conducting political negotiations with the envoys of the German Emperor; entertaining a gathering of scholars, poets and friends in his garden; receiving an epistle from the king of the Khazars; and as a judge and champion of his own people.

Hisdai grew up in Cordoba, the capital of the Caliphate in Spain, where his father was a wealthy and learned member of the Jewish community. Hisdai became an eminent physician and the chief diplomatic adviser to the Caliph. As such he received and dealt with the envoys from the emperor of Byzantium in 944 and the emperor of Germany in 953. In 958, as a Jew serving a Moslem ruler, he performed the remarkable political feat of mediating between the warring Christian kings of Leon and Navarre, and bringing them to Cordoba to negotiate and sign a peace treaty. While he was visiting Navarre on this mission, the Queen invoked his medical skills to cure her corpulent grandson of his weight problem – which he did successfully.

Hisdai used his prestige and influence to help his fellow-Jews in other lands. Two letters have recently come to light in which he addressed himself to the Byzantine emperor and empress, pleading for greater religious freedom to be given to the Jews in their domain. Inside the Spanish community Hisdai promoted the cause of Jewish learning. He sponsored a Talmudic academy in Cordoba, and he invited the noted Hebrew grammarian Menachem ben-Saruk from Tortosa in Christian Spain to come to Cordoba as his secretary. While occupying this position ben-Saruk published a famous Hebrew dictionary.

Hisdai heard stories of a Jewish kingdom of the Khazars on the shores of the Caspian Sea, ruled by a king

A model of Joseph, king of the Khazars, dictating to his scribe a letter addressed to Hisdai ibn Shaprut of Cordoba, in Spain.

called Joseph. When he questioned the envoys of the Byzantine emperor, they gave some confirmation to the story. Hisdai thereupon wrote Joseph a letter '...to ascertain...whether there indeed exists a place where the dispersed of Israel have retained a remnant of royal power, and where the Gentiles do not govern and oppress them.' He explained in the letter that the existence of such a kingdom would be of great importance as the absence of Jewish independence anywhere was regarded as evidence that the Jews were no longer the chosen people of God. The letter was carried by Jewish merchants via Hungary and Russia. Years later Hisdai received a reply from Joseph confirming the fact of his Jewish kingdom. The authenticity of these two letters has been the subject of much scholarly controversy.

The Khazar Kingdom

See above

Joseph was a 10th-century king of the Khazars, a nomadic people of Turkish stock in the region of the Volga River, the Caucasus and the Black Sea. There was a persistent legend

that Khazaria, which existed as a separate state from AD 740, was ruled by a Jewish king. Certainly the country had a large Jewish population, for the 10th-century Arab writer Mukaddasi says of Khazaria, 'sheep, honey and Jews exist in large quantities in that land'. According to the Arab historian al-Masudi, writing around 943, the Khazar king became a Jew between 786 and 809.

When word reached Hisdai ibn-Shaprut in Cordoba, Spain, that there was a Jewish king in Khazaria and that his name was Joseph, Hisdai determined to write to him to find out if it was true. Joseph's reply, which reached Cordoba in 955, recounts that his ancestor Bulan converted to Judaism around AD 740 with 4,000 of his nobles; and that Bulan's successor, Obadiah, invited to the country 'Jewish sages from all places who explained to him the Torah'. Synagogues and schools were founded throughout the country, although Christianity and Islam were still widespread.

In all probability only the king and his nobles converted to Judaism. The country's supreme court was a model commanding figure of Hisdai ibn-Shaprut, leading physician and counsellor to the Caliphate.

Early in the 11th century the Caliphate that had ruled over Moorish Spain collapsed, and was succeeded by a score or so of petty principalities, each under its own Arab or Berber ruler. The local Jewish communities were not seriously affected by this fragmentation, and continued to enjoy freedom and opportunities for advancement. Many of the minor Moslem kings relied heavily on Jewish political and financial advisers, emissaries, tax officials and physicians. In their internal affairs Jewish communities were dominated by an *élite* of courtiers, and there was a growing demand for a more democratic, elected structure of communal leadership. The outstanding Jewish personality of the time was Samuel ha-Nagid, the Vizier (chief minister) and military commander of the Berber kingdom of Granada from 1030 to 1056.

With the fragmentation of Moorish Spain the Christian Reconquista gained momentum. In 1085 the army of Castile won a notable victory in the capture of Toledo, that had been the old Visigoth capital before the Arab invasion.

The alarmed Moslem rulers appealed for help to their brethren in North Africa. That region was dominated at the time by the fanatical Berber sect of the Almoravids. They swept into Spain and defeated a Christian army in 1086, thereby halting the Reconquista for the next half-century. At first these extremist newcomers were hostile to the Jews, but in time they became attuned to the easy-going atmosphere of Andalusia and took up the benign attitude of the Ummayad Caliphate towards the Jews.

In 1146 renewed Christian pressure was countered by a fresh eruption of Berber tribesmen, this time belonging to the even more fanatical Moslem sect of the Almohads from the Atlas mountain area of Morocco. (This was one of the periodic upsurges of fundamentalist fervour that have occurred throughout the history of Islam, the most recent being that headed by the Ayatollah Khomeini in Iran.) The Almohad dynasty ruled Moslem Spain for the next century. It felt no indulgence for Jewish life and proceeded to eliminate it as far as possible. The practice of Judaism was banned; the synagogues and Talmudic academies were closed down; and the Jews were ordered to become Moslems. A great number of Jews streamed across the line into what had become, by a strange reversal, the relative security of Christian Spain. The Jews were discovering that in the Moslem-Christian struggle for the mastery of Spain, there was a shifting balance of tolerance as well as territory.

of religious tolerance. It comprised seven judges, two of whom were Jews, two Christians, two Moslems and one pagan. Joseph was nevertheless a resolute if rough defender of his faith. When he heard that Byzantine Jews had been forced to accept baptism, he exacted revenge from the Christians living in his country.

In Joseph's reply to Hisdai's letter he refers to raids which began around 913 on the kingdom of Khazaria from Russia along the Volga River. These attacks intensified in 965, and the kingdom did not survive for long after that, although there is some doubt about the date of its disappearance.

There is considerable difference of scholarly opinion concerning the authenticity of the Khazar Correspondence, as the exchange of letters between Joseph and Hisdai is called. Joseph's reply exists in two versions, one long, one short, and the existence of these texts has been known since the 16th century. From the style of the Hebrew in which they are written, it is evident that these letters could not possibly have been 16th-century forgeries. Moreover, there is a marked difference in style between the Hebrew of Hisdai's letter and that of Joseph's, and the language of the latter strongly suggests that it was composed in a non-Arabic-speaking environment. A number of scholars agree that these two texts were probably composed in the 11th century on the basis of an original letter written by the Khazarian king and no longer extant.

Samuel ha-Nagid

See colour pages 180 and 181

The brilliant and many-sided career of Samuel ibn-Nagrela marks the highest achievement of a Jew in Moorish Spain. He was born in Cordoba and received an all-round education not only in Jewish studies but also in Arabic and the Koran. Fleeing from Cordoba when it was occupied by fanatical Berber troops in 1013, he reached Granada in the south, and entered the service of its Berber ruler. According to the 12th-century Jewish historian Abraham

Above *The Exilarch in Babylonia and his court. A lawsuit is being heard at the gate of his residence.*

Right *The Byzantine Emperors and the Jews. The Emperior Justinian I (AD 527–565) seated on his throne.*

Benjamin de Tudela

We know of the journey made by Benjamin bar Jona (1), a merchant of Tudela in Spain, because he wrote an account of it.

(2). Rome. 'Rabbi Jechiel, who is the grandson of Rabbi Nathan, has the entry of the Pope's palace, for he is the steward of his house and all he hath.'

(3). Thebes. '2,000 Jews. They are the most skilful artificers in silk and purple cloth through all Greece.'

(4). Constantinople. 'No Jews live in the city, for they have been placed behind an inlet of the sea.'

(5). Jerusalem. When he reached Eretz Israel, he found Jerusalem still in the hands of the Christians.

4

5

(6). Baghdad. 'Over all the Jews of Babylon is
Daniel the son of Hisdai, who is styled our
Lord, the head of the captivity of all Israel.
(He possesses a book of pedigrees going back as
far as David, King of Israel.)'

(7). He travelled from the Persian Gulf to Aden,
and from there to Egypt.

(8). And, his journey ended, Benjamin bar
Yona sat down to write the full account of his
journey as we have it today.

6

7

8

Samuel ha-Nagid (AD 993–1055), vizier of the Moslem Berber kingdom of Granada in Spain, composing a farewell poem to his son Jehoseph on the eve of battle.

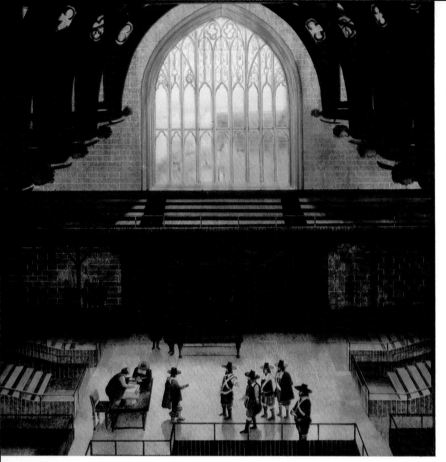

Left *The Return to England. A scene in Whitehall, London, during the negotiations for the return of the Jews to England.*

Right *Hisdai ibn-Shaprut. A mural painted in the style of mediaeval Spanish illuminated manuscripts.*

Overleaf *The Cairo Genizah. A diorama showing men gaining access by ladder to the Cairo Genizah.*

Below right *Kairouan. A diorama of a betrothal ceremony.*

Below *Saadiah Gaon and the Exilarch at the palace of the Caliph in Baghdad.*

Egypt and the Maghreb

ibn-Daud, Samuel had opened a spice-shop in Malaga, where he was asked by a maid-servant to write some letters for her master, an official at the court. The latter was so impressed by Samuel's elegant Arabic style that he obtained an appointment for him on the royal staff. His rise was meteoric. He became Vizier to the kingdom, and dominated its domestic, foreign and military affairs for nearly thirty years until his death. The Jews of Spain conferred on him the title of Nagid (Governor), to indicate their acceptance of him as their national leader.

For nearly the whole of his period of office, Samuel was involved in the military campaigns of Granada against the rival Moslem kingdom of Seville. The Jewish world took great pride in his victories, while the Islamic world became accustomed to the spectacle of a Moslem army being led into battle by a devout Jew.

His military experiences figured prominently in the large body of poetry he left. The epic battle poems among them are unique in Jewish literature. With all the manifold burdens of politics and war, this remarkably versatile man remained actively engaged in Jewish scholarship, and carried on a correspondence on legal and religious problems with eminent scholars in Babylonia and elsewhere. He endowed Talmudic academies in Spain and scholarships for poor students and carried out works of philanthropy among the Jews throughout the Moslem world, even including the supply of olive oil to the synagogues in Jerusalem. It is apparent from his poetry that in spite of his dazzling personal success he regarded Jewish life in exile as one of suffering and longed for the return of his people to Zion.

Samuel's awareness of the uncertainties of Jewish Diaspora life was tragically confirmed. He died on a military campaign in 1056, and his son Jehoseph succeeded him as head of the Granada Jewish community. Eleven years later, in 1066, there were Moslem riots against the Jews in which Jehoseph was murdered, together with some 1,500 local Jews.

Egypt

The Arab conquest of Egypt in AD 640 found there a relatively small and undistinguished Jewish community that had not recovered its vigour since the crushing of the great Alexandrian community in the 2nd century AD. Under Moslem rule the community concentrated mainly in the new city of Fostat (not far from the site of the later capital, Cairo), and became to a great extent Arabized in its language and mode of living. Little was known about Egyptian Jewish life during the ensuing centuries until it was illuminated by the documents found in the Cairo *Genizah* at the end of the 19th century.

The prestige of Cairo in the Jewish world was raised by the great Maimonides, who lived and worked there from 1165 to his death in 1204. The office of the Nagid, the head of Egyptian Jewry, was made a hereditary one occupied by the descendants of Maimonides.

In the 19th century the community grew and prospered as Western influence permeated Egypt. Wealthy and influential families emerged, such as the Cattauis and the Mosseris. Many of the Egyptian Jews had British, French, Italian or other foreign nationality and under the Capitulation treaties were protected persons enjoying certain privileges and immunities.

By the Second World War the community numbered 90,000 and was on the whole prosperous and well-established. But its position was undermined by the growth of Egyptian nationalism accompanied by pan-Arab, anti-Western and anti-Zionist feelings. With the proclamation of Israel's independence in 1948, and the Arab-Israel war that followed, the Egyptian authorities turned on the local Jews. Some of them were imprisoned, and some emigrated. By 1955, the number had dropped to 30,000.

After the Sinai campaign of 1956 the Nasser regime revenged itself for its defeat by putting 3,000 Jews in detention camps, expelling a number of others and taking over many Jewish businesses. The new Exodus from Egypt continued until the whole community had gone except for a few hundred elderly people. That ended the history of a community that went back to the 6th century BC.

The Maghreb

The Arab word *Maghreb* means 'west', and was applied to the adjoining North African states of Tunisia, Algeria and Morocco. Jewish settlements sprang up along this coast in ancient times, while Rome and Carthage vied for mastery of the western Mediterranean. When the area was conquered by the Arabs in the 7th century its Christian inhabitants were for the most part either eliminated or converted, but the Jewish communities were left intact and remained autonomous in their own internal affairs. During this period the leading centre of Jewish scholarship in the west was in Kairouan.

(continued on page 188)

Maimonides

'I dwell in Fostat and the Sultan resides in Cairo. These two places are two sabbath days journey from each other. My duties to the Sultan are very heavy. I am obliged to visit him daily early in the morning.'

'I am now getting hungry but I find the antechambers filled with people – Gentiles and Jews, important persons and common people, judges and bailiffs, friend and foe – a mixed multitude awaiting my return. I dismount from my animal, wash my hands, and request them to be patient until I have eaten a quick meal. I then go to attend to them, writing directions and prescriptions for their ailments. Patients come and go until night.'

'I have to lie down from sheer tiredness and when night falls I am so exhausted I can hardly speak.'

'When the Sultan, or one of his sons, or one of his concubines, is indisposed, I do not leave Cairo. Most of the day I am in the palace. If any of the royal officials fall sick, I have also to attend them.'

'As a consequence none of my fellow-Jews can get to speak with me or have a private interview except on the Sabbath. Then most of the congregation come to me after prayers. I instruct them as to what is to be done during the week. We stay together a little until noon when they leave. Some return and read with me again after the afternoon service until the evening prayer. This is how I spend my days.'

The above excerpts are from a letter in Judeo-Arabic written by Maimonides to his translator Samuel ibn-Tibbon. Ibn-Tibbon, a scholar and physician, translated Maimonides's *Guide of the Perplexed* and other of his works from Arabic into Hebrew under the author's guidance. (Four generations of the remarkable Tibbon family produced a large body of Hebrew translations and commentaries and played an important part in the development of the Hebrew language in the mediaeval period.)

Maimonides is the Greek form of the name of Moses ben-Maimon (1135–1204). In Hebrew writing he is generally known by the abbreviation *Rambam*. He was the intellectual giant of mediaeval Jewry and one of the most influential Jewish scholars and philosophers of all time. As a boy, he received an intensive education in Jewish and Arabic studies in his native city of Cordoba in Spain. When he was thirteen, his family fled from the persecution of the fanatical Moslem regime of the Almohads. After some years in Morocco and a short sojourn in Crusader Palestine, they settled in old Cairo. In due course Maimonides became the leader of the Egyptian community. He devoted himself to two parallel careers – medicine and Talmudic scholarship – with dazzling achievements in both.

As the excerpts from his letter to ibn-Tibbon show, he served as court physician to the Sultan of Egypt, while at the same time his medical reputation and skills drew a throng of patients, both Moslems and Jews, to his home. He produced a dozen treatises in Arabic on medical topics as varied as the art of healing, the therapeutic use of drugs, poisons, asthma, haemorrhoids and sexual hygiene. Some of these works were translated into Latin and used in European schools of medicine for centuries.

Maimonides's attitude to the physician's vocation strikes a relevant note today. He valued the human relationship between doctor and patient as much as professional skill,

and wrote: 'Medical practice is no knitting and weaving and the labour of hands, but it must be inspired with soul, filled with understanding and equipped with the gift of keen observation.'

It is astonishing that with all the demands upon his time and energy of his medical work and communal leadership, Maimonides should have been a major figure in the history of Jewish learning. While still a teenager he had published commentaries on the Hebrew calendar, the 613 precepts of Judaism and the technical terminology of logic. His monumental work was the Mishneh Torah, a codification of the whole of the Talmud, on which he spent the ten years from 1170 to 1180. Making use of both the Jerusalem and the Babylonian Talmuds and the commentaries of the Babylonian, Spanish and Franco-German scholars, he systematically clarified all the traditional doctrines. The Mishneh Torah was accepted as a standard work in the centuries to come.

As Maimonides's fame spread he was more and more consulted by Jewish communities all over the Moslem Diaspora, as far afield as Yemen in Arabia. In giving them guidance, he insisted on a rational approach to the problems of Jewish life and disapproved of the Messianic expectations that swept through the Jewish world. 'Let no one think', he wrote firmly, 'that in the days of the Messiah any of the laws of the world will be abolished or any innovation of nature will be introduced. The world will follow its normal course.'

Maimonides's epoch-making work of philosophy was the *Guide of the Perplexed*, produced in Arabic in 1190 when he was fifty-five years old. It set out to reconcile the tenets of Judaism with the logic and reason of Aristotle as transmuted through the leading Moslem philosophers. The work was widely-read and respected by Moslem scholars, and in Latin translation by Christian theologians. But the Hebrew translation stirred up fierce controversy in Jewish circles. It was bitterly attacked and even banned by Orthodox rabbis and

scholars, especially in the Franco-German region, on the ground that Maimonides's stress on reason as a source of religious belief would undermine the foundations of faith. The work was stoutly defended by other scholars (including its translator Samuel ibn-Tibbon) who formed the camp of the 'rationalists'. Only a century later was the study of philosophical works permitted by rabbinical authority, and even then it was confined to men over the age of twenty-five. In a later age Maimonides came to be accepted without reservation as one of the pillars of rabbinic Judaism, and revered as 'the second Moses'.

The Cairo Genizah
See colour page 184

Genizah is the Hebrew word for a hidden place used by synagogues from ancient times to store sacred writings and vessels that were no longer in use but could not be destroyed because they were regarded as holy. Such places have been found in the walls, foundations or attics of old synagogues in various countries. As a rule the documents have mouldered away in the course of time. A dramatic exception has been the Genizah found in the attic of the Ezra synagogue in Cairo, built in 882 on the site of a disused Coptic Church bought by the Jewish community. The attic is located at the end of the women's gallery, but it has no doors or windows, and can be entered only through an opening that is reached by ladder. The vast hoard of written material, accumulated over many centuries, was preserved in darkness in the dry desert air of Cairo, just as the Dead Sea Scrolls were preserved in Judean caves under similar conditions. Entry into the Genizah was discouraged because of the local superstition that any disturbance of its contents would bring ill-fortune to the congregation. Nevertheless, from time to time pages or fragments were stolen and sold to Western visitors. The first case on record was in 1763. It was only in 1896 that material was

The Jewish population suffered under the repressive Almohad regime in the 12th and 13th centuries. The communities were revitalized by the influx of Spanish Jews after the 1391 pogroms in Christian Spain and the Expulsion of 1492. The Sephardi newcomers soon dominated Jewish business and intellectual life in the Maghreb. They developed the type of communal leadership that had been the custom in Spain – through wealthy and important families.

In the 16th century the Ottoman empire expanded to take in the whole of North Africa – except Morocco, which remained independent under its own sultan. But the Ottoman overlord was remote and lax, and in practice the Bey of Algiers and the Bey of Tunis were rulers in their own right. In the 17th and 18th centuries all three Maghreb countries, together with Tripolitania (later part of Libya) were known as the Barbary Coast – that is, the coast of the Berbers. They were the indigenous tribes who had been conquered by the Arabs but remained the majority of the inhabitants. The chief source of revenue for these countries was piracy, preying on the Mediterranean sea-lanes with rich rewards in booty, slaves, and ransom for captives. The Jews were frequent travellers through these waters on business, family or religious affairs. The communities were constantly called upon to find ransom money for captured Jews – a *mitzvah*, religious duty. It was not until the beginning of the 19th century that the navies of the Western powers were able to suppress the Barbary corsair industry and secure the Mediterranean route.

With the local Moslem regimes in the Maghreb weakened and the Ottoman empire disintegrating, the power vacuum was filled by France. In 1830 French forces occupied Algeria and made it a province of Metropolitan France. French citizenship was conferred on all the Algerian Jews under the so-called Crémieux Decree of 1870 (Adolphe Crémieux was at the time the Minister of Justice in Paris and also the leader of French Jewry). Tunisia was made a French protectorate in 1881. The kingdom of Morocco came under French administration in 1912.

The Maghreb Jewish communities felt increasingly insecure in the face of rising Arab nationalism. They welcomed French control and their educated classes eagerly imbibed the French language and culture. The Moslem population resented the Jewish identification with their French masters. In Algeria there were a number of anti-Jewish outbreaks in the last two decades of the 19th century. In the Algerian Revolt that started in 1954, the Jews found themselves caught in the middle, and their emigration increased. After Algerian independence was conceded by General de Gaulle there was a general exodus of the Jewish population, mainly to France, which they were entitled to enter as citizens. Conditions in Morocco and Tunisia were less tense and hostile for the Jewish community, but here too emigration was stimulated by a feeling of insecurity. After Israel was established in 1948 the bulk of the Jewish population of Morocco and Tunisia settled there.

removed on a large scale and examined. This came about by chance.

Two Scottish ladies on a visit to Egypt were offered some old pages of Hebrew writing and bought them as a souvenir. On their return they showed the fragments to the renowned Jewish scholar, Dr Solomon Schechter, at Cambridge University (later President of the Jewish Theological Seminary in New York). To his amazement, he found himself looking at a portion of a manuscript copy in Hebrew of the Apocryphal work *Ecclesiasticus* or *The Wisdom of Ben Sirach*. Originally written in Hebrew in the 2nd century BC, it was known till then only in a Greek translation. The document was traced to the Genizah. With the support of Cambridge University and the consent of the synagogue, Schechter spent some months in Cairo extracting and crating documents for study at Cambridge. They comprised about 100,000 manuscript pages. A similar quantity was later removed by other scholars and acquired by large libraries around the world. The task of deciphering and analyzing this great mass of old documents has not yet been completed.

Among the finds of special historical and literary value are most of the Ben-Sirach Hebrew manuscript; portions of the Greek translation of the Hebrew Bible made in the 2nd century AD by Aquila (a Roman scholar who converted to Christianity and then to Judaism, and studied under the great Rabbi Akiba); many old liturgical poems ('piyyutim') previously unknown, composed in Eretz Israel, Babylonia and Spain; and a great number of letters and papers relating to important individuals. The oldest dated document is from 750 AD.

The Genizah material has thrown light on Jewish life in Egypt and Palestine during the period between the Arab Conquest in the 7th century and the Crusaders in the 12th century. Much valuable information has also been gleaned about the Karaite movement.

Kairouan

See colour page 183

The betrothal ceremony of the daughter of Nissim, the rabbi of Kairouan in North Africa, to Jehoseph, son of Samuel ha-Nagid, the chief minister in the Moslem kingdom of Granada in Spain and the acknowledged leader of Spanish Jewry in the 11th century. The union cemented the close ties that existed between Kairouan, an important centre of Jewish commerce and learning in what is today Tunisia, and the Jewish community of Spain. In 1056 Jehoseph succeeded his father as Nagid or head of Granada Jewry, but eleven years later he was killed in anti-Jewish riots. The following year Kairouan was destroyed by Bedouin tribes.

The Ottoman Empire

In the 11th century, nomadic Turkish tribes that had embraced Islam started moving into the Middle East and overran portions of the Byzantine and Arab empires. One of these tribes was the Ottoman Turks, so called after their leader Othman. In the 13th century they occupied an area of Asia Minor south of the Bosphorus and established a state ruled by a sultan. The small Jewish community in this area had been there from Roman times and were known as Romaniots. They were treated much better by the Turks than they had been by their previous Byzantine masters. They were permitted to practise their religion, carry on trade and own property without restriction. On the other hand, they were required to pay a poll-tax that the community leaders were responsible for collecting.

In the 15th and 16th centuries the Ottoman domain expanded by conquest in every direction to form a huge empire. The crucial event was the fall of Constantinople in 1453 – the death-knell of the Byzantine empire. The Ottoman empire reached its zenith under its greatest sultan, Suleiman the Magnificent (1520–66). It then extended into the Balkans and Eastern Europe, including Hungary and Rumania; over the whole Arab Middle East; and along North Africa from Egypt to Algeria.

The Holy Land was now under Turkish rule, as well as a great proportion of Diaspora Jewry – probably more than a million in number. In practice the Empire was loosely organized, and in most countries the local rulers were free to carry out their own domestic policies, while acknowledging Turkish suzerainty. That explains the variations in the treatment of the Jewish communities in different regions of the empire.

In Palestine the Ottoman regime came as a relief from Mamluk repression. The Jewish community increased by immigration and its conditions improved. Safad in the Galilee became of particular importance for its scholarship. Suleiman rebuilt the walls that still surround the Old City of Jerusalem.

In the heartland of the empire (roughly corresponding to modern Turkey) the major Jewish centres were in Constantinople, Salonika, Adrianople and Smyrna (Izmir). The Jews of this region enjoyed economic prosperity and a high level of culture, and developed important Talmudic academies. The first printing press in the Ottoman empire was a Hebrew one in Constantinople. The Islamic restrictions under the Covenant of Omar were not strictly observed, though Jews were required to wear yellow headgear to distinguish them from the Moslems, who wore green. There was little social or cultural integration with the Turkish majority, and no 'Judeo-Turkish' language evolved on the analogy of Judeo-Arabic, Ladino (Judeo-Spanish) or Yiddish (Judeo-German).

Eager to increase the beneficial economic activities of their Jewish subjects, the Ottoman rulers encouraged the immigration of Jews from Christian lands where they were oppressed or had been expelled. In the mediaeval period there was a steady settlement of Jewish refugees from Germany, France, Hungary and elsewhere. The most significant influx occurred after the 1492 expulsions from Spain and the exodus from Portugal in 1497. The Ottoman Sultan at the time, Bayazid II, is reported to have remarked that the Spanish king, Ferdinand (who together with his queen Isabella had signed the expulsion decree), could not be very intelligent since he was impoverishing his country and enriching that of the Sultan. A score of Sephardi (Spanish) congregations sprang up in mainland Turkey, while small numbers of the Spanish and Portuguese immigrants settled in Safad and Jerusalem, and in Egypt. Some of them were Marranos who reverted to Judaism.

Jewish medical skill (especially that of the Spanish Jews) was so highly regarded that it was customary for the Sultans to have Jewish physicians. As a mark of distinction they were allowed to wear tall red hats instead of the yellow headgear of their fellow-Jews. It was also common for Jews to hold high public office in the financial services, as directors of customs, tax officials and advisers.

The most influential Jewish figure in the history of the Ottoman empire was Don Joseph Nasi (1524–79), a Portuguese Marrano who settled in Constantinople at the age of thirty and returned to Judaism. He rose to be the diplomatic counsellor and friend of the powerful Sultan Selim II, who made him Duke of Naxos and the Cyclades.

The status of the non-Moslem religious communities was governed by the 'millet system'. Each creed had internal autonomy in the religious, administrative, legal, educational and taxation spheres. The religious leaders were the official heads of the respective millets and were responsible for them to the authorities.

Before the 19th century there was no centralized leadership for all of Turkish Jewry. Jewish communities were organized according to their places of origin. By the end of the 16th century there were over forty such congregations in Constantinople alone. In the 17th and 18th centuries the communal separation started breaking down. The original Jewish settlers, the Ashkenazim and the Sephardim, mingled and intermarried.

In the 19th century the structure of the millets was re-organized and given a detailed legislative framework. The official regulations were approved for the Greeks in 1862, the Armenians in 1863 and the Jews in 1865.

Internal and external trade in Turkey was concentrated mainly in the hands of these three non-Moslem minorities. On the whole the Jews were favoured by the authorities, since the Christian communities were regarded as sympathetic to the European Christian powers, of whose intentions the Ottoman rulers were always suspicious.

The Ottoman empire was at the time a land of opportunity for commerce. It was spread over three continents and lay astride the

(continued on page 192)

Donna Gracia Mendes

Donna Gracia Mendes (1510–69) was the aunt of the famous Don Joseph Nasi and the outstanding Jewess of her day. She is seen here holding a meeting in her Constantinople home in the year 1556, to discuss a possible Jewish boycott against the Italian port of Ancona, where twenty-five Portuguese Marranos have been burnt at the stake as heretics.

It was natural for Donna Gracia to react strongly to this grim event. She had been born into a distinguished Marrano family in Lisbon, and had grown up with the Spanish name of Beatrice de Luna. She married Francisco Mendes, also a Marrano, a wealthy banker and dealer in gems.

A meeting in Donna Gracia's home in Constantinople.

When her husband died, she left Portugal with her family, including her young nephew who later became Don Joseph Nasi, and settled in Antwerp, where her husband's brother and partner was running the branch of the family business. From this base she organized the flights and helped the resettlement of Marrano families fleeing from the Inquisition in Portugal. Moving to Venice in 1545, she carried on with this task until she was denounced by her own sister as a secret Jew, and flung into prison. Her nephew obtained her release through diplomatic intervention.

Undaunted, Donna Gracia went to Ferrara in Italy where she openly professed Judaism and renounced her Spanish name. The Ferrara Spanish Bible published in 1553 was dedicated to her. In that year she finally settled in Constantinople, where she was joined by her nephew and took him into partnership in her business enterprises. She was associated with him in the lease from the Ottoman authorities in 1558 of the ruined town of Tiberias and its surrounding land on the Sea of Galilee, for the purpose of settling Jews in the Holy Land. Don Joseph Nasi had the tumbledown walls restored, took initial steps to introduce wool and silk industries, and wrote to Marrano refugee groups in Italy, inviting them to settle in Tiberias; but apparently nothing came of this project.

In Constantinople Donna Gracia became a patron of Jewish religious life, promoting the establishment of new synagogues and yeshivas there and in Salonika. She was so renowned in the Jewish community by this time that everyone referred to her simply as 'La Senora' or, in Hebrew, *Ha-Geveret*. One of the Constantinople synagogues bore this name in her honour.

*Ottoman Jewish Types. Three
pictures of 16th-century Ottoman
Jews from the book of travels by N.
Nikolai,* Les Quatre Premiers Livres
des navigations et pérégrinations
orientales, *Lyons 1568: a rich Jewess
from Adrianople; a Jewish physician;
a Jewish cloth merchant from
Constantinople.*

main international trade routes. As merchants the Jews had certain advantages. They had widespread contacts in Christian Europe, and the immigrants had brought in with them the main European languages – German, French, Spanish and Italian. In addition, Jewish merchants and shippers were long established in the principal Moslem ports and cities in the Empire outside Turkey, including Alexandria, Cairo, Damascus, Baghdad and Basra on the Persian Gulf.

The Ottoman Jews developed certain types of industry. The most important was the weaving and dyeing of woollen cloth and the manufacture of the finished garments. The major centre for this textile industry was Salonika. The community there even paid part of its taxes in kind by the supply of blue uniforms to the Ottoman army. Jews were predominant in the leather trade, especially in the tanning of hides and skins. They were also expert wine-makers and traditional craftsmen in gold and silver jewellery. The Spanish Jews brought with them an expertise in the manufacture of fire-arms that contributed to Ottoman military strength.

As a rule Jewish commerce, industry and finance were conducted as tight family businesses. When branches were opened in different centres, members of the family were usually sent to run them.

The 'Capitulations' were the treaty concessions made in favour of

foreign nationals living in the Ottoman empire. They included a variety of privileges, legal immunities and tax exemptions. The first such treaty was signed with the republic of Venice in 1521, followed in due course by all the European powers. Large numbers of Christian and Jewish residents managed to acquire or buy 'berats' (certificates of nationality) from foreign consuls, and thus became protected persons of the European states concerned. As the Ottoman empire weakened, the Capitulations became a wedge for European intervention in internal Ottoman affairs.

From the late 17th century onwards the Ottoman empire declined. Its borders were steadily pushed back by the wars with Russia and by successful rebellions in vassal states. Internal decay set in. The rulers and pashas lived in indolence and extravagance. The civil service and provincial governors became corrupt, with bribery an accepted practice of government. The armed forces were disaffected, and some Sultans were dependent on the 'janissaries', the Turkish conscript militia. The maximum taxes were squeezed from subject peoples.

The position of the Jews deteriorated in the context of the general decline. The religious tolerance for non-Moslems, that had been such a redeeming feature of the earlier Ottoman regime, started to be less evident. There were no longer Jews with positions of influence at the

(continued on page 196)

Salonika

Salonika (or Thessalonike, the official name) is a large port-city in Macedonia, the north-eastern province of Greece. Its early importance lay in its location at the head of the Aegean Sea and on the Via Egnatia, the main highway from Rome to Asia.

Founded in 315 BC by the king of Macedon, it passed through many hands: Roman, Byzantine, Crusader, Greek, Venetian, Ottoman (from 1430) and again Greek (from 1912).

One constant factor in the history of the city was its Jewish community, which went back over twenty centuries. St Paul preached in its synagogue on three consecutive Sabbaths in the year AD 50 during his second missionary journey, and later wrote to Jewish and pagan converts to Christianity in his two Epistles to the Thessalonians (i.e. Salonikans).

From the beginning of the Turkish occupation, the old Romaniot Jewish community was swelled by refugees from elsewhere. The first immigrant group came from Bavaria in 1470. Since these German Jews had little in common with their local brethren, they set up a separate Ashkenazi community. In the 15th and 16th centuries there was a stream of newcomers who had been expelled from Spain, France, Italy and Portugal. They set up their own Sephardi synagogues and congregations. These were named after their places of origin. By the middle of the 17th

Salonika Jews being deported to the Nazi death camps in March 1943.

century there were about 30,000 Jews, organized in thirty congregations. They united in 1680 and set up a joint council of three rabbis elected for life, and seven lay leaders.

The Jewish population inhabited three different quarters – the original one at the port, next to the city wall; the more elegant quarter of the *Francos* (Europeans); and the quarter of the Greek Jews.

In the 16th and 17th centuries Salonika was an important centre of Talmudic learning, and attracted a number of prominent rabbis and

scholars. It was also renowned for the study of the Kabbalah. The most dramatic event in the life of the community during this period was the arrival in the town of the false messiah Shabbetai Zevi. At first he was welcomed, but when he proclaimed himself as the Messiah, the local rabbis took a collective decision to expel him. After his death Salonika was the religious centre for a group of his followers who copied his example by converting to Islam. They were called *Doenmeh*, from the Turkish word for 'apostates'. It was the upheaval caused by the Shabbetai Zevi affair that induced the different congregations in the town to unite.

The Salonika community pursued a remarkable variety of occupations. The well-to-do merchant class was engaged in the export trade in grain, textiles, cotton, wool and silk. The major industry lay in the weaving and dyeing of woollen cloth and the manufacture of woollen garments. Jews had their own guilds of skilled craftsmen, such as the goldsmiths, silversmiths and jewellers. At the port the stevedores and porters were largely Jewish. There were also Jewish workers in the gold and silver mines further inland, and in tobacco growing. Since about half the population of Salonika was Jewish from about the 17th century, the port and most of the business area were closed on the Sabbath and on Jewish festivals.

In 1900 the Jewish community numbered 80,000. It was already declining owing to the general stagnation in the Ottoman Empire. There was a steady stream of emigration, especially of younger people, to Palestine, the United States and Western Europe. By the outbreak of the Second World War the Jews constituted only a fifth of the city's population.

On 9 April 1941, the first German panzer columns rolled into Salonika. In the opening phase of the Nazi occupation Jewish adult males were sent to forced labour camps, where many of them died of malaria and malnutrition. Jewish businesses and

property were confiscated; the Nuremberg race laws were applied; the contents of Jewish libraries and the ritual objects from synagogues were crated and sent to Germany. The centuries-old cemetery, with its graves, was turned into a quarry, and the tombstones used for building stones, and for lining army latrines.

By the beginning of 1943, the 'final solution' stage of the Holocaust programme got under way in Nazi-occupied Europe. Between 14 March and 7 August, 43,880 of the Salonika Jews were transported in nineteen train convoys to the death-camps of Auschwitz and Birkenau. A small number managed to escape to the countryside and to Athens, and survived. When the war was over a remnant returned to find their homes occupied, their property looted, and all but two out of nineteen synagogues destroyed. They started to pick up their lives in the ruins of what had been a sturdy and creative community for over 2,000 years.

Sublime Porte, as the Sultan's court was called. Jewish economic and intellectual activity failed to maintain the levels that had been reached in the previous century. The community was shaken by the meteoric rise in the 17th century of the false messiah Shabbetai Zevi from Smyrna, and the shattering anti-climax when he saved himself by converting to Islam.

Blood-libel charges crept in from Christian Europe and reached a dramatic high point in the notorious Damascus Affair of 1840. A number of leading Syrian Jews were imprisoned and tortured (two of them to death) on charges of having murdered two missing persons and used their blood for ritual purposes on the Passover. The prisoners were released through the efforts of a delegation of Western Jewish leaders headed by Sir Moses Montefiore of England and including Adolphe Crémieux of France. The delegation obtained from the Sultan a decree making the blood-libel a punishable offence. Though blood-libel charges recurred after that in a number of places in the Ottoman empire, their consequences were usually averted through European Jewish intervention and judicious bribery.

It was in this, the 19th century, that a shrunken and bankrupt Ottoman empire was called 'the sick man of Europe'. The statesmen of the leading Western powers (including Disraeli in England) were much concerned with the Eastern Question, which in essence meant propping up the Ottoman empire in order to preserve the European status quo and to block the southward expansion of Czarist Russia. Unable to repay its huge debt to Western countries, the Empire became financially dependent on its creditors; it had to permit the duty-free import of European goods and the taking over of public utilities by European capital. The result was a further erosion in the local economy, and therefore in the situation of the Jewish community.

By the Young Turk Revolution of 1908 the despotic Sultan Abdul Hamid II was overthrown and a republic proclaimed. Six years later the First World War broke out. It led to the defeat and dissolution of the Ottoman empire and the emergence of the present-day Turkish Republic, shorn of imperial possessions.

Yemen

Yemen occupies the south-western corner of the Arabian Peninsula, at the entrance to the Red Sea. It is a poor and primitive land, with the coastal strip barren and humid and the interior a high plateau cut up by mountain ranges. The beginnings of Jewish settlement here are shrouded in legend. One romantic but unlikely version is that the first Jewish sojourners arrived after the famous visit of the Queen of Sheba to King Solomon, in the 10th century BC (the country of Sheba or Saba was in the Red Sea area). The Yemenite Jews believe that their community began after the destruction of Solomon's Temple at the beginning of the 6th century BC, and that their sufferings were God's punishment for their failure to join the Return in the days of Ezra and

The Jews of San'a

See above *A street in San'a c. 1900. In the background is Jebel Nuqum, a mountain 7,790 feet high and seven miles east of San'a.*

The earliest Jewish settlement in this area was on its slope, where the remains of two ancient synagogues still exist. A Jewish quarter was later established next to the city gate, on the site of the present bazaar of the coppersmiths. The San'a community remained the centre of Jewish life in Yemen.

In 1678 the Imam exiled the whole community, together with most of the Jews in other parts of Yemen, to Mawza in the desolate coastal region. Many of them died of hunger and disease. A year or so later they were allowed to return, but not to their

(continued on page 199)

previous homes. Instead, they were assigned to another Jewish quarter (*Qa al-Yhud*) outside the city wall.

Disaster again struck the community in 1905, when the Imam revolted against Ottoman rule, and conducted a prolonged siege of San'a. It was reported that only 150 Jews were left alive when the city fell. One traveller wrote: 'During the siege entire families died stolidly in the street, or turning their faces to the wall in their own house, for it was little use begging when bread was sold at thirty shillings per pound.'

In 1948 there were an estimated 6,000 Jews in San'a. They were permitted to leave for Israel on payment to the Imam of a large ransom.

Maimonides's letter to Yemen

The letter arose out of a major crisis in the history of the Yemenite Jewish community. About 1160, the Imam (ruler) of Yemen launched a religious persecution of the Jews, giving them a choice between conversion to Islam or death. Some of them did convert. The rest clutched desperately at the words of a pseudo-messiah who told them that these tribulations were sent by God to mark the advent of the Messianic Age.

The head of Yemenite Jewry, Rabbi Jacob ben-Nathanel al-Fayyummi, turned for help to Maimonides in Old Cairo. The great scholar and communal leader used his behind-the-scenes influence, as the personal physician to the Egyptian sultan, to alleviate the burdens on his brethren in Yemen. His reply to Rabbi Jacob was designed to strengthen their faith and hope. It was deliberately written in simple terms, and he requested that it be distributed to every local community in Yemen. In his letter Maimonides told them to reject the pseudo-messiah.

The letter had a powerful impact on the Yemenite Jews, who stood firm until the crisis passed. They showed their gratitude by introducing into the Kaddish, the prayer recited by mourners, which is a plea for 'the life of our teacher Moses ben-Maimon' (Maimonides). This unique tribute had until then been reserved only for the Exilarch in Babylonia, who was regarded as the representative of all the Jews in Islamic lands.

ובורא עולם במדת רחמים יזכור אותנו ואתכם לקבץ גלויות נחלתו וחברו, לחזות בנעם ה' ולבקר בהיכלו, ויוציאנו מגיא הצלמות אשר הושיבנו בו

(מתוך "אגרת תימן" להרמב"ם)

Messianism in Yemen

There is a Yemenite Jewish folk-tale about a devout woman who lived alone. At night she slept tied to a rope with its end fastened to the leg of a donkey standing at her door. She relied on the donkey to awaken her when he heard the approaching footsteps of the Messiah.

The naive story illustrates how deep-rooted in the consciousness of the Yemenite Jews was the belief in the Messianic advent that would redeem them from their hard life and degrading status, and lead them back to the Promised Land. That fervent hope explains why the Yemenite community was even more vulnerable to Messianic movements than Jews in other countries.

The appearance of the pseudo-messiah Shabbetai Zevi in the late 17th century, which caused an upheaval throughout the Jewish world, swept the Yemenite community into a state of ecstasy. They paid dearly for their expectations in bloody persecution by the Imam of Yemen.

In the second half of the 19th century at least three pseudo-messiahs appeared in Yemen. The most serious of them was Judah ben-Shalom of San'a, who called himself by the Arab name of Shukr Kuhail. In a dream he was called upon by the prophet Elijah to be the Redeemer. During 1862–4 he travelled through the villages and gained a large following from among both Jews and Moslems. The Imam had him murdered, but his followers believed he would return. Three years later they accepted for a while an impostor who proclaimed himself the resurrected Shukr. He even took Shukr's widow to himself and had a son by her.

Another pseudo-messiah, Joseph ben-Abdallah, appeared in Yemen in 1893, and gained wide influence until he was exposed as a confidence man, out to make money from Jewish hopes. By that time the migration of Yemenite Jews to Eretz Israel was already on the increase. The promised Return had in fact begun, and would be completed by 1950.

Nehemiah. Another possibility is that among the earliest settlers there may have been soldiers from the Judean contingent attached by Herod the Great to the Roman expedition that came to conquer South Arabia in 25 BC. Jewish traders may also have taken root in Yemen at that time. What seems certain is that by the 3rd century AD a community of some thousands of Jews had already been living in Yemen for a long time. They sent the bodies of some of the leaders by camel caravan all the way to the catacomb of Beit She'arim in the valley of Jezreel for burial.

The country was then called the kingdom of Himyar. Some of its rulers and a number of its tribesmen were converted to Judaism. According to Arab traditions, one such Jewish ruler was Ab Karib As'ad (AD 385–420). The last king of Himyar, Dhu Nuwas, was also a convert to Judaism, and took the name of Joseph. At that time there was increasing pressure on Himyar from Abyssinia across the Red Sea. The Abyssinians had adopted Christianity and been drawn into the orbit of the Byzantine empire. With Byzantine support they invaded Yemen in 525 AD. Its Jewish king was killed and the kingdom of Himyar came to an end.

After its conquest by the Moslems in the 7th century, the country went into a decline. The Jews were granted freedom to practise their religion, but were subjected to degrading restrictions and at times persecuted. They lived in segregated quarters in the towns, or were scattered in small groups among the mountain villages. They were not allowed to ride a camel or a horse, and had to dismount even from a donkey when a Moslem passed. The men were forbidden to wear coloured robes, or to carry the mediaeval weapons of the area, flintlock guns and ornamental daggers. Ironically, these weapons were brought to the Jews for repair and adornment, for they were considered the best craftsmen in Yemen. They excelled as goldsmiths and silver-smiths, jewellers, basket-weavers, potters, carpenters, blacksmiths, gunsmiths and saddlers. The embroidered garments made by the Yemenite Jewish women were unique.

These craftsmen earned a humble living, as did the petty traders and peddlers. With few exceptions, the Yemenite Jews were in-credibly poor and ill-nourished, and were kept down to a subsistence level by the poll taxes collected for the Imam (the ruler) and the protection money paid to local Arab notables who were their 'patrons'.

During century after century of existence under these wretched conditions the Yemenite Jews never faltered in their faith, or gave up their hope of an ultimate return to Zion. Every boy was educated in a religious elementary school, where he studied the sacred books. Since there was seldom more than one book to a class, the pupils could read it just as well upside-down or sideways as right-side-up. Amidst surroundings of squalor they kept their homes and persons clean and hygienic, in strict accordance with the religious precepts. Their love of beauty was expressed in their delicate handiwork and in poetry, songs and folk-dances. Somehow their culture remained closer in spirit to

Jews of Yemen, South Arabia, being taken to Israel in 'Operation Magic Carpet', 1950.

Yemenite immigrants in 1950

When the news reached the Jews in Yemen that the State of Israel had come into existence, thousands of them started making their way to Aden, the British-held port on the Red Sea. They arrived exhausted, hungry and carrying their sick, after weeks of trekking by foot or on

donkeys for hundreds of miles across mountains and desert. Their possessions had been stripped from them by hostile tribes, but they clung fiercely to their holy Scrolls of the Law.

The British authorities in Aden collected them in an abandoned military camp, where they were fed and cared for by Jewish welfare agencies. Since Egypt had blockaded the normal sea route through the Suez

Canal, the Israel Government and the Jewish Agency decided to fly these refugees to Israel by an air shuttle service, using stripped-down American Skymasters. Each plane was loaded with more than the normal complement of passengers, which was possible since the average weight of the adults was only 86 lbs and their possessions were meagre. They had never seen a plane before, and simply

that of their biblical ancestors than that of more sophisticated communities elsewhere.

While they lived in a backwater, out of the mainstream of Jewish life, contact was maintained with the centres of learning and commerce in Babylonia, Egypt and North Africa. Some mediaeval correspondence survives with the capital of Yemen, San'a, where its largest Jewish community lived.

The lot of the Jews, the only non-Moslem community in Yemen, became more precarious when the country was annexed to the Ottoman Empire in the 16th century. There were recurrent attempts by the native population, who belonged to the dissident Zaydi sect of Islam, to throw off the shaky Turkish rule. As usual in such conflicts, the Jews were distrusted by both sides and suffered from both.

One point of contact with this remote community was through the port of Aden, where Jewish merchants were engaged in the transit trade between the Near East and India. The route acquired world importance with the opening of the Suez Canal in 1869. The Western presence greatly increased in the strategic Red Sea area, and Yemen (including its Jews) were drawn into closer touch with the outside world. At that time there were about 80,000 Jews in Yemen, most of them living in the rural villages.

When the Yemenite Jews heard of the Zionist settlement that started in Palestine in the 1880s, they were convinced that this was the beginning of God's redemption, and began to make their way in increasing numbers to the Holy Land.

When Yemen became independent in 1911, all the anti-Jewish measures from the past were enforced with greater severity. The worst blow was an ordinance of 1925 requiring Jewish orphans to be brought up as Moslems. As many of them as possible were adopted into Jewish families or smuggled out of the country.

These events further stimulated the urge to leave the country for Eretz Israel. By 1948, when the State of Israel was proclaimed, some 18,000 Yemenite Jews had already settled there. In 1949–50 almost the whole of the remaining community was evacuated from Aden to Israel by an airlift, in what was known as 'Operation Magic Carpet'.

The Yemenites were in certain respects unlike any other immigrant group. They had emerged into the modern world from conditions more primitive than those prevailing in any other Diaspora community. They had never known beds, chairs or toilets, electric light or piped water, a railway, a bus or an aeroplane. Yet by common consent, these hardworking pious people of slender build are one of the most appealing of Jewish communities. Their artistic traditions in the dance, jewellery and embroidery have made a distinctive contribution to Israeli culture.

related their journey to the biblical promise that the Lord would bring them to Israel 'on eagles' wings' (*Exod. 19:4*).

By the end of the airborne operation in September 1950, nearly 49,000 Yemenite Jews had been brought to Israel in 430 flights. Operation Magic Carpet had transported to the homeland the whole of a Diaspora community whose beginnings were shrouded in the mists of antiquity.

Important Events

The Covenant of Omar

624–8	Mohammed destroys Jewish tribes in Arabia.
638	Caliph Omar takes Jerusalem.
762	Beginning of events leading to Karaite schism.
930	Dispute between Saadiah Gaon and Exilarch.
1099	Jerusalem captured by Crusaders.

Moorish Spain

711	Moorish conquest of Spain.
955	Supposed letter from Joseph king of the Khazars to Hisdai ibn Shaprut.
1026(?)	Samuel ha-Nagid, vizier of Granada, appointed Nagid.
1146	Start of fanatical Almohad rule.

Egypt and the Maghreb
Egypt

640	Arab Conquest.
1165	Maimonides settles in Cairo.
1896	Schechter recovers material from Cairo Genizah
From 1948	Exodus of Egyptian community.

Maghreb

1830	French occupation of Algeria.
1881	Tunisia made French protectorate.
1912	Morocco under French administration.
1950–62	Most Maghreb Jews emigrate.

Ottoman Empire

1453	Constantinople captured by Ottoman Turks.
From 1492	Influx of Spanish and Portuguese refugees.
1562	Lease of Tiberias to Don Joseph Nasi.
1840	Damascus blood-libel case.

Yemen

c. 1172	Maimonides letter to Yemen.
1678	Jews exiled to coast.
1949–50	Operation Magic Carpet – airlift to Israel.

Chapter Fourteen

Eastern European Jewry

Poland – Lithuania: 15th–18th centuries

Eastern European Jewry started as an offshoot from the communities of mediaeval Germany and other countries of the Balkans.

In the early 13th century the towns of Poland were devastated by the incursions of the Mongols and Tartars, Central Asian peoples that had conquered Russia. The country was left with a backward and stagnant economy, based on landowning nobles and their serfs. The Polish princes became eager to create a new urban middle class that would revive both trade and skilled crafts. For this purpose they gave inducements to Germans to repopulate Polish towns. Among the new settlers were a number of Jews escaping persecution in Germany and seeking a more secure life in Eastern Europe. They were promised protection and economic opportunities by the Polish rulers.

The basic document determining their status was the Charter of Privileges granted to them in 1264 by Prince Boleslav the Pious of Kalisz. After Poland became a united country in the 14th century its outstanding sovereign, Casimir the Great, reconfirmed and amplified the Charter of Boleslav. The Polish Jews were therefore under royal protection, on the analogy of the *servi camerae regis* ('servants of the royal chamber') in the German empire. In 1388 a similar charter was granted by the Grand Duke of Lithuania to the Jews settling in his country (later united with Poland). The Lithuanian charter expressly granted the Jews full economic equality with Christians.

However, life for the Jewish immigrants in Poland was far from tranquil. There were sporadic outbreaks of violence against them. The Polish clergy was hostile, and pressed for repeal of the privileges granted to Jews in royal charters. Some of the nobles too were infected by anti-semitism. In the towns the Christian merchants and craftsmen, organized into exclusive guilds on the German model, resented Jewish competition and in a number of cases succeeded in expelling or excluding Jews. Blood-libel charges cropped up in several places. Nevertheless, the Jews were on the whole much better off in Poland-Lithuania than they were in mediaeval Western Europe, where the

(continued on page 205)

Jewish Occupations in Poland–Lithuania

The original Jewish immigrants from Germany into Poland were mainly money-lenders. They were welcomed by the Polish princes for the financial services they could render in reviving the towns. With the growth in numbers of the Jewish community, its occupations became diversified. A large number moved into all branches of trade, particularly in horses and cattle, cloth, dyes, liquor and spices. Through their links with their brethren in the Ottoman empire, Polish Jewish merchants played an important part in the overland transit trade between the Eastern Mediterranean and Western Europe. Jews served as collectors of taxes and customs dues. They obtained concessions for working salt-mines and forests. They were involved in agricultural life as the stewards or lessees of large estates by the 'arenda' system. In this capacity they helped to open up and settle tracts of undeveloped land in Eastern Poland, which included the western district of the Ukraine and White Russia. They were engaged in a wide range of crafts and service occupations, as doctors and chemists, goldsmiths, tailors, shoemakers, furriers, weavers, butchers and soapmakers. The poorest class of Jews were the peddlers.

Six illustrations in the style of 16th-century woodcuts, showing some Jewish occupations of that period: a physician, a silversmith, a tailor, a shoemaker, a furrier, and a weaver.

A model of a Jewish innkeeper being threatened by a village crowd.

appalling tale of repression, massacres, and expulsions was unfolding itself. Thus a steady stream of migration continued into Eastern Europe. By the end of the 15th century there were about sixty organized Jewish communities in Poland-Lithuania, containing a total of up to 30,000 souls. By the middle of the 17th century, the figure had risen to half a million.

The contacts of the Jews with non-Jews were confined to what was required for earning a living. Apart from that, the Jews lived an intense and inward-looking life of their own. With an unprecedented degree of self-government, they formed self-contained communities regulated by the Halachah. There was little integration with Polish society or culture. Among themselves the Jews continued to speak only Yiddish. Their intellectual life focused on Jewish religious learning and study. Numerous yeshivot sprang up and some of them gained a fame for their scholarship. In brief, Polish Jewry was a world within a world. By the 16th century it was a main centre of Ashkenazi life and culture. In spite of the pressures in the cities from Christian businessmen, the economic base of Polish Jewry was relatively broad and secure, and

The Arenda System

A Jewish tax-collector was a familiar feature of Polish village life. It tended to be an unpopular and sometimes dangerous occupation.

The Polish term 'arenda' covered leases and concessions of various kinds: landed property, mills, salt mines, timber forests, inns, tax-farming, collection of customs and the minting of the coinage. Some of these rights were derived from royal prerogatives. In the 15th and 16th centuries Jews obtained such concessions on a large scale in Eastern Poland, which was still 'an open frontier' for economic development. The lands leased to Jews might include villages and small towns. In Western Poland the nobles demanded these profitable concessions

A 17th-century painted jug with the head of a Jewish 'arenda' and a mocking inscription below it.

Above *Bogdan Chmielnicki, the leader of the Cossacks.*

was expanding eastward. The general picture was that of a vital and buoyant society.

That picture changed drastically for the worse from 1648, a watershed year in the history of Polish Jewry. A great part of the community was overrun and destroyed in the massacres that accompanied the Cossack revolt against Polish rule led by Bogdan Chmielnicki. Thirty years of war followed between Poland and its neighbours, with invasions by Swedish, Russian, and Tartar armies. From then on the kingdom of Poland started disintegrating, until it was partitioned among neighbouring powers towards the end of the 18th century. During this period the Jewish community became poorer, and subject to greater intolerance and restriction. Internally, it was shaken by the aftermath of the Shabbetai Zevi messianic movement, and the bitter conflict provoked by the rise of Chassidism.

(continued on page 209)

of the Crown for themselves and exerted strong pressure against their grant to Jews. At the same time, Jewish lessees, agents and managers were extensively used by nobles to run their agricultural estates

The 'agricultural arenda' in the countryside became an important aspect of the Jewish occupational structure in Poland. The Council of the Four Lands, the representative body of Polish Jewry, laid down regulations to obviate unfair competition between Jews in this field. The attitude of Jewish estate managers towards the peasants was often more humane than that of the landowning Polish nobility. Nevertheless, the Jews became the natural target for the resentment of the downtrodden serfs.

The Chmielnicki Massacres

In 1648 the Cossack leader Chmielnicki headed an uprising in the Ukraine against Polish rule. The Jews, identified with the Polish regime and blamed for economic difficulties, became the main victims of the violence. Bands of Cossack horsemen devastated and looted hundreds of communities and butchered tens of thousands of defenceless Jews. These occurrences sent a shock of horror through the Jewish world. In later Russian history, the Cossack on his horse would remain for Jews a savage and recurrent symbol of the pogrom.

Cracow and Kasimierz

Cracow was an important trading centre on the Vistula river and the capital of the Polish kingdom until 1609.

By 1350 there was an organized

community of German Jews in Cracow with a synagogue and a cemetery. It encountered fierce hostility from the Christian townspeople, many of them also settlers from Germany. The reasons were resentment at Jewish competition reinforced by a religious bigotry that was fanned by the clergy. Throughout the 15th century the community was harassed by periodic outbreaks of violence, commercial restrictions and money extortion. In 1495 the king ordered all the Cracow Jews to move into nearby Kasimierz, where they were permitted to live and work unhindered. It had been founded as a separate town in the 14th century. Increased by refugees from Bohemia-Moravia, Germany, Italy, Spain and Portugal, Kasimierz became predominantly Jewish. Some of the Jews living there continued to own shops and property in Cracow, in the face of every effort to prevent them from doing so.

Below *Cracow and the adjacent town of Kazimierz. A 15th-century engraving.*

A street scene in the Jewish quarter of Lublin, Poland. The wall-poster in the street refers to a ban on the followers of the false messiah, Shabbetai Zevi.

The Jews of Lublin

Lublin was one of a number of Polish cities that in the early period of Jewish migration from Germany obtained from the Crown the privilege *de non tolerandis Judaeis* – that is, the right to ban Jews. In the 14th century a community nevertheless started on a site outside the city wall called 'Jewish Sands', placed at its disposal by the sympathetic Polish king, Casimir the Great. Later a Jewish quarter developed inside the city in the vicinity of the castle, by royal permission. This was a typical example of the way Polish kings encouraged Jewish settlement while the Christian city burghers resisted it.

Lublin was the venue of a great annual spring fair, where the Council of the Four Lands, the representative body of Polish Jewry, met regularly. In the 18th century the local community became a centre of the Chassidic movement and produced one of its leading 'Tzaddikim', Jacob Isaac, 'the Seer of Lublin'.

'Private Townships'

Above right A drawing of the town of Rzeszow, 1762.

The town of Rzeszow in south-east Poland was located on the estates belonging to the Lubomirsky princes. In 1657 they issued a charter of privileges to the Jews to induce more of them to settle in the town. In due course a thriving Jewish community developed that formed seventy-five per cent of the inhabitants. It became well known for its cloth, the work of its goldsmiths and its engraved seals. Some of the latter were supplied to the imperial courts in Moscow and Stockholm.

Rzeszow was one of hundreds of 'private townships' belonging to Polish noblemen, as distinct from the 'royal townships' – the older Polish cities established under charter from the Crown. For the most part, these newer towns were situated in the territories in eastern and southeastern Poland and eastern Lithuania that were opened up to development in the 16th–17th century. Large tracts of land had been acquired by aristocratic Polish families. They offered favourable conditions to Jews to settle in the local towns, in order to promote commerce and industry. Many Jews were attracted by the fresh opportunities proffered to them, and the relief from the pressures of Gentile merchants and craftsmen in the older cities. A number of these 'private townships' became predominantly Jewish, and in some cases wholly so. They also served as centres for Jews scattered in villages in the surrounding countryside as innkeepers, estate agents and other occupations under the arenda system.

Settlement in these private townships brought about a general shift of the Jewish population from Western to Eastern Poland.

In 1662 a proposal put before the Sejm (the Polish parliament) to expel the Jews from the country was defeated by nobles who had an interest in protecting the Jewish population living on their estates.

The Czars and the Jews

When Czarist Russia swallowed up most of Poland towards the end of the 18th century, she took over a million Polish Jews. It was for her an unwelcome acquisition. Since the days of Ivan the Terrible in the 15th century, Russia had firmly hung out a 'No Jew Wanted' sign. Requests from Polish-Jewish merchants for permission to come in, even for a temporary sojourn, were rejected. When Catherine the Great (ruled 1762–96) mounted the throne of Russia, she demonstrated her urge to westernize the country by issuing an imperial decree permitting foreigners to travel or live there. But the document expressly added the phrase 'except for Jews'. Now, after the dismemberment of Poland, the Czars found themselves ruling over the largest Jewish minority of any country in the world. It was the same Catherine, otherwise proud of her enlightened image, who in 1795 decreed the confinement of the Jews to the Pale of Settlement – that is, to the annexed Polish territories – and debarred them from moving into the rest of Russia.

Throughout the 19th and early 20th century the Jews of Russia were caught up in the wider struggle between liberalism and reaction. There were interludes when Catherine and her successors seemed willing to accept reforms and to bring their backward semi-Oriental realm into the modern age. But such tendencies were invariably crushed by an alignment of reactionary forces. The autocratic Czarist regime feared the revolutionary ideas spread by Napoleon's armies and they used the apparatus of a police state to resist change. The main pillar of the status quo was the Russian Orthodox Church, with its vast congregation of ignorant and superstitious serfs and its Byzantine legacy of anti-Jewish doctrines. The 19th century also saw the emergence of an emotional Slav nationalism that invoked an idealized Russian folk-past and spurned the liberal and democratic concepts in Western Europe.

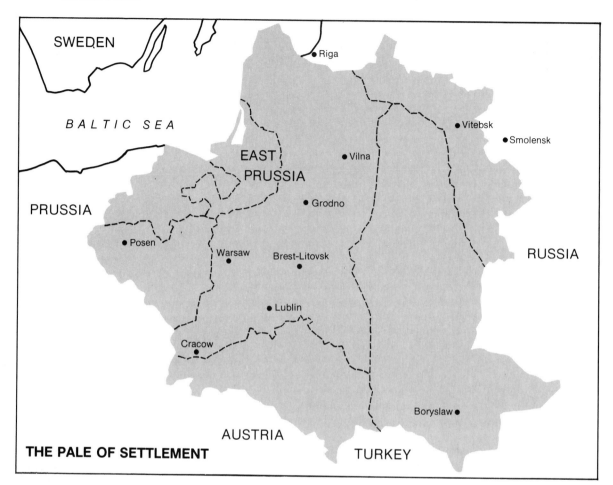

THE PALE OF SETTLEMENT

This was the background to the erratic Jewish policy of the Czars. The overall objective was to break down the separate identity of the Jews and 'amalgamate' them with the rest of the Russian population. This aim was sought at times by relaxing restrictions on the Jews, but more often by harsh coercion. Both approaches were self-defeating. Czarist 'Liberalism' stopped far short of real emancipation; while Czarist repression simply reinforced the barriers between Jews and Russians.

These conflicting trends could impinge on policy in the same reign, as was the case with Catherine's grandson Alexander I (ruled 1801–25). The young and handsome Czar had been given a progressive education at the insistence of his grandmother, and at the beginning was filled with reforming zeal. One of his first projects was to alleviate the hardships of the Jews, and to help them integrate into Russian life. A committee set up to study the problem raised Jewish hopes by proposing relief from certain disabilities. But in 1804 Alexander dashed these hopes with a statute that became known as the Constitution of the Jews. It had some well-meaning features. Russian

The Pale of Settlement

The Pale of Settlement, to which the Russian Jews were confined, covered the Polish territories annexed by Russia in the partitions of 1772, 1793 and 1795. ('Pale' is the accepted English equivalent for the Russian term 'Cheta'. It is an old English word for an enclosed area, and in the late mediaeval period was used to denote the districts of Ireland and of France that came under the jurisdiction of England.)

The Pale of Settlement was 386,000 square miles (a million square kilometres) in extent. So vast was the land mass of the Russian empire that the Pale represented only four per cent of its area. It stretched from the Baltic Sea to the Black Sea, through Lithuania, White Russia, the

Ukraine and Bessarabia.

At the Congress of Vienna in 1815, after the Napoleonic wars, the Duchy of Warsaw was made a small semi-independent Polish kingdom under the suzerainty of the Russian Czars. Not long afterwards this so-called 'Congress Poland' was absorbed into Russia, adding 200,000 Jews to those already in the Pale. Poland would not re-emerge as an independent country until 1918, at the end of the First World War.

The Russian census of 1897 provides an interesting statistical analysis of Jewish life in the Pale of Settlement at the end of the 19th century. In spite of the large-scale emigration from 1882 onwards, there were nearly five million Jews in the Pale, forming eleven per cent of its general population. Among the other national groups were Poles, Russians, Lithuanians, Ukrainians, Moldavians (in Bessarabia) and Germans. Since some eighty per cent of the Jews lived in towns, they formed more than one-third of the urban population of the Pale, and were the majority in many of the smaller towns.

In the second half of the 19th century a certain number of Jews received permits to reside outside the Pale. They included wealthy bankers and business magnates; students admitted to universities under the *numerus clausus* (the tiny percentage of places allotted to Jews); medical personnel; certain categories of skilled craftsmen who were in short supply; and Jewish army conscripts who had completed their twenty-five years of military service. Between 300,000 and 400,000 Jews lived in Russian cities outside the Pale, many of them illegally. As part of the sweeping anti-Jewish measures initiated by the May Laws of 1882, some 200,000 of these Jews were rounded up and deported back to the Pale. In 1891 the total Jewish community of Moscow was expelled in a single night. This was followed by the expulsion of the Jews from Leningrad and several other cities.

The Pale of Settlement was abolished in the Russian Revolution of 1917.

universities and schools would be open to Jews. They would be encouraged to enter productive occupations, especially as farmers in the territories in South Russia recently gained from Turkey. As against that, they were to be driven out of the villages and rural areas and concentrated in the towns – allegedly in the interests of the peasants.

The programme produced little change in practice. The Jews showed no desire to become peasants in distant areas, or to send their children to Russian schools where they would be brain-washed by the Orthodox Church. In resisting expulsion from the villages, they found allies in the Christian estate-owners and squires for whom the Jews provided essential economic services. But the shock of Napoleon's 1812 invasion of Russia, and especially the burning of Moscow, wiped away any liberal impulses in Alexander's unstable mind. He became reactionary and intensely religious, and his attitude to the Jews hardened. At the end of his reign they were suffering greater restrictions than they had at its beginning.

Alexander was succeeded by his brother Nicholas I (ruled 1825–55). He had imbibed none of the ambivalent liberal leanings of Catherine or Alexander I. A rigid military martinet, he sought to force the diverse elements in his realm into one disciplined Russian people, and to stamp out national and religious separation. The brutal way he crushed national uprisings in Poland and Hungary earned him the title of 'the policeman of Europe'.

Nicholas enacted scores of repressive laws against the Jews. They were expelled from the western border areas of the Pale, as they were considered an unreliable security factor. Restrictions were imposed on their domicile and their movements inside the Pale. They were not allowed to keep Christian servants. The use of Yiddish was forbidden for public purposes. Censorship was imposed on Jewish books and papers, including religious literature. Thousands of Jews were transported as colonists to Siberia, where most of them died in the bleak conditions.

No imposition on the Jews was as feared and hated as the special form of military conscription applied to them. For other national groups the draft was for a period of twenty-five years, from the age of eighteen. Jewish boys, however, were seized at the age of twelve and sent for a preliminary six years to 'cantonments', where they were forced to be baptized, and where as a rule they suffered starvation and ill-treatment. Few of these 'cantonists' or 'Nicholas-soldiers' were ever seen again by their families. Jewish parents were willing to do anything to save their children from the recruitment – hiding them in the woods, changing their names, or even maiming them. One abominable aspect of this system was that the responsibility for handing over the boys was placed on the 'kahals', the Jewish community councils, who hired Jews for this invidious task. They were known by the Yiddish word 'chappers' ('snatchers').

By 1840 it was clear to the regime that its repressive anti-Jewish

(continued on page 213)

The Shtetl

The Kremierniec Jewish community is first mentioned in 1438 in a charter granted by the Grand Duke of Lithuania. The Russian census of 1897 showed that the community at that time numbered 6,539 and formed thirty-seven per cent of the population of the town. With the Nazi occupation in June 1941, all Jews with academic degrees were rounded up and shot, the synagogue was burnt down, and a ghetto was imposed. In August 1942, 1,500 able-bodied Jews were despatched to a slave labour camp, where they later met their death. The rest of the community was murdered. They were brought to the edge of trenches dug outside the town and shot.

Shtetl is the diminutive form of *Shtot*, the Yiddish word for a town. It stands for the smaller Jewish communities that grew up in Poland-Lithuania from about the 16th century, and continued to exist in the Russian Pale of Settlement after the partition of Poland. The shtetl had no fixed size. It could hold anything from a few score to a few thousand families. But there was a distinction, however ill-defined, between the shtetl communities and the large urban ghettoes in cities like Warsaw, Odessa, Lodz, Vilna, Kishinev, Minsk or Bialystok.

Whatever their size, the shtetl communities shared a roughly similar religious, social, cultural and economic pattern. In Czarist times they suffered hardship and insecurity. The overwhelming majority of shtetl dwellers were desperately poor, eking out a bare living as peddlers, stallholders in the market, tailors and cobblers. The market-place was the centre of the daily struggle, and the arena of contact with the Gentile world.

With all that, the atmosphere within the community was warm and intimate, and not without gaiety on Sabbaths and festivals. The shtetl strongholds were the synagogue, the study-house and above all the home. The authority of the rabbi was paramount. The two fundamental values of shtetl life were 'Yiddishkeit' ('Jewishness') and 'menshlichkeit' ('human decency').

In the 19th century the winds of change started to blow through the traditional fabric of shtetl life. The Haskalah movement introduced modern European culture. The liberal, socialist and revolutionary movements in Russia drew in many Jewish intellectuals. The Zionist movement quickened Jewish national sentiment. To a younger generation the shtetl seemed a cramped and arid prison from which they sought to escape through these new movements, or by migration to the United States and elsewhere in the Western world.

Long after the shtetl had been swept away by the Russian Revolution and the Holocaust, there was a revived nostalgic interest in its way of life, expressed in the novels of S.Y. Agnon, Isaac Bashevis Singer and others; in the pictures of Chagall; and in the re-reading of the Yiddish writers Sholem Aleichem and Mendele Mocher Seforim.

Right *Market day in the shtetl of Kremierniec, 1925. This town, one of the oldest settlements in eastern Poland, fell within the Russian Pale of Settlement.*

policy had wholly failed to 'Russianize' the Jews. The highly intelligent Minister of Education, Count Uvarov, gained the Czar's endorsement for a different and more sophisticated approach. Jewish stubbornness, it was argued, was rooted in their faith and their traditional Talmudic way of life. This could be broken down only if the young generation was given a secular education and exposed to the Russian language and culture. Experience showed that the Jews would not voluntarily send their children to Russian state schools (a survey at the time showed that out of 80,000 pupils in these schools, 48 were

Jews). The solution was to promote a secular school network *within* the Jewish community and under Jewish direction. As the overall director of the plan, Uvarov selected Dr Max Lilienthal, a brilliant twenty-five-year-old German rabbi and educator who had established secular schools in the community of Riga in Latvia. Lilienthal accepted the appointment in the sincere belief that the road had at last been opened to Jewish emancipation in Russia.

The adherents of the Haskalah (the Enlightenment movement) in Russia as well as the emancipated Jews in Western countries, hailed the plan as an important step forward. It took Lilienthal, with Uvarov's personal backing, three years to overcome the distrust of the local Jewish leaders in the Pale, who found it hard to believe that any good could come from a proposal put forward by a reactionary anti-Jewish regime. The new school system was launched in 1844.

The suspicion that there were ulterior motives behind the Uvarov plan was soon confirmed. An exchange of confidential memoranda between Uvarov and the Czar leaked out. It showed that the real intention was to phase out the Jewish content of the school curriculum and to pave the way for eventual conversion. By then Lilienthal had become disillusioned with the whole project and emigrated to the United States, where he became a Reform rabbi. In an article that appeared in a German-Jewish journal he wrote that 'only when the Jews will bow down to the Greek cross will the Czar be satisfied ...' Uvarov's educational reforms soon faded away.

With Czar Alexander II (ruled 1855–81) there was again a shift towards liberal reform in general, accompanied by a more benevolent attitude to the Jews. The cantonist recruitment system for Jews was abolished; educated Jews were given greater freedom of movement and employment outside the Pale of Settlement. The Czar won the esteem of the Jewish community for his good deeds and intentions, but there was no basic change in the Jewish situation.

In 1881 Alexander II was assassinated by a bomb planted by the Nihilists, an underground revolutionary group. He was succeeded by his son Alexander III (ruled 1881–94). Once more there was an abrupt swing back to a reactionary anti-Jewish policy. Alexander III was a stern old-fashioned Russian nationalist, opposed to reform of any kind and determined to undo the liberal influences introduced by his father. His prescription for Russia contained three ingredients: an unquestioned autocracy, the Russian Orthodox faith and Slavophile patriotism.

Alexander believed that Jewish intellectuals were stirring up revolutionary ferment and he decided to be ruthless with the Jews. The first year of his reign saw the beginning of a series of ugly pogroms in the Pale of Settlement, instigated by agents of the Russian secret police. The official reports stated that the cause of the disturbances was Jewish exploitation of the local inhabitants, and called for economic curbs on the Jews. In 1882 the Czar signed a set of 'temporary regulations' called the May Laws, from the month in

Jews in Russian Left-wing Movements

Socialist doctrines had a strong appeal for the poor and repressed Jewish masses in Eastern Europe. Their aspirations for a free and progressive society found expression in three different directions: Communism, the Bund, and Zionist Socialism.

Jewish intellectuals who threw themselves into the Communist underground did so as individuals, breaking their ties with organized Jewish community life. They believed that anti-semitism was a by-product of capitalism, and would automatically disappear in the classless society of the future.

There were Jews among the leaders of the Russian Revolution of 1917. Outstanding among them was Leon Trotsky, a brilliant orator and writer who organized and led the Red Army in the revolutionary war, and was next in importance to Lenin. In the power-struggle after Lenin's death, Trotsky was ousted and driven into exile by Stalin, who later arranged for him to be murdered.

The Bund, a Jewish workers' party, was part of the general socialist movement in Eastern Europe, but differed sharply from the Communists in one vital respect. The Bund insisted on the distinctive identity of the Jews and their right to retain their national and Yiddish cultural autonomy in Eastern European states.

A third group was the Poale Zion (Zionist Socialist Party). It was an integral part of the Jewish national movement that sought to rebuild the ancient homeland in Palestine. It envisaged that homeland as a labour commonwealth, embodying socialist ideals of equality and co-operation.

The Jewish influence in the Communist parties behind the Iron Curtain was virtually eliminated in the Stalinist period. The Bund faded out with the Holocaust. Only the Zionist Socialists achieved some practical fulfilment of their socialist philosophy, in the State of Israel.

Leon Trotsky (1879–1940), revolutionary leader and founder of the Red Army. A contemporary drawing, 1919.

which they were promulgated. Jewish residence was to be restricted to the towns, as was Jewish ownership or lease of property. Jews already living in the villages were allowed to remain, but they were later stopped from moving their residence from one village to another. These provisions caused in effect a drastic contraction of the Pale of Settlement. They dealt a heavy economic blow to an already impoverished Jewish community. They also led to local expulsions, police harassment and further overcrowding in the Jewish quarters of the towns.

The pogroms and May Laws were a major cause of the massive westward migration of Jews from the Pale of Settlement. In talking to a Jewish deputation, the Czar's chief adviser bluntly expressed the solution of the Jewish problem in Russia desired by the regime: 'One-third will die out, one-third will leave the country, and one-third will be completely dissolved in the surrounding population.' On 9 August 1890, the English satirical weekly *Punch* published a famous political cartoon. It showed Alexander III drawing a sword marked 'persecution', with his jackboot on a bound and prostrate Jew. Behind him loomed the shade of the Egyptian Pharaoh at the time of the Exodus, saying: 'Forbear! That weapon always wounds the hand that wields it.'

Alexander III was succeeded by his son Nicholas II (ruled 1894–1917), the last of the Russian Czars. He was a weak man, who had inherited much of the reactionary and anti-Jewish outlook of his father. His regime tried to make of the Jews a scapegoat for the seething discontent in the country and the underground revolutionary movement it produced. The wave of pogroms that started in Kishinev in 1903 (once more stirred up by the secret police) caused a storm of international protest. During the ensuing years the authorities connived at physical attacks on the Jews by the notorious 'Black Hundreds', armed bands organized by an anti-semitic right-wing society. In 1905 there appeared for the first time a pamphlet known as *The Protocols of the Elders of Zion*, disseminated by the authorities to 'prove' that the leaders of international Jewry were engaged in a conspiracy to conquer the Christian world. Although exposed as a crude forgery, the *Protocols* have continued to circulate elsewhere in the world, including the Arab countries. In 1911 the Czar's police even stooped to reviving the mediaeval blood-libel in the Beilis trial, which again drew international protest. With the Russian Revolution of 1917, Nicholas III was deposed and later murdered together with his family. The whole Czarist edifice, with its anti-Jewish laws and decrees, came tumbling down.

Important Events

Poland-Lithuania

1264	Charter of Bolislav the Pious.
1334	Casimir III extends the Charter.
1388	Charter of Grand Duke of Lithuania.
1648	Chmielnicki massacres.

The Czars and the Jews

1772, 1793, 1795	Partitions of Poland create the Pale of Settlement.
1804	Alexander I's Constitution of the Jews.
1827	'Cantonist' military service introduced for Jews.
1881–2	Widespread pogroms. May Laws. Beginning of mass emigration westward.
1903	Kishinev pogroms.
1913	Beilis blood-libel trial.
1917	Russian Revolution. Pale of Settlement abolished.

Chapter Fifteen

The Age of Emancipation

The rationalist philosophers in the 18th-century Western world evolved the explosive doctrine of Natural Rights, that would in due course lead to the emancipation of all repressed and exploited groups – slaves, working-men, women, children, coloured races, religious minorities and subject peoples. In this process the Jews too would be emancipated. Some of them were psychologically prepared for it by the Haskalah launched in 18th-century Germany by the philosopher, Moses Mendelssohn.

In the last quarter of the 18th century the concept of inherent human rights was enshrined in two epoch-making revolutionary documents. In 1776 the American Declaration of Independence declared: 'We hold these truths to be self-evident, that all men are created equal, that they are endowed by their Creator with certain inalienable rights, that among these are Life, Liberty and the Pursuit of Happiness ...' These bold principles were echoed in the Declaration of the Rights of Man that formed a preamble to the French Constitution of 1791. In the same year the French National Assembly granted the Jews equal citizenship, a status they had last enjoyed in the Roman empire about 1,500 years earlier. Wherever the revolutionary armies went, – Italy, Holland, Germany – the walls of feudal anti-Jewish discrimination came tumbling down.

In 1815 the statesmen of Europe met at the Congress of Vienna to reconstruct the map of the Continent after the Napoleonic upheaval. The goal was the establishment of a stable political order. The mood was conservative, even reactionary; the majority of the participants were concerned with containing the forces of change unleashed by the French Revolution. In France and Holland the Jews kept their new-won freedom. In other European countries anti-Jewish disabilities were partly restored in the backlash of reaction. This relapse was most evident in Italy. The Papal States went so far as to reimpose the ghetto in Rome and elsewhere, as well as the Jewish badge of shame.

In the next half-century the issue of Jewish emancipation was involved in the European struggle for liberalism and parliamentary democracy. The pressure came from the urban middle class that had grown out of the Industrial Revolution. Progress was uneven, with royalist, clerical and landowning elements fighting a rearguard action.

Moses Mendelssohn. From a painting by D. Rode.

Moses Mendelssohn

Moses Mendelssohn (1729–86) was the key figure in the 18th-century movement known as the Haskalah (Enlightenment). It aimed at drawing German Jews out of their ghetto isolation and into the mainstream of European culture and society. His own remarkable career bridged these two worlds and exemplified the first steps toward Jewish emancipation in Germany.

He was the son of a struggling Torah scribe in the ghetto of Dessau in Germany. At the age of fourteen he followed on foot to Berlin the erudite rabbi who had been his teacher. A hunchback (because of rickets in his childhood) and without means, he nevertheless rose to be a favourite of Berlin intellectual society. Moses became fluent in German, Hebrew, Latin, Greek, English, French and Italian, and achieved renown as a rationalist philosopher, a literary critic and a master of German style. Mendelssohn's mentor and close friend, the Christian poet and dramatist Gotthold Lessing, modelled on him the hero of the play *Nathan the Wise* (1779) with its message of respect and tolerance for the Jews.

It was surprising that a man devoted to the 18th-century cult of Reason, and accepted in German intellectual society, should choose to remain so attached to Judaism. Yet in controversies with Christian theologians Mendelssohn stoutly asserted his Jewishness. He also used his prestige on behalf of oppressed Jewish communities, and in support of the demand to grant the German Jew civic rights. In his book *Jerusalem* (1783) and other works, Mendelssohn presented his own view of Judaism as a non-dogmatic and humane faith which could be reconciled with the fashionable rationalist philosophy of the time.

One of Mendelssohn's most important undertakings, with a team of assistants, was a translation of the Old Testament into German written in Hebrew characters. It was meant to wean Jews away from Yiddish (also written in Hebrew characters) to the

In England the only real barrier left for Jews to overcome in this period was representation in parliament. In 1847 Lionel Rothschild, the head of the English family, was elected to the House of Commons by the City of London. He could not be seated because new members had to take an oath 'on the true faith of a Christian'. It took eleven years and five re-elections before a change in the rules allowed him to take an oath without reference to Christianity, and with his head covered. Yet prejudice died hard. In 1869 Gladstone, then Prime Minister, proposed to Queen Victoria that Lionel Rothschild be elevated to the House of Lords. The Queen refused, stating that she could not bring herself to make a Jew a peer. But sixteen years later the Queen granted a peerage to Lionel's son and successor Nathaniel, who became the first Lord Rothschild.

By the 1880s the emancipation of the Jews in Europe was an accomplished fact, except in Czarist Russia and Roumania. Russia remained feudal and despotic and kept its Jews in poverty and

(continued on page 224)

German language; and to lay stress on the Bible rather than the Talmud as the foundation of the Jewish faith.

Mendelssohn undoubtedly helped to break down the ghetto walls and open wider cultural horizons for the Jews. On the other hand his stress on the German language and culture paved the way for the complete assimilation of many German Jews in the 19th century.

The French Revolution
See colour page 252

In 1791 the Declaration of the Rights of Man was adopted by the revolutionary National Assembly in Paris. It guaranteed to everyone the rights to liberty, property, security, resistance to oppression and freedom of speech and the press. The Declaration had a decisive effect on the European liberal movement during the 19th century.

In September 1791 full rights of citizenship were granted to the French Jews – though not without opposition, and two years after equality was extended to other non-Catholics. French Jews responded with fervour. They joined the army and the National Guard in thousands, and contributed lavishly to the cost of the military campaigns. In the next decade they made important strides towards integration into French life, entering professions previously closed to them, gaining public offices and in many cases sending their children to public schools.

As the French armies marched into neighbouring countries they carried with them the potent slogan of 'Liberté, Égalité, Fraternité'. They abolished the system of restrictions that had confined and degraded the Jews for centuries. The army battering-rams that knocked down ghetto gates were the symbol of the new order.

Though the French Jews had gained civil equality as individuals, the relations between the Jewish community and the State remained to be clarified. In 1806 the Emperor Napoleon convened an Assembly of 112 Jewish notables in Paris. It elected as president Abraham Fur-

tado, a wealthy and cultured Bordeaux Jew of Marrano descent. The Emperor's representative confronted the delegates with a set of twelve questions covering a variety of topics: Jewish marriage and divorce, intermarriage with Christians, the judicial and administrative powers of the organized community and the Jewish attitude to usury. The key question was: did Jews regard France as their country and were they willing to obey its laws and defend it? When the answers were handed in, Napoleon made a breathtaking announcement. He would convene a Sanhedrin modelled on the supreme Jewish body of that name in ancient Israel, which had remained dormant for 1,400 years.

The revived Sanhedrin was composed of the traditional number of seventy-one members, the majority of them rabbis, with the respected Rabbi Sinzheim of Strasbourg as its chairman. (Strasbourg was the main centre of Alsace-Lorraine, where three-quarters of the French Jews lived at that time.) The Sanhedrin gave its religious endorsement to the answers elicited from the Assembly of Notables, and was then adjourned. Soon after, Judaism was given the status of an officially-recognized faith in France.

In the enthusiasm engendered among the Jews by the dramatic Sanhedrin gesture, Napoleon was able to bring about certain reforms that they might otherwise have resisted. The French Jewish community lost its corporate autonomy, and was reorganized in a manner that made it virtually state-controlled. Much of the jurisdiction of Jewish rabbinical courts was transferred to the secular French courts. Crippling limitations were imposed on Jewish (but not Christian) money-lending, and on Jewish domicile in certain areas. These latter measures met some of the complaints made to Napoleon against the Jews by the Gentile population of Alsace.

With all that, the convening of the Assembly of Notables and the Sanhedrin highlighted the equal civic status accorded to the Jews in the wake of the French Revolution. Nap-

oleon was hailed by Jews everywhere as the Great Liberator.

The results of these two gatherings had a marked impact on the way emancipated Jews in the Western world would define their own identity for some time to come. The French Jews had pledged their exclusive allegiance to the nation, and agreed to regard themselves purely as a religious group. In effect, they had renounced the concept of a separate Jewish people or nation. Only in the 20th century would it become generally accepted that Jews could be loyal citizens of their countries and at the same time feel identified with the Jewish people and its revived National Home.

Crossroads

With the transition from mediaeval to modern times, the path to civic equality opened for European Jews. Each Jew had to redefine the nature of his relationship to the Jewish people and to the country in which he lived. He faced crucial dilemmas at every stage.

1

1 The French Revolution

After the French Revolution this French Jew is confronted with the thesis that emancipation gives him equal rights as an individual but denies him the right to be part of a wider Jewish nation. In accepting emancipation, should he

A abandon his Jewish heritage? or
B preserve it?

The outcome:

Choice A: He will throw himself fervently into the struggle for democratic rights, as a revolutionary rather than as a Jew. He believes that his loyalty to the cause will bring him and his children equal opportunities with all other Frenchmen. He will regard the Jewish community as an antiquated relic, and support the abolition of its autonomous status and privileges. His children will be sent to secular state schools and get the same education as non-Jewish children.

Choice B: He will dissociate himself from the ultra-Orthodox and seek a middle way between assimilation and traditional Judaism. In the synagogue on the Sabbath he will pronounce a prayer for the welfare of the new France. He will find an educational framework for his children that will teach them both French patriotism and Jewish values. Among Frenchmen he will be a Frenchman, at home he will be an observant Jew. Most French Jews will take this path.

2 Liberalism

After the defeat of Napoleon and the Congress of Vienna in 1815, there is a period of reaction against liberalism among European rulers. But by the middle of the century the process of emancipation for the Jews of Western Europe is breaking down the remaining barriers. This Viennese Jewish banker is embarrassed by traditional Judaism, which he feels is an obstacle to his social and economic advancement. His choice lies between

A Total assimilation; and
B Reform Judaism.

2

The outcome:

Choice A: He decides to embrace Christianity, in the belief that this is the way to escape the fate of a humiliated people. He sees baptism as the key to acceptance into European civilization.

Choice B: He refuses to abandon his faith but decides that acceptance in modern society requires the adjustment of religious law and customs to the needs of the times. He chooses Reform Judaism.

3

3 Reaction in Russia

The upsurge of modern nationalism in Europe has given rise to a fresh wave of anti-semitism towards the end of the 19th century. The world of this Jewish intellectual living in Odessa in 1883 has been shaken by a fresh outbreak of pogroms in 1881 and the anti-Jewish May Laws that follow. The impotence or indifference of his non-Jewish Russian liberal friends has undermined his confidence in the possibility of a Jewish future in Russia. He decides to emigrate. He must choose between

A America; or
B Palestine

The outcome:

Choice A: In New York he suffers hunger and toil in the sweatshops. But he also helps to build up the Jewish workers' movement and a lively Yiddish culture in the New World.

Choice B: He decides that the only solution is to be free in his own homeland. He sets out for a pioneering life in the land of Israel – but few join him there.

4 Radicalism

The year is 1920, in the wake of the First World War. Revolution and civil war sweep through Eastern Europe. The Jewish masses are impoverished and insecure. This young working-class Jewish mother in Vilna, Lithuania, deeply worried about the future of her children, joins a radical movement, together with many of her fellow-Jews. She, like them, is faced with the dilemma of choosing between

A The path of world revolution; and

B The path of Jewish socialism.

The outcome:

Choice A: She joins the underground Communist Party, in the belief that world revolution and a classless society will solve the Jewish problem as well. Fleeing the local police, she finds refuge in Soviet Russia. In one of the Stalinist purges she may be arrested and sent to a labour camp.

Choice B: She regards Zionists as mere dreamers and detests religious orthodoxy, but she wants the Jews to retain their Jewish identity and Yiddish culture in a socialist society. She therefore joins the Bund. The end of the Second World War finds her surviving as a destitute refugee,

4

searching the world for a new home. The Bund has vanished and the Yiddish culture has faded.

5

5 Crisis of Democracy

This is a 'German citizen of the Mosaic Faith.' In 1930 his hometown of Breslau is already a Nazi stronghold. He can still emigrate but refuses to believe that Hitler can come to power in Germany. He recognizes that Nazism must be fought, but should he

A Retain his faith in the democratic process? or

B Become a militant activist?

The outcome:

Choice A: Each time he goes to the polling booth to cast his vote, the Social Democrats assure him that the progressive forces in Germany will defend the constitution and withstand the Nazi challenge. He is therefore shocked when Hitler wins the election in 1933 and becomes Chancellor of Germany. He still pins his hopes on the intervention of the great democracies, but that will come too late for him.

Choice B: In his youth he was active in a left-wing socialist youth movement. He regards anti-semitism as a class problem and the Jewish question as marginal to the class struggle. In January 1933 he sees 25,000 Nazi

torch-bearers triumphantly parade through Berlin. The great working-class parties collapse. His socialist comrades are thrown into concentration camps. He escapes to Italy and joins a Zionist pioneering group.

6 Post-War Survivors

This Auschwitz survivor is one of the tragic remnants that has known at first hand how millions of helpless Jews were abandoned to their fate by the nations of the world. His faith in humanity and progress has been shattered. He is torn between

A Concern for his personal rehabilitation; or

B The struggle for Jewish national survival.

6

The outcome:

Choice A: He seeks a refuge as far from Europe as possible. He reaches San Francisco where he returns to his old occupation. He feels isolated and stays away from Jewish communal affairs – until his sense of identification is restored on the day the State of Israel is established in 1948.

Choice B: He joins in organizing groups of DPs (Displaced Persons) in the camps and leads them illegally across borders and seas, in an effort to burst open the closed gates of Eretz Israel. He and his fellow survivors from the concentration camps and the Jewish partisan bands are on their way to help build the Jewish homeland.

Heinrich Heine (1797–1856), poet and writer, Germany.

Above *Felix Mendelssohn-Bartholdy (1809–47), composer, Germany.*

Below *Benjamin Disraeli (1804–81), statesman, England.*

Some Famous Jews in Modern Western Europe

In the modern age, the Jewish contribution to general European culture has been phenomenal. The Emancipation produced an outburst of creative achievement in every field – in politics, in banking, finance, commerce and industry, in literature, art, music, theatre, film, publishing and the press, in medicine and law, and in the socialist and labour movements. Three German-speaking Jews – Karl Marx, Sigmund Freud and Albert Einstein – have each had a profound influence on the modern world.

The Nobel Prize, initiated in 1901, has been the world's most prestigious award for outstanding achievement in the fields of physics, chemistry, physiology, medicine, peace and literature – to which economics was added in 1969. It is a striking fact that about a fifth of the total number of Nobel Laureates have been Jews.

Sigmund Freud (1856–1939), founder of psychoanalysis, Austria.

Top *Sarah Bernhardt (1844–1923), actress, France.*

Above *Artur Rubenstein (1886–   ), pianist, Poland and America.*

Six Jews have been the elected prime ministers of major Western governments: Benjamin Disraeli in Britain, Léon Blum, Pierre Mendes-France and René Mayer in France, Luigi Luzzatti in Italy, and Bruno Kreisky in Austria.

Camille Pissarro (1830–1903), painter, France.

Zweig, Franz Kafka, André Maurois, Lion Feuchtwanger, Eugène Ionesco, and the Nobel Laureate poetess, Nelly Sachs.

Art
The painters Camille Pissarro, Amedeo Modigliani, Max Liebermann, Jules Pascin, Chaim Soutine, Marc Chagall and Leon Bakst; and the sculptors Jacob Epstein and Jacques Lipchitz.

Music
The composers Felix Mendelssohn, Giacomo Meyerbeer, Jacques Offenbach, Gustav Mahler and Darius Milhaud; the conductors Serge Koussevitsky, Otto Klemperer, Bruno Walter; the violinists Joseph Joachim, Mischa Elman, Jascha Heifetz, Bronislaw Huberman, Isaac Stern, Yehudi Menuhin; and the pianists Vladimir Horovitz, Artur Rubinstein and Artur Schnabel.

Theatre
Rachel, Sarah Bernhardt, Max Reinhardt and Marcel Marceau.

Jewish pioneers in other fields have included Henri Bergson in philosophy, Alfred Adler in psychiatry, Paul Ehrlich in medical research, Emile Durkheim in sociology and Claude Levi-Strauss in anthropology.

Top Franz Kafka (1883–1924), writer, Czechoslovakia.

Above Jacob Epstein (1880–1959), sculptor, America and England.

A selected list of other names will indicate the extensive Jewish role in the intellectual and artistic life of Europe:

Literature
Heinrich Heine, Franz Werfel, Marcel Proust, Arnold and Stefan

Above Marc Chagall (1887–   ), painter, Russia and France.

Below Albert Einstein (1879–1955), physicist, Germany and America.

oppression, penned up in the Pale of Settlement. Their emancipation would come about only with the Russian Revolution of 1917. In Western and Central Europe, the Jews had as a rule attained full citizenship, religious freedom and access to all occupations. They assumed, rashly, that Jew-hatred was a hang-over from mediaeval religious bigotry and would disappear in the modern world.

But already dark forces were gathering for a virulent new onslaught on the emancipated Jew. Revived anti-semitism was a dangerous beast that in the 20th century would devour the Jews of Europe.

In France a warning note was sounded with the success of a violently anti-Jewish book, *La France Juive* (1886) by Edouard Drumont. It was a best-seller, and serialized in the right-wing press. It helped to pave the way for the extraordinary Dreyfus Affair that projected the Jewish question into the centre of French political, intellectual and social life for a number of years.

But it was Germany that became the home of modern anti-semitism as it had been in the Middle Ages. (The term 'anti-semitism' was first coined in 1879 by a rabid German anti-Jewish pamphleteer.) Conservative and Catholic circles in Germany had by no means reconciled themselves to the egalitarian spirit of the age, nor to the rising power of the middle class. They resented rich, Germanized Jews and tried to prevent their social acceptance. This attitude was reinforced by the pan-German nationalism that emerged after the unification of Germany in 1870.

The anti-semitism of the old privileged classes in Central Europe was curiously paralleled in the lower middle classes. This stratum of society contained the struggling and frustrated mass of small shopkeepers, white-collar workers, petty officials and school teachers, who felt themselves above the working class but were unable to rise on the economic and social ladder. The depression of the middle 1870s hit this group particularly hard. A new political faction, the Christian Social Workers Party, promised them welfare benefits and pointed to the Jewish capitalists as the source of their woes. Another body called the National Anti-Semitic League presented to the German Chancellor, Bismarck, a petition demanding that the Jews be disfranchised. It had a quarter of a million signatures.

In Austria the Christian Social leader was the formidable Karl Lueger, repeatedly elected as Mayor of Vienna on an anti-semitic platform. An ill-educated and complex-ridden youth who listened avidly to Lueger was called Adolf Hitler. His father was a petty customs clerk and his mother a domestic servant. His mind became filled with fantasies of Germanic grandeur and a pathological hatred for Communists and Jews.

The late 19th century produced a whole pseudo-scientific literature on the theme that the Germans were the descendants of a mythical Aryan or Nordic super-race, with flaxen hair and blue eyes. Their tribal ancestors out of the Teutonic forests were glorified in the thunderous operas of Richard Wagner, and in a distorted interpre-

(continued on page 230)

Ferdinand Lasalle (1825–64).

Karl Marx (1818–83).

Rosa Luxemburg (1871–1919)'

Jews in Western European Socialism

In 19th-century Europe it was natural that a number of Jews should be drawn into socialist and revolutionary movements. They lived under reactionary regimes, and antisemitism was rife in their countries. Although some Jewish radicals (including Karl Marx) spurned their Jewish roots, they were heirs to the profound concern for social justice that has pervaded Judaism from biblical times.

Marx's monumental work *Das Kapital* laid the theoretical foundations for socialism and communism. It was probably the most influential political-economic treatise to be published in the modern age.

Ferdinand Lassalle was for a while associated with Marx, but rejected his concept of a revolutionary class struggle and sought the attainment of a socialist society by democratic means. He became the father of the German Social Democratic movement. Another Jew, Victor Adler, founded the Austrian Social Democratic Party, headed in recent years by Chancellor Bruno Kreisky, also a Jew.

Rosa Luxemburg, a small crippled Polish Jewess, was a fiery leader of left-wing socialism in Germany and the founder of the German Communist Party in 1918 at the end of the First World War. She was arrested and murdered shortly afterwards by German army officers.

Maier Amschel Rothschild

(Gründer des Welthauses)

The House of Rothschild

See left and colour page 252

The Industrial Revolution propelled the Western World into an era of economic growth, population expansion and rising standards of life without parallel in human history. There was an unquenchable thirst for loan capital to finance the new industrial cities, railway construction, steamships, housing projects and mechanical equipment for the armies. It was the heyday for Jewish financial and merchant-banking houses that operated on an undreamt-of international scale. They included the Péreire Brothers and Baron Maurice de Hirsch in Paris, Lazard Brothers of Paris and New York, the Hambros of Copenhagen and London, the Goldsmid family in England – and above all the House of Rothschild. It has for nearly two centuries been a financial dynasty without precedent. In the remotest 'shtetl' of the Russian Pale of Settlement the name Rothschild stood for unimaginable wealth, a life-style of oriental splendour, benefactions on a vast scale – and with it a stubborn Jewishness. In the demonology of the anti-semites, the Rothschilds stood for a sinister 'Jew-power', manipulating thrones, currency systems and the press. Throughout it all the family went its own exotic and cohesive way. In point of fact, no Diaspora Jews have ever wielded more real power than the Rothschilds did in the 19th century.

The story starts in the 18th-century Frankfurt ghetto, where a Jewish community of some 3,000 souls lived together in crowded quarters. Here **Mayer Amschel Rothschild** was born in one of the meaner houses. Formerly the family had been in a better house, marked above the front door with a red shield – in German, *rothschild* – and that name stuck.

The young Mayer Amschel began to prosper, selling old coins to local nobles and cashing drafts for the princes of Hesse-Cassel. He married

Left *Mayer Amschel Rothschild (1744–1812), banker, Germany.*

THE AGE OF EMANCIPATION

and in due course had twenty children, of whom ten survived – five sons and five daughters. In his will he enjoined his sons always to work together and trust each other. Later, when they became barons, their crests contained a cluster of five arrows held together by a fist. Their family solidarity was their most important asset, after the brothers had settled as bankers in different countries. The eldest, **Amschel**, remained in Frankfurt, **Nathan** went to London, **James** (Jacob) to Paris, **Salomon** to Vienna and **Karl** to Naples.

The services the brothers rendered to the rulers in these countries were quite extraordinary. In Frankfurt, Amschel became the most powerful banker in Germany and the treasurer to the German Federation. Throughout, he remained a pious Jew, wearing traditional ghetto garb and keeping strict kashrut. In Italy Karl was the financial mainstay of the Bourbon dynasty, restored to the throne of Naples. In Austria, Salomon's state loans and financing of railway construction made his the wealthiest private family in the country. At the request of the powerful Chancellor, Prince Metternich, he was able to perform a signal and delicate personal service for the Emperor Francis I.

The Emperor's daughter, Marie Louise, was married to Napoleon, then languishing in exile on the island of St Helena. She consoled herself with an affair that produced two illegitimate offspring. Salomon devised a round-about method whereby the Emperor could provide for these bastard grandchildren without the connection being traced to him. As a reward Metternich obtained from the Emperor a grant of the hereditary title of Baron, not just for Salomon but also for his four brothers. In France, James adroitly kept the regimes that succeeded each other after Napoleon as his banking clients. Nathan, in London, managed on behalf of the British Government to transfer huge amounts of funds and gold bullion to finance Wellington's Peninsular campaign in Spain. The transfers actually took place through the enemy country, France! Since the Rothschilds's means of communication with their agents were more rapid than those of any government, Nathan was the first man in England to get news of Napoleon's defeat at Waterloo in 1815. He informed the government before repairing to the Stock Exchange to buy up government bonds.

During the forty-year reign of Nathan's son **Lionel** as head of the English family, the bank was involved in many historic loans to the government. They included those connected with the emancipation of the slaves, the Irish famine of 1847, the Crimean War of 1854 and the dramatic off-the-cuff loan to the Disraeli government in 1875 to buy the Suez Canal shares from the Khedive of Egypt. Lionel was the first professing Jew to be seated in the House of Commons, and his son Nathaniel the first Jewish peer.

Baron Edmond de Rothschild (1845–1934), of the French branch of the family, played a unique role in the early Zionist settlement in Palestine. He provided the financial and technical assistance without which the struggling pioneer colonies could hardly have survived.

The German Rothschild bank was dissolved in 1901, since there were no male heirs in that branch of the family. The Italian bank was wound up after the unification of Italy in 1860. When Hitler's troops occupied Austria in 1938 the head of the Viennese branch, Baron Louis, was imprisoned and released against the surrender of all his assets to the Germans. He emigrated to the United States. Only the English and French branches of the House of Rothschild remain intact today.

Mayer Amschel and his Five Sons

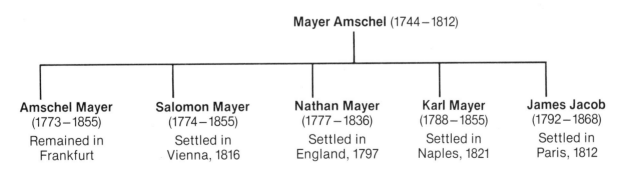

Mayer Amschel (1744–1812)

| Amschel Mayer (1773–1855) Remained in Frankfurt | Salomon Mayer (1774–1855) Settled in Vienna, 1816 | Nathan Mayer (1777–1836) Settled in England, 1797 | Karl Mayer (1788–1855) Settled in Naples, 1821 | James Jacob (1792–1868) Settled in Paris, 1812 |

Alfred Dreyfus being stripped of his rank. The cover picture of Petit Journal Illustré, *5 January 1895.*

The Dreyfus Affair

Alfred Dreyfus (1859–1935) was the son of an assimilated middle-class Jewish family in Alsace. He took up the army as a career, and was posted as a captain to the General Staff in Paris. Earnest, serious, hardworking and withdrawn, of medium height and wearing pince-nez, he was a wholly unremarkable man. Yet he was suddenly propelled into world attention as the central figure in a drama that would obsess France for many years.

In 1894, the French counter-intelligence discovered that defence secrets were being passed on to Germany through its military attaché in Paris. Dreyfus was arrested, charged with treason and condemned *in camera* by a military tribunal. The

evidence against him was flimsy, but the judges had been shown a secret file produced by the counter-espionage bureau of the army. It transpired later that the document in the file incriminating Dreyfus had been forged by an officer in the bureau. Dreyfus was publicly stripped of his rank and sentenced to life imprisonment. He was shipped to Devil's Island, a rocky islet off the coast of French Guiana, South America, where he was kept in chains under guard. To all intents and purposes the case was closed, and the prisoner was left to rot in isolation for the rest of his life.

However, his brother and a few other individuals in Paris continued to agitate for his release, insisting that there had been a miscarriage of justice. One of them was Bernard

Lazare, a Jew and a distinguished man of letters who, in 1896, almost two years after the trial, published and distributed a pamphlet called *The Truth about the Dreyfus Affair*. Evidence came to light that the real culprit was another officer, Major Esterhazy, who was in the pay of the Germans. Important public figures took up the cause of 'revision' – the re-opening of the trial. They included the vice-president of the Senate, the leader of the Socialist party, the most formidable debater in the French parliament, Clemenceau, and the two famous writers Anatole France and Emile Zola.

At the beginning of 1898, the French government was obliged to put Esterhazy on trial; but he was acquitted, as a result of heavy army pressure behind the scenes. The next day Zola published, in Clemenceau's newspaper, a powerful indictment of the political and military establishment, under the banner headline *J'accuse*. In it he named the men whom he charged with an act of injustice and a subsequent cover-up, challenging them to sue him for libel. A case was brought against Zola and he was fined and condemned to a year in prison but escaped to England.

By now, however, the Dreyfus Affair had become a *cause célèbre* in the world press. In France it was the subject of the most bitter and divisive controversy that had rent the nation since the Revolution a century earlier. The honour and prestige of the army was now committed to the proposition that Dreyfus was guilty. Behind the army was ranged a powerful alignment of forces: right-wing conservatives, the Church, the upper classes and almost the entire press. Those political figures and intellectuals who fought for justice were reviled and attacked in the name of patriotism. It was an atmosphere in which families were split apart and old friends cut each other dead in the street.

The ugliest and most frightening aspect of the Affair was the anti-semitism it brought to the surface. Its spokesman was Edouard-Adolphe Drumont, author of a widely-read anti-Jewish book *La France Juive* (1886), and founder of the National Anti-Semitic League. The opponents of revision became infected with the belief that behind the Jew Dreyfus was a mysterious and powerful syndicate, organized by international Jewish finance to destroy France. This alleged syndicate, it was said, was in league with the Germans, the Freemasons, the atheists and every other enemy of the established order.

These fantasies dredged up from the Dark Ages were personified in the popular press by the stereotype of a fat, hooked-nose Jewish money-lender. After a century of emancipation, anti-semitism was once more politically and socially a potent force in France, as it was in Germany and Russia.

A French cartoon of Alfred Dreyfus, 1894.

In 1898 an independent examination established that the document incriminating Dreyfus had been forged by a Major Henry. He was arrested and committed suicide in his cell. A re-trial before a new military court could no longer be refused and it received world coverage. All in the court were shocked when Dreyfus appeared. Only forty years of age, he seemed an old man, bent and shrunken, with prematurely white hair. The most poignant irony was that he had been totally cut off from the world for nearly five years and was the only person present who was ignorant of the developments in the Dreyfus Affair during that time.

Once more the judges were presented with the uncompromising view that a verdict for Dreyfus was a verdict against the French army. The military court was unable to stand up to such pressure. It took the easy way out by reaffirming Dreyfus's guilt but recommended that his sentence be shortened. Soon after he was given a presidential pardon. It was only in 1906, when a Leftist government came into power, that the original conviction was set aside. Dreyfus was reinstated in the army with a higher rank and awarded the Order of the Legion of Honour.

The first Dreyfus trial in 1894 was covered by a Viennese Jewish press correspondent, Dr Theodor Herzl. Later, he witnessed the military ceremony in which Dreyfus was degraded, and heard the crowd screaming 'Death to the Jew!' Herzl wrote sadly: 'Where? In France. In republican, modern, civilized France, a hundred years after the Declaration of the Rights of Man.' The experience crystallized the distress that Herzl had felt for a long time over the Jewish question, and his disillusionment with assimilation as an answer. In 1897 he convened the first Zionist Congress in Basle. The Dreyfus Affair had been part of the backcloth to the emergence of the modern Zionist Movement.

tation of the superman motif in the works of Germany's most influential philosopher, Nietzche. The corollary of these intoxicating theories was that the Jews were an inferior race that threatened to contaminate the purity of German blood and morals. There was thus nothing very original about Nazi doctrines. They only had to await the proper historical moment before they could be translated into power. That situation came after the First World War. Germany had suffered a crushing defeat. Added to this humiliation were the punitive terms of the Treaty of Versailles. The German economy was in ruins. Hitler and his National Socialist Party, making full use of the anti-semitic weapon, appealed above all to the 'little men' of the submerged lower middle class. They found an emotional outlet in the parades and heady rhetoric of the Nazis, and their sons became the swastika-wearing thugs of the Nazi storm-troopers.

When Hitler came to power in 1933, anti-semitism was converted from a personal obsession and a propaganda weapon into the policy of a great State. It was systematically used to manipulate the mass psyche of the German people, to provide them with an age-old scapegoat, to make them submissive to totalitarian rule and to prepare them for the war to come.

The Nuremberg Laws of 1935 were a systematic programme for the economic, cultural and social elimination of the Jews from the general life of Germany. Many of its details were familiar from mediaeval times, but the basis had shifted. The only criterion now was genetic. A Jew could no longer escape by becoming a Christian. Nor did it matter whether his occupation was that of a peddlar or a professor; if he had had a Jewish grandparent, it was enough. The Western democracies failed to intervene. In this appeasement period, it was convenient to regard the persecution of the German Jews as an internal matter of the German Reich.

In the first two years of the Second World War many millions of Jews were trapped in Nazi-occupied Europe, which stretched from the English Channel to the heart of Russia. They were rounded up and transported to concentration camps, walled into ghettoes or used as slave labour in the German war industries. In the Spring of 1941 Hitler gave his approval for the 'Final Solution of the Jewish Question' – that is, the physical liquidation of the Jews. From the summer of 1941 trained mobile units were used for this mass murder. On 20 January 1942, a meeting was held at Wannsee, a suburb of Berlin, to adopt a detailed programme for the gigantic project. This was later to include the installation of specially designed gas-chambers in a number of concentration camps. The implementation was entrusted to the SS, the security apparatus headed by Himmler. In the midst of all the war pressures upon him, Hitler gave his personal attention to the extermination of Europe's Jews. In country after country the horror of genocide unfolded itself.

As the advancing Allied armies liberated one death camp after another in the last phase of the war, they found in them the pitiful

The Memorial Column in the Museum of the Jewish Diaspora, Tel Aviv, a reminder of Jewish martyrdom through the ages.

living skeletons of those inmates who still survived. By the time Hitler lay dead in a Berlin bunker, beneath the rubble of his Third Reich, the 'final solution' had accounted for the slaughter of six million Jews – one out of every three Jews on earth. The Holocaust was by far the greatest disaster in Jewish history.

Important Events

1776	American Declaration of Independence proclaims that 'all men are created equal'.
1783	Moses Mendelssohn's *Jerusalem* published.
1789	French Declaration of The Rights of Man.
1791	French Jews granted equal citizenship.
1807	Paris Sanhedrin convened.
1815	Congress of Vienna stimulates reaction.
1847	Lionel Rothschild elected to House of Commons.
1886	Drumont's *La France Juive* published.
1894	Dreyfus condemned. Start of Dreyfus Affair.
1933	Hitler comes to power.
1935	Nuremberg Laws.
1938	'Kristallnacht.' Economic ruin of German Jews.
1939–45	The Second World War. The destruction of European Jewry.

Chapter Sixteen

The New World
The United States of America

History seems to have its own peculiar sense of irony. In 1492 Ferdinand and Isabella signed the decree expelling all the Jews from Spain. Four days after the last professing Jew left the country, Christopher Columbus set sail from there under the patronage of the same monarchs. The New World he was about to discover would in time contain the largest and freest Jewish community the Diaspora has ever known.

To add another artistic touch to the story, the first member of the expedition to set foot in the New World was its only Jew, Columbus's interpreter Luis de Torres, who had hurriedly been baptized just before sailing. Whether Columbus himself was of Marrano extraction remains uncertain. It is remarkable that his account of the voyage begins with a reference to the Expulsion Decree.

During more than a century of English colonial rule, the small number of Jews in the American colonies had freedom of worship and trading. By the outbreak of the American Revolution in 1776 they numbered about 2500, organized in communities along the Atlantic regions such as New York, Newport, Philadelphia, Charleston, Savannah and Montreal. Practically all of them were engaged in trade. Most were small shopkeepers, but some were occupied in shipping, import-export, and the fur trade. In dress and language they were the same as other settlers, and intermarriage was not uncommon.

During the American Revolution the majority of the Jews threw in their lot with the rebels. They fought as officers, soldiers and militiamen, and one of them, Haym Solomon, had a key role in financing the American forces. In spite of the equality for all guaranteed in the Declaration of Independence, it took some time before the American Jews gained full civic rights, a matter under the jurisdiction of the individual States. By 1820 the Jews enjoyed citizenship in several of the thirteen original States. Disabilities remained concerning the requirement to take a Christian oath for public office. These were overcome by the middle of the 19th century.

In the Civil War (1861–5) an estimated 7,000 Jews fought on the side of the North and 3,000 on the side of the South. In 1862, General

NIEUW AMSTERDAM.
Op 't Eylandt Manhattans.

de Kerck. 303 C. de Wintmolen. 304 D. dese Vlagge wort op gehaelt als daer Schepen in de haven komen. 305 E. 't gevangen huys. 306 F. de Hr Generaels hu 307 308

Above *A view of Manhattan Island, c.1664.*
Right *A model of the Touro synagogue in Newport, R.I.*

Grant's Order No. 11 called for the expulsion of Jewish cotton traders from the border areas, but it was revoked personally by President Lincoln.

From about 1840 there was an increasing influx of Jews from Germany, driven by political reaction and economic difficulties in that country. By 1881 the American Jewish community numbered some 300,000. The bulk of these Jews belonged to Reform congregations modified from the German model. They spread inland from the Eastern seaboard into the cities growing up along the Great Lakes and the Ohio and Mississippi rivers, and into Northern California after the Gold Rush of 1849. Reform Temples proliferated in the pleasant new residential areas of these cities.

From 1881 onwards this comfortable semi-assimilated American Jewry was confronted (somewhat to its dismay) by an avalanche of poor Yiddish-speaking Orthodox 'Ostjuden' (Eastern European Jews) streaming out of the Russian Pale of Settlement. Life was hard for this immigrant generation, but their children entered the mainstream of American life. They gained an education in the public schools, entered wider business, professional and academic fields, and moved out of the ghettoes. The difference between the 'uptown' and the 'downtown' Jews disappeared, and the American Jewish community became more cohesive.

The energy and talent released by the integration of the American Jews produced remarkable results. They have played a part in the public, economic, intellectual and artistic life of the country that is comparable to that of the Jewish communities in the Golden Age of mediaeval Spain or in modern pre-Hitler Germany.

As a community, American Jewry can be said to have come of age at the time of the First World War. A quarter of a million Jews served in the US Armed Forces. By that time the Jewish community of the

(continued on page 239)

Arrival at New Amsterdam

In the summer of 1654, a ragged band of twenty-three Jewish refugees – four men, two women and seventeen children – arrived at New Amsterdam, the settlement on Manhattan Island established by the Dutch West India Company. They were ending a journey that had begun some five months earlier in Recife, northeastern Brazil. That area had been taken by the Dutch from Portugal in 1633, and some Dutch Jews, formerly Portuguese Marranos, had settled there. They fled when Portugal recaptured the area twenty-one years later. (Portugal and its possessions were barred to Jews, and Marranos who professed Christianity were subject to the Inquisition.)

Peter Stuyvesant, the autocratic governor of New Amsterdam, was unwilling to absorb these destitute newcomers but he was over-ruled by the Company. The party remained, but subject to restrictions. These were removed in 1664 when an English fleet took the settlement and renamed it New York.

The Touro Synagogue

The town of Newport, in the State of Rhode Island, was founded in 1639. Its Jewish community started in 1677, when a number of Jews arrived

H. de Kaeck I. Compagnies Pachuys. K
309   310

from the island of Barbados in the West Indies. They started to trade, and bought a plot of ground for a cemetery.

Not long afterwards the community disbanded, and was not revived until the middle of the 18th century. A congregation was organized; a Cantor, Isaac Touro, came from Amsterdam, and in 1763 the congregation, then about twenty families, dedicated a handsome small synagogue, designed by the Colonial architect Peter Harrison.

Within a decade, the town had a flourishing community of about 200 Jews. Its leading (and wealthiest) member was Aaron Lopez. He had arrived as a young Portuguese Mar-

rano, openly embraced Judaism, had himself circumcised and remarried his wife in a Jewish ceremony.

In the American War of Independence the trade of Newport was ruined, and its Jewish congregation began to dwindle. It was already a dying community when President George Washington received an address of welcome from it on a visit to the town. By 1822 there were no Jews left in Newport. The synagogue building was preserved from funds bequeathed for the purpose by the son of Isaac Touro. It has since been declared a national historic site, as the oldest extant synagogue in North America.

The Newport community was not re-established until the 1880s.

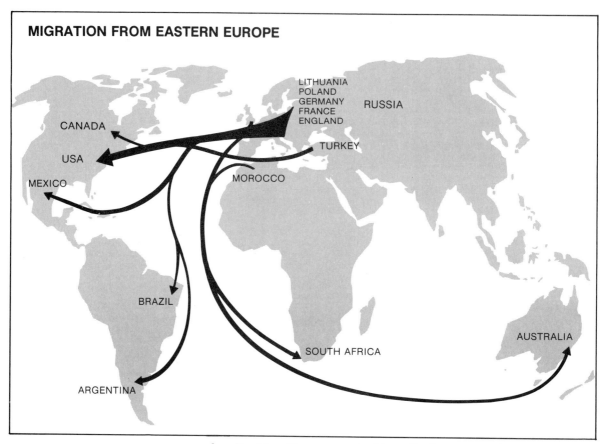

MIGRATION FROM EASTERN EUROPE

The German-Jewish Immigrants

Thousands of the German-Jewish immigrants in the 19th century started their new lives as peddlers, foot-slogging with packs on their backs through the rural areas and the Indian territories. Moving up the ladder meant the acquisition of a horse and buggy and then a store or trading-post.

The prosperity of the post-Civil War years established the Jewish community as a solid middle class, with an elite of German-Jewish banking and merchant families of wealth and importance, who distinguished themselves as philanthropists and patrons of the arts.

The banker Joseph Seligman handled the placing of US government securities in Europe during the Civil War, and later declined an offer from President Grant to appoint him Secretary of the Treasury. Jacob Schiff headed the investment house of Kuhn, Loeb and Company that financed much of the railroad construction. Through his great wealth, philanthropy and devotion to Jewish affairs, he was regarded as the most influential Jew in the United States at the turn of the century. His position in the bank and the community later devolved on his son-in-law, Felix Warburg. Julius Rosenwald developed the huge mail order business of Sears, Roebuck that distributed forty million copies annually of its famous catalogue. Levi Strauss started making blue denim pants, 'Levis', for the gold-miners in California, and made them the basis of a multi-million-dollar industry. Adam Gimbel and the Strauss family built up retailing empires and pioneered the department store. These men and others like them had one biographical

fact in common: they had all come to the United States as penniless young Jewish immigrants from Germany.

Migration from Eastern Europe

In the forty-odd years from 1880 onwards, four million Jews moved westward out of the Russian Pale of Settlement and the adjacent areas of Rumania and Hungary. Nearly three million of them would reach what they hopefully called the 'Golden Land' of the United States. The rest would augment the declining Jewry of Western Europe and Britain, and expand the small communities of the New World in Latin America (especially the Argentine) and in the British Empire (Canada, South Africa, Australia). This was by far the most massive population shift in Jewish history. It transformed the shape and character of the Diaspora.

To the 'Golden Land'

From 1880 the Jews of Eastern Europe moved away in increasing numbers from abject poverty, over-crowding and persecution. Across the Atlantic the vast half-empty United States was experiencing the most rapid economic growth in the world. With an insatiable demand for immigrant labour, it had opened its gates to the surplus population of Europe. The Russian Jews joined a great flood of transatlantic immigrants – Irish, Swedes, Germans, Italians, Poles, Slavs, and many others. In the sixty years before the First World War the United States took in thirty million immigrants. (The Italians alone accounted for some eight million.)

The gigantic Statue of Liberty, erected in New York Harbour in 1882, carried the words of the

Below *Before leaving port at Liverpool, the ship's doctor (in the bowler hat) examines Russian Jews embarking for the United States, 1891.*

American Jewish poet Emma Lazarus:

Give me your tired, your poor
Your huddled masses yearning to
breathe free
The wretched refuse of your teeming
shore
Send these, the homeless, tempest-
tossed to me
I lift my lamp beside the golden door

The mass movement was made possible by the revolutionary developments in transportation in the industrial age. One of the points of exit for the Jews from the Pale of Settlement was the town of Brody, on the Austrian side of the border. From there they could travel by train and ship to New York in about two weeks. Shipping companies found it profitable to cram these cut-rate passengers into the steerage holds of their transatlantic liners. About two-thirds of the Jewish migrants were carried on German liners from Hamburg and Bremen, and the rest by British Cunard liners from Liverpool.

The Gateway

See colour pages 270 and 271

During the first decade after 1880, the immigrants arriving in New York were cleared at Castle Garden, at the southern tip of Manhattan. In 1890 an important US Supreme Court judgment transferred responsibility for immigration from State to Federal Authorities. A new immigrant centre was opened on Ellis Island, used until then for harbour defence. For millions of immigrants thereafter, Ellis Island was the gateway to America and their first exposure to bureaucracy in the New World. They spent days or even weeks on the Island being questioned by immigration officers, undergoing medical examinations and filling in forms. Local Jewish organizations, especially the Hebrew Immigrant Aid Society (HIAS), helped the bewildered newcomers to cope with the red tape, trace relatives and find a place to live. Between a third and a half of them arrived penniless, having spent all they had on their tickets.

Lower East Side, New York

See colour pages 270 and 271

The Jewish immigrants arriving in the United States found the reality much bleaker than the dream. Other immigrant groups were drawn from the peasant communities of Europe, and a proportion of them could be settled on the land. But the Jews of Eastern Europe had been divorced from the soil for centuries. The old-established American Jewish community could help them but not absorb them, owing to their sheer numbers and the wide gap in culture and religious practice. They concentrated in specific slum quarters of the major cities – mostly in New York's Lower East Side and on a smaller scale in similar districts of Boston, Philadelphia, Chicago and elsewhere. They now 'breathed free', as the inscription on the Statue of Liberty had promised them – but in conditions of overcrowding and poverty little better than those they had left behind in the Old Country.

At one stage 350,000 Jews were huddled together in a square mile of teeming, dilapidated tenement houses on the Lower East Side. Some of them eked out a living as petty traders in the Jewish quarters, mostly with street-stalls and barrows. Their main occupation was in the sweatshops. There was an expanding market for cheap ready-to-wear clothing. Parts of garments were cut and sewn in thousands of little workshops, each with a handful of employees. The conditions were appalling. The rooms were crowded and dirty, with no proper ventilation, light or heating in winter. In the busy periods men, women and young girls worked sixteen hours a day for low wages.

However poor, these Eastern European immigrants were restless, ar-

Above *A sweatshop in Ludlow Street, 1890.*
Left *Market day in the Jewish quarter of New York, by J. Durkin. Derived from photographs of Jewish pedlars, 1891.*

ticulate and with a strong intellectual tradition. They created their own self-contained society. Yiddish was the language of the home and the street. The whole neighbourhood closed down on the Sabbath and Jewish festivals. According to their places of origin they belonged to *landsmanshaften* ('home-town associations'), that served as social clubs and mutual benefit societies. There was a flourishing Yiddish theatre and press. A vigorous struggle against sweatshop and factory conditions produced progressive labour unions.

United States was rapidly growing in size, influence and wealth. Its leadership moved out of an American parochial framework into the wider international concerns of the Jewish people. Louis Brandeis, Stephen Wise and others worked hard to gain endorsement from President Wilson for the Balfour Declaration of 1917 that promised a Jewish National Home in Palestine. At the Paris Peace Conference of 1919 Louis Marshall led a strong American Jewish delegation that fought for guarantees of minority rights for the Jewish communities in the new successor states in Europe. The American Joint Distribution Committee was set up as a relief agency for the Jews of Eastern Europe, victims of civil war, revolutions and pogroms sweeping through that region. Prominent American Jews like Marshall and Felix Warburg, though non-Zionist, nevertheless agreed to support Jewish immigration and economic development in Palestine, through Dr Weizmann's Jewish Agency created in 1929. There was growing Zionist sentiment in America, and some leading personalities came to settle in Palestine – including Henrietta Szold, the founder of Hadassah (the American Women's Zionist Organization), and Rabbi Judah Magnes, who became the first President of the Hebrew University of Jerusalem.

Three different trends developed in the contemporary religious practice of the American Jews : Modern Orthodoxy ; Reform Judaism and Conservative Judaism. *Modern Orthodoxy*: For the majority of the Jews in the modern period the Talmud waned as the framework of a separate Jewish way of life. The ghetto and the shtetl were gone for good. Jews became citizens of the countries in which they lived and

Jews in American Public Life

The Jews have been one of the most politically conscious and active groups in the United States. Hundreds have held public office as Cabinet members, Senators, Congressmen, State Governors and Mayors of major cities. As President Roosevelt's Secretary of the Treasury (1934–45), Henry Morgenthau Jr helped bring the United States out of the Depression, and had a major share in the country's economic mobilization during the Second World War.

The highest public position held by an American Jew was that of Henry Kissinger as Secretary of

Henry Kissinger (b.1923), Secretary of State.

State. He became a world figure through his negotiation of the Vietnam peace (for which he was awarded the Nobel Peace Prize) and his 'shuttle diplomacy' in the Israel-Arab conflict.

The United States Supreme Court Justices Benjamin Cardozo, Louis Brandeis, Felix Frankfurter, Arthur Goldberg and Abe Fortas all belonged to the liberal wing of the Court. Cardozo and Brandeis in particular had a marked impact on contemporary American jurisprudence.

The Day of Atonement Service in a New York synagogue. From Frank Leslie's Popular Monthly, August 1877.

largely adapted themselves to the life-style of their neighbours. Traditional Judaism in the western world had been thrown onto the defensive by the Emancipation, the general secular temper of the age and the rise of the Reform movement.

The term 'Orthodox' came into use at the beginning of the 19th century. It embraced all those Jews who continued to accept that the Old Testament was the revealed will of God, and that the Halachah was the divinely-inspired guide for Jewish life. Yet that common premise could not in itself make of Orthodoxy a monolithic camp. It faced its own dilemmas, with different groups finding different answers to them.

The ultra-Orthodox wing, including certain Chassidic sects, have resisted change. They have tried to preserve a traditional Eastern

Louis Dembitz Brandeis (1856–1941), Supreme Court Justice.

Jews have played an important part in the American Labour movement. The grim conditions in the sweat-shops, the socialist ideals the Eastern European Jews brought with them, the age-old Jewish demand for social justice that went back to the Hebrew Prophets – all these produced progressive Jewish labour unions in the garment industry that were models of their kind. One was the International Ladies Garment Workers' Union, led by David Dubinsky. Another was the Chicago-based Amalgamated Clothing Workers of America – its leader, Sidney Hillman, was Roosevelt's chief adviser on labour affairs during the Second World War. Samuel Gompers, the architect of the American Federation of Labour, promoted a worker-employer co-operation that was attacked by more militant unionists but became the cornerstone of American labour relations.

European way of life. Yiddish remains their spoken tongue. The men wear beards and earlocks (*pevot*), and a garb that dates back to 16th-century Poland, while their married women shave their heads and use a wig (*sheitel*). The sexes are kept segregated in public places.

Such rigid traditionalism is today confined to relatively small enclaves. While striving to maintain traditional observance, the bulk of Orthodox Jews resemble Jews of other trends, as well as their non-Jewish fellow-citizens, in dress, language, occupations, leisure activities and political affiliations. A modern, educated Jew who is also an Orthodox Jew has to reconcile his faith with the culture and society in which he lives, and to accept the need for change. Even within the Orthodox fold, there is no consensus on the degree of change which is permissible. It is a far cry from the Yeshiva University in the Bronx to the Lubavitcher Yeshivah a few miles away in Brooklyn, yet both are expressions of Orthodox Judaism. Proposals to recreate an authoritative central body, as the Sanhedrin was in ancient Judea, have proved abortive.

One Orthodox faction became part of the modern Zionist Movement and called itself the Mizrachi Party. More fundamentalist factions, like Agudat Israel, rejected Zionism. They contended the Return to the Homeland depended on the coming of the Messiah in God's good time. However, when the State of Israel came in to existence in 1948 it was accepted as a fact by most of Orthodox Jewry including Agudat Israel, but still not by a few extremist groups like the Satmar Sect in New York or the Naturei Carta Sect in Jerusalem.

The European Emancipation from the end of the 18th century brought in its wake a large-scale drift away from traditional Judaism. The Reform movement started in Germany in the early 19th century. Its initial aim was to make the synagogue service more attractive to modern minds, as an antidote to assimilation. The liturgy was shortened, and most of it translated into German. A choir and an organ were introduced. Strict decorum replaced the informal and easygoing club atmosphere of the traditional *shul* (synagogue).

In the early phase, the object was simply to modify the service from within. But by the middle of the century, Reform had evolved into a new and separate movement in Judaism. It also became known as Liberal or Progressive Judaism, and spread to other Western countries, particularly the United States, Britain, France and Hungary. The break with Orthodox practices became more marked – for instance, in synagogue men and women were no longer seated separately, nor did men keep their heads covered.

With the innovation in observance went a deeper doctrinal spirit. The Reform movement rejected the concept that the Jews were still a national entity, and insisted that they were no more than Germans of the Jewish faith, or the equivalent in other lands. All reference to the hope of a Return to Zion was deleted from the prayer books. Instead, Reform acclaimed the belief of the time that an era of universal progress and brotherhood was dawning for Jew and Gentile alike.

(continued on page 244)

Jews in American Intellectual and Cultural Life

Top left Jonas Salk (b.1914), microbiologist.
Top right Saul Bellow (b.1915), novelist, receiving the Nobel Prize for Literature from King Carl Gustav of Sweden, 10 December 1976.
Bottom left Leonard Bernstein (b.1918), conductor and composer.
Bottom right Jeremiah, 1968, a watercolour and gouache by Ben Shahn (1898–1969).
Below The Marx Brothers.

Jews have been prominent in every field of American intellectual, scientific and cultural life, as indicated by these examples:

Nuclear Science: J. Robert Oppenheimer, Isidor Rabi, Edward Teller.
Medical Research: Jonas Salk and Albert Sabin (anti-polio vaccine), Selman Waksman (antibiotics)
The Novel: Saul Bellow, Edna Ferber, Norman Mailer, Bernard Malamud, Herman Wouk, Leon Uris
Playwrights: Arthur Miller, Clifford Odets, Lillian Hellman, Moss Hart, Ben Hecht
Music: Leonard Bernstein, Isaac Stern, Aaron Copland, George Gershwin, Irving Berlin

Art and Architecture: Ben Shahn, Mark Rothko, Louis Kahn
Theatre: Shubert Brothers, Flo Ziegfield, George S. Kaufman, Jerome Robbins
Press and Advertising: Adolph Ochs, Joseph Pulitzer, Albert Lasker
Radio and Television: David Sarnoff (RCA and NBC), William Paley (CBS), Leonard Goldenson (ABC)

Jews have had a dominant role in the general entertainment industry:

Motion Pictures

Motion Pictures may well have been the most important technological advance in the spread of culture since the invention of the printing press. In its infancy, the Hollywood industry was a new field, open to the talents and enterprise of Jewish immigrants. For the most part, the leading studios were founded and built up by Jews. That was the case with Metro-Goldwyn-Mayer (Sam Goldwyn and Louis B. Mayer), Warner Brothers (the four sons of an immigrant family from Poland), Paramount Pictures (Adolph Zukor), Universal Studios (Carl Laemmle), and 20th Century-Fox (William Fox and Sol Brill). (Several European film-makers have also been Jews. They include Sir Alexander Korda in Britain, Fritz Lang in Germany, Sergei Eisenstein in Russia, and Jan Kadar and Milos Forman in Czechoslovakia.)

Most of the well-known Hollywood producers and directors have been Jewish, as has been a galaxy of famous stars. Against the background of Jewish suffering, it may seem strange that so many of the great comic talents should be Jews – such as the Marx Brothers, Eddie Cantor, Danny Kaye, Zero Mostel and Woody Allen. Yet by tradition the jester is a licensed critic of society, and the clown's fooling is rooted in pathos.

The Musical

The musical has been a distinctive American contribution to the history of the theatre. It has been created mainly by gifted Jewish writers of songs and lyrics. The most successful has been the partnership of Richard Rodgers and Oscar Hammerstein II (*Oklahoma, South Pacific, The King and I, The Sound of Music*). Others have been George Gershwin (*Porgy & Bess*); Alan J. Lerner and Frederick Loewe (*My Fair Lady*); Frank Loesser (*Guys and Dolls*); Leonard Bernstein and Stephen Sondheim (*West Side Story*); and Gerry Bock and Sheldon Harnick (*Fiddler on the Roof*). Through film versions and foreign language stage productions, this form of American mass culture has reached a global audience.

The *Reform Movement* found fertile ground in the 19th-century United States, where the community was still dominated by affluent German-Jewish merchants and bankers. Of almost 200 American synagogues that existed in 1880, before the great influx from Eastern Europe, all but a dozen were Reform.

The ideology of the movement in the United States was formulated in the Pittsburgh Platform of 1885. It declared flatly that 'we consider ourselves no longer a nation but a religious community.' The Bible, the document continued, was not sacred revelation, but a record of the Jewish spiritual mission, and an instrument of moral instruction. In the Mosaic Code, only those laws that had moral value were binding, and only such ceremonies as were adapted to the views and habits of modern civilization. The prevailing trend towards universal culture and intellect would lead to the fulfilment of Israel's Messianic hope for a kingdom of truth, justice and peace among all men.

This optimistic view of the Jewish future was to be shattered by the realities of the 20th century. A revised platform adopted at Columbus, Ohio, in 1937 showed a far-reaching change in the outlook of American Reform during little more than a half-century from the Pittsburgh document. There was a shift back to more traditional Jewish tenets, a sympathetic attitude to the Zionist aim of a Jewish homeland in Palestine, and a call for the revival of the Hebrew language.

Reform congregations in twenty-six countries have a common framework in the World Union of Progressive Judaism. American Reform rabbis are trained at the Hebrew Union College that has its main campus in Cincinnati, Ohio, and European Reform rabbis at the Leo Baeck College in London.

The *Conservative Movement* in the United States sprang up in the second half of the 19th century as a kind of half-way house between Orthodoxy and Reform. It followed such basic elements of tradition as the Hebrew prayer book, the dietary laws and strict Sabbath observance. At the same time, the attitude to change was more open and revolutionary than that of Orthodoxy.

The Conservative philosophy derived from the Jewish historical school in 19th-century Europe. The Jewish people was depicted as a living organism, adapting itself to the challenges of each period without losing its special character. In keeping with its theme of historical continuity, the Conservative movement was, from its inception, pro-Zionist.

With the mass influx of Eastern European Jews into the United States from 1880 onwards, Conservative Judaism filled an important role. It helped the children of the immigrants to integrate into American life without jettisoning the strong Jewish traditions their parents had brought from the Old Country. The Conservative movement is today the largest of the three major Jewish trends in the United States.

The dominant figure in Conservative Judaism in the early years of

Abba Hillel Silver addressing a mass rally in Madison Square Garden, New York, in a salute to the new State of Israel, 16 May 1948.

The Israel Commitment

An overwhelming commitment to the survival and progress of Israel unites all sections of American Jewry, and has swept away earlier sensitivity to the charge of dual loyalty. This commitment finds an outlet in massive financial support; in the united front presented on political issues affecting Israel, through the Conference of Presidents of Major American Jewish Organizations, popularly known as the 'Presidents' Club'; and in the wave of excitement and anguish that sweeps through the community when Israel is in danger, as it was before the Six-Day War of 1967 and in the Yom Kippur War of 1973.

the 20th century was the renowned European scholar, Solomon Schechter, who headed the movement's teaching centre, the Jewish Theological Seminary of America. Schechter developed the institutions of the movement and shaped its ideas in his published works.

One off-shoot of Conservative Judaism was the Reconstructionist movement founded by Mordecai M. Kaplan, for many years the dean of the Teachers Institute of the Jewish Theological Seminary. In Kaplan's view, Judaism was an 'evolving religious civilization' and its perception of God changed as the scope of human knowledge expanded.

The major divisions of contemporary Judaism are by no means clearcut. Each has in its own way tried to hold a balance between Jewish tradition and the needs of modern societies. All of them face the same factors that threaten to erode present-day Jewish identity in the Diaspora: religious apathy, assimilation and intermarriage. Moreover, the distinctions between different trends have been overshadowed by the shared Jewish experiences of our time – the horror of the Holocaust, the birth of Israel and its battle for survival, and concern for Soviet Jewry and for threatened communities elsewhere. It has become accepted that Diaspora Judaism is and will remain a pluralistic faith, and that there is today peaceful co-existence between different trends. In 1926 the Orthodox, Reform and Conservative

245

movements in the United States jointly set up the Synagogue Council of America to represent the whole community in inter-faith activities and other fields of common interest.

The conflict is developing inside the State of Israel, where organized religion is firmly controlled by the Orthodox establishment. Reform and Conservative congregations, as yet small, are striving for equal status.

The period of mass immigration into the United States had produced the concept of the 'melting-pot'. The immigrant groups were expected to shed their foreign tongues and ways and become Americanized. In effect, that meant assimilation into the dominant WASP (White Anglo-Saxon Protestant) culture. However, that idea has been replaced by a concept more flexible and more suited to a predominantly immigrant nation – that of Cultural Pluralism.

American Jewry today is six million strong – half the world's Jews in the post-Holocaust era. It is a highly-organized community, with an elaborate network of institutions: synagogues and temples, welfare federations, community centres, Hebrew schools, recreation clubs and a spectrum of national organizations. At first glance it seems to be the traditional Jewish community writ large, but its relationship with its non-Jewish environment is quite different. The challenge it faces is whether it can maintain a strong Jewish identity in conditions of equality and assimilation.

The pessimists point to certain negative factors. For all but a small minority, the religious commitment is much weaker than the Judaism that sustained their ancestors in previous centuries. This is not an Age of Faith, for either Jew or Gentile. The intensely Jewish way of life and the Yiddish culture brought with them by the Eastern European immigrants have all but disappeared. Three-quarters of American Jewish youth go to college, where they share campus life with non-Jews; intermarriage among them is at a rate of 30-40 per cent. Large-scale Jewish immigration was stopped more than fifty years ago, and by the Second World War the majority of American Jews were native-born. The basic fact is that the immigrants found in America an open society, free of the mediaeval and feudal past that bedevilled even post-emancipation Europe. Assimilation would seem to be an inevitable process.

Yet in spite of the successful integration of the Jews in American life, there is less talk today of the Vanishing American Jew than there was a generation ago. The community has gained a marked self-confidence, and asserts its Jewish identity without feeling defensive or inhibited about it. It has been profoundly influenced by the Holocaust and the rise of Israel. Inside the community there is a revival of interest in its roots, in rediscovering its Jewish heritage. It has been said: 'What the son wished to forget the grandson wishes to remember.'

Moreover, though the American Jew feels secure, he has long lost the illusion that anti-semitism was something he left behind when he sailed from the shores of Europe. It has flared up from time to time on the American scene, even in the 20th century. The Jews have not forgotten the isolationist and xenophobic years after the First World War, when the Ku Klux Klan was riding high and Henry Ford was spending millions of dollars on attacking the 'Jewish menace' through his newspaper, *The Dearborn Independent*, and on propagating the *Protocols of the Elders of Zion*. The immigration quota act of 1924 was largely inspired by race theories – by the demand to preserve the Anglo-Saxon character of the American nation and prevent it from becoming 'a mongrel race'. In the Thirties there was the anti-semitism of the Depression years, and the rash of Nazi 'shirt-movements' brandishing swastikas. Today, the community is concerned about the potential backlash of the energy crisis with American dependence on Arab oil, and of a possible economic recession. In brief, while the American Jews are not seriously threatened by anti-semitism, they recognize the need to remain vigilant. They feel secure – but not totally so.

Over the years, the majority of American Jews have evolved a balanced attitude towards their own identity. They are not 'Americans of the Jewish persuasion', taking at best a philanthropic interest in less fortunate Jews elsewhere. They have come to accept that as Jews they belong to an historical community that is held together by profound ties of faith, emotion, and mutual responsibility, that cut across national frontiers and that have their centre in Israel. On the other hand, the United States is their country; they feel firmly rooted in it.

Canada

Jewish settlement in Canada started after the British conquest of New France (French Canada) in 1759. The community grew very slowly; in 1881, on the eve of the transatlantic migration from Eastern Europe, it numbered just over 2,000 with the largest congregation in Montreal. After that it expanded rapidly. Today the community numbers 280,000, a little more than one per cent of the total Canadian population.

Canadian Jewry is a cohesive community. It is predominantly Orthodox in synagogue affiliation and has always been strongly Zionist in sentiment. One representative national body, the Canadian Jewish Congress, is responsible for Jewish concerns in Canada and elsewhere in the Diaspora. All Zionist groups are included in the Canadian Zionist Organization. These two major bodies are closely co-ordinated and make joint representations to the government on political issues affecting the State of Israel.

Canadian Jewry has developed an outstanding network of Jewish day schools. There is a special reason for this in Montreal, Quebec Province – one of the two major Jewish communities in the country (the other is Toronto). There are two separate public school systems in that province, one Catholic and the other Protestant. The Jewish community belongs to the Protestant system, a situation that has given

rise to certain difficulties. This factor has encouraged the development of separate Jewish schools in Montreal.

Canadian Jews are fully integrated into the general life of the country. In the business world, they are concentrated in commerce and light industry, though there is still little Jewish representation in heavy industry or in the leading banking and insurance institutions. A number of Jews have held top positions in public service and the judiciary. Jewish poets and novelists have been prominent in Canadian literature.

The main area of concern for Canadian Jewry relates to the growth of French-Canadian nationalism in Quebec Province. In the past this separatist movement has had anti-semitic overtones, notably under the leadership of Adrian Arcand in the 1930s. The central question in Canadian political life – whether Quebec Province will secede from the Dominion – may have disturbing implications for the future of the Montreal community.

Jewish
Occupations
in
Spain

The Jews played an important role in all spheres of government, economics and public administration. The diversity of their occupations indicates their deep involvement in the economic life of the country. Although comprising only 4 per cent of the population, they paid 20 per cent of the taxes. The Jews had many varied professions in Spain; they worked as scribes, translators, ambassadors, wine merchants, pharmacists, physicians, surveyors, astronomers and money-lenders.

Above *The French Revolution. A collage depicting the main events and protagonists.*

Below *The House of Rothschild. The famous zebras of Lord Lionel Walter Rothschild (the second baron) of England, based on a photograph.*

הוברות לבית רוטשילד
LORD ROTHSCHILD'S ZEBRAS

Nobiliſſimos, y magnificos ſeñores,

El ſeñor DAVID SENIOR Coronel;

El ſeñor Doctor ABRAHAM de MERCADO;

El ſeñor JAHACOB MVCATE;

El ſeñor ISHAC CASTANHO;

Y MAS

Señores de nueſtra naſcion, habitantes enel Recife de
PHERNAMBVCO, Salud.

I Los de menor calidad, pueden, y ..... ſi
avn les es licito imitar los grandes, parua b-
ſegun el principe delos Poëtas Lati- cet com-
nos, ſeame licito tambien en algun magnis.
modo imitar los Reyes y generoſos principes. Y
como eſtos ſuelen, quando dela patria ſalen a otras
prouincias, mandar a los Reyes, o Magiſtrados del-
las, vn Embaxador, q̃ de ſu parte les dé a entender
y certifique ſu venida: del miſmo modo yo, (nobiliſſimos ſeñores) partiendome de la florentiſſima
Batauia a tan logincas partes del Braſil, determiné
primero, no digo mandar Embaxador, nobis non li- Ex Mer-
cet eſſe tam beatis, mas ſegun nueſtro humilde eſta- tiale pa-
do, vn ſeñal de mi doctrina e ingenio, el qual ten- tydia.
dra por hora la vez de Embaxador. Eſpero ſea re-
cebido

The title page of part of Conciliador,
*1651, a biblical commentary by the
Amsterdam scholar Manasseh ben-
Israel. It is dedicated to four leading
Jewish residents of Recife, capital of
the province of Pernambuco.*

Latin America

None of the Jews who had been expelled from Spain and Portugal
was allowed to settle in the new World colonies of these two powers.
(These former colonies are now known as Latin America.) A number
of Marranos, however, migrated across the Atlantic and some of them
became prominent in the colonial administration, trade and the
professions. The Inquisition followed them overseas and started
operating in the New World from 1570. During the next century
Marranos condemned of secret Jewish practices were periodically
burnt at the stake.

In the first two decades of the 19th century, in the wake of the
American War of Independence, the Spanish colonies in Latin
America and the Portuguese colony of Brazil rebelled against the
mother countries and gained their freedom. They abolished the
Inquisition, partly because it was one of the institutions associated
with the colonial regimes, partly under the influence of the American
and French Revolutions. Jewish communities were established from
the 1860s onwards and benefitted from the tolerance that had been
gained for the Protestant minorities in these Catholic countries.

Substantial Jewish immigration into Latin America began only
after 1880. Of the 670,000 Jews living in the region today, at least
ninety per cent have an Ashkenazi background, mainly Eastern
European. The Russian Jews introduced their Yiddish culture,
schools and 'landsmanschaften', as in the United States. The Sephardi
immigrants – Ladino-speaking Jews from the Balkans, and Arabic-
speaking Jews from Syria and North Africa – tended to form their own
separate congregations.

The main country of immigration was the Argentine. It was the
most European in population, had the most advanced economy and
highest literacy rate, and actively encouraged newcomers. The Jewish
community of the Argentine today numbers about 300,000, almost
fifty per cent of the total for Latin America.

Since the Jews are predominantly occupied in commerce and
industry, they naturally concentrated in the biggest and busiest Latin
American cities: Buenos Aires in the Argentine (c.250,000); Rio de
Janeiro (55,000), and Sao Paulo (75,000) in Brazil; Montevideo
(48,000) in Uruguay; Mexico City (32,000) ; Santiago, in Chile
(25,000); Caracas in Venezuela (9,000). The majority of the twenty-
four states in the Latin American-Carribean region have fewer than
2,000 Jews each.

While many Latin American Jews have prospered and some have
achieved positions of distinction, the overall situation of the Jewish
communities has been more insecure and vulnerable than in the case of
Western democratic countries. With few exceptions, the Latin
American lands have been politically unstable, with one-man dictator-
ships or government by military juntas more the rule than the
exception. The Jews belong to a middle class which is relatively small

by Western norms and is sandwiched between a landowning oligarchy and a depressed mass of workers and peons (farm labourers). The resultant economic and social tensions have produced an endemic anti-semitism, that flares up in different times and places. It was exploited and inflamed by the Nazi movements in the years preceding the Second World War. Today the Jewish leadership has to be vigilant concerning the influence of Arab oil, petro-dollars and propaganda drives. There is a steady, though not massive, re-emigration to the United States and to Israel, where an estimated 8,000 Latin American families have settled.

The Jewish communities were very active in the crucial period of 1947–9 in helping to secure Latin American backing for the establishment of Israel. At the United Nations, Latin American support was decisive in securing the adoption of the Partition Resolution of 1947, and in Israel's admission to the Organization in 1949.

South Africa

After England had acquired the Cape of Good Hope from the Dutch at the beginning of the 19th century, Jewish settlers came in from Britain, and a smaller number from Germany. In time, prosperous Jewish businesses grew up in the larger towns, and Jews played a leading part in the export of agricultural products such as wool, mohair, hides and skins, and wine.

South Africa entered a new economic era with the dramatic discoveries of the Kimberley diamond mines (1879) and the Rand goldfields (1886). Among the newcomers attracted to the country were several young London Jews who became leading mining magnates. The most prominent and colourful of them was Barney Barnato. He contended with Cecil Rhodes for control of the diamond fields and then went into partnership with Rhodes in setting up the De Beers Consolidated Mines, which has dominated the world diamond market ever since. It was later headed by a German Jew, Sir Ernest Oppenheimer, followed by his son Harry.

In 1880 there were 4,000 Jews in South Africa. In the next thirty years 40,000 Jewish immigrants came in, nearly all from Eastern Europe. More than seventy per cent were 'Litvaks' (Lithuanian Jews). That fact gave the South African community its distinctive character. It has been unusually close-knit, and imbued with the Litvak pragmatism, reverence for scholarship and wholehearted devotion to Zionism. South African Jewry has proportionally a higher level of Zionist fund-raising and a larger number of settlers in Israel than any other Free World community, while the South African Zionist Federation is regarded as a model of its kind.

A considerable number of the newcomers made their way into the rural districts, first as itinerant peddlers and then as village and small-town shopkeepers. On the whole they were well received by the

Recife, Brazil, in the 17th Century

Pernambuco had been a Dutch colony from 1630, and was the only place in Latin America where Jews could practise their religion openly. Recife had an organized congregation with a synagogue, two religious schools and a cemetery. As the effusive tone of his dedication implies, Manasseh Ben-Israel was interested in being appointed the rabbi of that community.

From 1652 the colony reverted to Portuguese rule, and its Jews and Marranos were again persecuted. Nearly all of them left, and the congregation disintegrated. One small group of twenty-three souls

(continued on page 256)

Jewish gauchos pose with Argentine colleagues, Mauricio, Buenos Aires Province, Argentina.

reached New Amsterdam and were the first Jews to settle in what became the United States of America.

Jewish Agricultural Colonies in Argentina

In 1891, the Jewish banker and philanthropist Baron Maurice de Hirsch, who had been born in Bavaria and settled in Paris, established the Jewish Colonization Association (ICA). Its main objective was to promote the settling of Russian Jews on the land in the New World. With the assent of the Czar's government a network of committees was set up throughout Russia and a number of farm and vocational schools operated for training the prospective emigrants. The main area of settlement was in Argentina, where a Jewish farm colony, Moisésville, had been founded two years earlier. Three small colonies were also started in Brazil but failed to develop. The colonization in Argentina reached its peak by about 1930, when 20,000 Jews were living from grain farming and cattle ranching on a million and a half acres. The Jewish gaucho on horseback was a familiar figure in certain districts of the Argentinian pampas. The Jewish colonies pioneered agrarian co-operatives, diversified farming methods and the cultivation of new crops.

As time passed there was a steady drift to the cities and the Jewish farming community dwindled to a few thousand. To a large extent this was part of the general process of urbanization, and the impact of the depression years on rural life. Other reasons were friction between the settlers and ICA overseers, losses from periodic droughts and locust swarms in marginal semi-arid areas, fluctuation in the market prices of beef and grain, and the chronic land shortage from which some of the Jewish colonies suffered.

255

Afrikaner (Boer) farmers – stern Calvinists who lived by the Old Testament. But the next Jewish generation tended to move to the big towns, where there were more opportunities and a better chance to bring up children in a Jewish environment. In the urban centres Jews pioneered modern methods of retailing and dominated certain fields of light industry, especially clothing and textiles. A considerable number of the sons of the Jewish immigrant merchants entered the free professions of law and medicine.

One interesting field in Jewish hands was the ostrich feather industry before the First World War, with its world centre in the Cape town of Oudtshoorn.

Jewish immigration into South Africa met with strong public resistance at certain times, and provoked a backlash of anti-semitism. The Eastern European immigration was virtually halted by the Quota Act of 1930. That Act, based on geographical quotas, did not block the entry of German-Jewish refugees after Hitler came to power, so in 1937 it was replaced by a new Aliens Act. Under its terms a selection board was given power to reject any individual immigrant, and few Jews satisfied its criteria. At that time Nazi propaganda was fomenting anti-Jewish feeling among the Afrikaners, and 'shirt movements' were sprouting in the country. With the curtailment of immigration, the low birth-rate and some younger Jews leaving the country, the size of the community has remained static, at a figure of about 120,000, and its percentage of the population has declined.

The South African Jews are part of a complex multi-racial society. They are half of one per cent of the population, but the significant statistic is that they are three per cent of the white ('European') minority that alone enjoys full political, economic and residential rights. Within the white community most of the Jews are identified with the English-speaking group in language, culture and urban life-style. The Nationalist Party, that represents the Afrikaner majority among the whites, has been in power since 1948. Initial Jewish fears have been allayed, since the government has shown itself well-disposed to the Jewish community, and has staunchly supported the State of Israel. South African Jews are not under any political or economic pressure, and overt anti-semitism died down after the fall of Hitler. But it is difficult for them to feel completely secure in a country where the racial problems remain unresolved and the future is unpredictable.

Smuts and Zionism. Field Marshal Jan Smuts, Prime Minister until 1948, on Table Mountain. Smuts was an eloquent supporter of the Zionist cause from the time he became a personal friend of Dr Chaim Weizmann while he was a member of the Imperial War Cabinet in London during the First World War. He had a hand in formulating the Balfour Declaration of 1917 and was one of the authors of the Palestine Mandate after the war.

Top *Sir Isaac Isaacs as Governor-General of Australia. From a painting by Sir John Longstaff, 1936.*

Above *Sir John Monash, general, commander of the Australian army corps in France during the First World War.*

Australia and New Zealand

European settlement in Australia started in 1788 with a British penal colony, where Sydney now stands. The first Jews were six convicts, who remained as settlers. With characteristic Jewish resilience, one of them became a policeman!

By the mid-19th century there were established congregations in Sydney, Melbourne and several smaller towns, with about one-quarter of the Jewish citizens scattered in the rural areas. The Jewish community had no problems of integration, and encountered no restrictions.

In the first half of the 20th century the small and semi-assimilated community was greatly expanded and revitalized by an influx of European Jews. In the years before and after the First World War they came from Eastern Europe. In the late 1930s Australia took in about 8,000 refugees from Nazi Germany. After the Second World War thousands of Holocaust survivors were admitted from the DP camps. Today there is an active and well-organized Jewish community numbering approximately 70,000, represented by the Executive Council of Australian Jewry. Although only five per cent of the total population, the Jews have a respected place in Australian life, and a number of them have been prominent in politics, business and the professions. Eminent Australian Jews have included Sir Isaac Isaacs, Chief Justice of Australia and its first native-born Governor-General; General Sir John Monash, who commanded the Australian and New Zealand forces on the Western Front in the First World War, and who was the highest-ranking Jew in any modern army; and Sir Zelman Cowen was appointed Governor-General in 1977.

The 4,000 Jews in New Zealand (two per cent of the population) are nearly all from families who originated in England. (New Zealand immigration laws have been designed to preserve the British character of the Dominion.) They have enjoyed complete freedom since the community started in 1829, and are well established in farming, business and the professions. The three main congregations are in Auckland, Wellington and Christchurch. The public offices held by Jews have included a Premier, Sir Julius Vogel; a Chief Justice, Sir Michael Myers; and a number of MPs and mayors of the main cities.

Important Events

United States

1492	Columbus discovers America.
1654	Marrano group reaches New Amsterdam.
1776	Outbreak of American Revolution.
1835	Beginning of German-Jewish immigration.
1861–5	7,000 Jews fight in Civil War.
1873	Union of American Congregations (Reform) founded.
1881	Beginning of mass immigration from Eastern Europe.
1890	Ellis Island immigration centre opened.
1898	Union of Orthodox Jewish Congregations founded.
1913	United Synagogue of America (Conservative) founded.
1917–18	Quarter-million American Jews serve in the First World War.
1919	American Jewish Delegation to Paris Peace Treaty.
1924	Immigration quota Act restricts Jewish immigration.
1948	United States recognizes Israel (14 May).

Latin America

1570	Inquisition introduced to New World.
1881	Beginning of substantial Eastern European immigration.
1891	ICA colonies launched in Argentina.

British Commonwealth

1759	First Jewish settlers in Canada.
1788	First Jews arrive in Australia (as convicts).
1820	British Jews settle in South Africa.
1820	Start of New Zealand community.
c.1882	Beginning of Eastern European Jewish immigration to Canada, South Africa, Australia and New Zealand.

Chapter Seventeen

The Return

One of the most powerful factors that held the Jewish people together in the Diaspora, and sustained them under stress, was the hope of a Messianic Return to the ancestral homeland.

The term 'Messiah' comes from the Hebrew word *mashiach*, meaning 'the anointed one'. In biblical times it was used for the Hebrew kings and high priests who, on taking office, were consecrated to God by the formal anointing of their heads with holy oil.

The Hebrew prophets foretold that the Jewish kingdom would be restored under a descendant of King David. This belief was further developed in the post-biblical period. There would be a time of convulsion in human affairs, 'the end of days'. A divinely-appointed Messiah would bring the Jews back to the Land of Israel. A kingdom of God would arise there, ushering in for all mankind a new era of peace, justice and national harmony. The Messiah was pictured as riding into Jerusalem on a donkey, in accordance with the prophecy in the *Book of Zechariah*:

> *Lo, your king comes to you;*
> *triumphant and victorious is he,*
> *humble and riding on an ass.*

(Zech. 9:9)

Messianic expectations arose sharply in periods of general upheaval and Jewish persecution. Such a period was the 1st century BC and the 1st century AD. It saw the emergence of Rome as the imperial master of the Middle East, the birth of Christianity and the crushing of the Jewish State. The time produced a flood of apocalyptic literature – mystic revelations of the future – and a number of preachers who claimed that the redemption was approaching. The Gospels present Jesus as the awaited Messiah, a descendant of David, proclaiming that the kingdom of God was at hand. (The appellation 'Christ' is from the Greek word meaning 'the anointed one' – that is, the Messiah.) Jesus is described as entering Jerusalem on a donkey.

The Messianic theme runs throughout Diaspora history, but was most marked during the centuries of Jewish suffering in mediaeval Europe and in Moslem lands. The bloody massacres that attended the First Crusade (1096), the Black Death (1348), the Spanish pogroms

Jerusalem
See colour page 269

> *If I forget you, O Jerusalem,*
> *let my right hand wither!*
> *Let my tongue cleave to the roof of*
> *my mouth,*
> *if I do not remember you,*
> *if I do not set Jerusalem*
> *above my highest joy!*
> (Psalm 137:5, 6)

> *For out of Zion shall go forth*
> *law,*
> *and the word of the Lord from*
> *Jerusalem.*
> (Isaiah 2:3)

One cannot enter Jerusalem for the first time without feeling the impact of forty centuries of continuous history. The very name 'Jerusalem' has a profoundly emotional sound to hundreds of millions of Christians, Jews and Moslems throughout the world. This is the city the kings David and Solomon, of the prophets Isaiah and Jeremiah, of Ezra and Nehemiah in the Return, of Judah the Maccabee

 (continued on page 264)

The Wailing Wall. An engraving by W.H. Bartlett, 1842.

and his brothers. This is the city of Jesus's Ministry and the Crucifixion. And Moslems hold this city to be the place from which Mohammed ascended to heaven; for them it is next after Mecca and Medina in holiness.

Many different breeds of men have sat in the seat of power in Jerusalem – Jebusites, Hebrews, Babylonians and Persians; Greeks and Romans; Arabs, Crusaders, Ottoman Turks and British. But throughout the flux of these thousands of years there runs one constant thread – the unique attachment of the Jewish people to Jerusalem. Only for that people has the city been the national centre. The attachment has remained unbroken from the time when King David made Jerusalem the capital of the Hebrew State to the time when David Ben-Gurion did likewise, 3,000 years later.

Through all the centuries of dispersion, from the farthest corners of the earth, Jews have prayed for the Return to Zion, and built the sacred Ark on the synagogue wall facing the direction of Jerusalem. History has no parallel to this mystic bond.

The Temple

Down the ages imaginative visions of the Temple of Jerusalem have been a frequent theme of Jewish and Christian art. King Solomon's Temple was completed in the 11th year of his reign, that is about 950 BC. The site was the threshing-floor that Solomon's father David had bought from Araunah the Jebusite for fifty shekels of silver. The fame and splendour of Solomon's Temple would suggest an imposing structure, but actually it was small. Scholars have calculated that the outside dimensions were about fifty metres long, twenty-five metres wide and fifteen metres high. It must be borne in mind that the interior was not a place of assembly; the congregation gathered in the great courtyard outside. The shrine itself was 'God's house', a dwelling for the Divine Presence.

The First Temple lasted nearly four centuries, until it was destroyed and Jerusalem sacked by a Babylonian army in 586 BC.

The Second Temple was constructed on the foundations of the previous one by a group of Jews that returned from the Babylonian Exile. It was completed around 515 BC. This must have been a more modest building, with none of the sumptuous adornments Solomon had lavished on the original one. The new Temple was no longer the shrine of an independent kingdom, but the house of worship of a small and struggling sect in an obscure corner of the Persian empire. However, it was of profound importance for the survival of the Jewish people that they should once more possess a focus of faith in their ancestral homeland and their holy city.

Herod the Great (37–4 BC) was the finest royal builder in Jewish history after King Solomon, a thousand years earlier. In 22 BC he convened a national assembly and announced a sweeping plan to reconstruct the Second Temple that had served for five centuries. Herod gathered together a great labour force for the project, and hundreds of wagons to transport the materials. The building itself was put up in eighteen months. The ground plan and location remained the same, but Herod's Temple was higher and far more luxurious than the one it replaced. Herod's major change was to construct a huge platform on the Temple Mount, surrounded by massive retaining walls of enormous limestone blocks. The completion of the whole complex of buildings and courtyards on the enlarged platform took forty-six years in all – in fact, a generation beyond Herod's death. It was to be destroyed a few decades after it was finished.

After the destruction by the Romans in AD 70, Judaism survived and continued to develop, but the loss of the Temple remained a searing memory. For centuries the Jewish farmers had brought their first fruits to the sanctuary. On the great pilgrimage festivals thousands of worshippers had gathered in the courtyards from all over the Jewish world. They had been emotionally uplifted by the splendour of the Temple and by its time-hallowed rituals. Now the focus of their religious experience had been removed. The transition to a life without the Temple was painful.

For the next nineteen centuries Jews would come to pray and mourn at the Western (Wailing) Wall, an exposed section of Herod's great retaining wall. This was the closest they could get to the site of the demolished Temple, where, according to the rabbis, the Divine Presence still lingered. The Western Wall served as the holiest shrine of Judaism, and the tangible symbol of the First and Second Temples. Their destruction is commemorated by the annual fast day of Tisha b'Av (the ninth day of the month of Av, in July or August). On that day, the approximate date of both these national calamities, the biblical *Book of Lamentations* is recited in synagogues.

Jews cling to the mystical 3,000-year memory of the sanctuary that once stood on Mount Moriah. They believe with the biblical Prophets that in God's good time the Temple will rise again at the centre of a Messianic kingdom.

False Messiahs
See colour page 269

The most remarkable of the false messiahs in the mediaeval period were David Alroy in the 12th century, David Reuveni and Shlomo Molcho early in the 16th century, and Shabbetai Zevi in the 17th century.

David Alroy
David Alroy was the leader of a Messianic movement that sprang up in Kurdistan about twenty-five years after the Crusader capture of Jerusalem in 1099. The background to the movement was the struggle between Christianity and Islam for possession of the Holy Land. Alroy, whose real first name was Menachem, took the name of David when he claimed to be the king of the Jews. He was an exceptionally handsome young man who excelled in religious and mystical studies and was credited with possessing magic powers. His pretensions were promoted by his father Solomon, who himself claimed to be the prophet Elijah.

Alroy established his headquarters in the fortified town of Amadiya, astride the road leading to the Crusader kingdom of Edessa in Mesopotamia. Letters were sent to the Jewish communities throughout the region, calling upon them to prepare themselves by fasting and prayer for his return to Jerusalem. According to one tradition, the Jews of Baghdad spent a night waiting on their rooftops because of a story that they would be transported to Jerusalem by winged angels.

Alroy's expectations came to an abrupt end when he was murdered. A number of his followers, known as Menachemites, continued to believe he would reappear. Benjamin Disraeli's novel, *The Wondrous Tale of Alroy* (1839) is a largely fictional account of the episode.

David Reuveni
David Reuveni first appeared in Western Europe in 1522. He claimed that his brother was the ruler of a Jewish kingdom in the desert, inhabited by the descendants of the Lost Israelite tribes of Reuven – hence his name – Gad and part of Manasseh. (These were the tribes that had settled east of the Jordan River at the time of Joshua's Conquest.) Reuveni stated that he had come to offer an alliance to the Christian leaders against the Moslem Turks, who had recently conquered the Holy Land in 1516. With Christian support and weapons, an army from the Jewish kingdom under Reuveni's command would regain the Holy Land. That would be followed by the Return of the Jews to their homeland and the inception of the Messianic age.

Reuveni was at first regarded with scepticism by the Jewish leaders, but to their surprise he was taken seriously by the Church hierarchy. The influential Cardinal da Viterbo welcomed him and arranged an audience for him with the Pope. Armed with a letter from the Pope, Reuveni arrived in Lisbon in 1525 and was given ambassadorial treatment by the King of Portugal. His advent caused great excitement among the Portuguese Marranos (crypto-Jews), and speculation was rife among them concerning the Messianic redemption. For that reason Reuveni provoked the hostility of the powerful Inquisition and had to leave the country. It is likely that he spent the next few years in Spanish and North African prisons.

Shlomo Molcho
One of Reuveni's Portuguese disciples was an intellectual young Marrano called Diogo Pires (1500–32), who as a boy had secretly learnt Hebrew and studied Jewish religious books. With Reuveni's advent in Lisbon, Pires was swept by Messianic fervour. He publicly announced himself a Jew, circumcised himself and took the name of *Shlomo Molcho* (Molcho is from the Hebrew word for a king). He fled from the Inquisition and settled in Salonika,

Turkey. Having become convinced of his divine mission, he went to Rome, dressed in rags and lived for a month among the beggars gathered on a bridge over the River Tiber – acting out a Talmudic legend that the Messiah would emerge from these conditions. After that he started preaching in public and gained renown by predicting a flood in Rome and an earthquake in Lisbon. Arrested by the Inquisition, he was saved from death at the instance of the Pope.

Molcho renewed contact with Reuveni, who had emerged again in Venice. In 1532 the two of them set off on a visit to Emperor Charles V in Regensburg, Germany, for some unspecified purpose. But the Emperor had been turned against them by Church circles. He sent them back in chains to Mantua in Italy. Here Molcho was burnt at the stake by the Inquisition. Reuveni lingered on in prison, and died in about 1538.

The main source of information about Reuveni is a diary he kept in Hebrew. His real name and origin remain a mystery. Some scholars believe he was a Falasha, one of a black Jewish community in Ethiopia.

Shabbetai Zevi

Shabbetai Zevi (1626–76) caused a far greater upheaval in Jewish life than any other false messiah in Diaspora history. The son of a prosperous Jewish merchant of Smyrna, in Turkish Asia Minor, he was subject to strange moods of euphoria and melancholy, and would probably be diagnosed today as a manic-depressive. From his boyhood he was intensely religious, and absorbed himself in Kabbalistic studies. At the age of twenty-two he publicly declared himself the Messiah, purported to utter the forbidden name of God and announced that the redemption was imminent. He was not taken seriously, but some years later his recurrent Messianic claims and his eccentric behaviour during ecstatic spells, led to his being banned by the rabbis. After years of wandering he settled in Jerusalem. In 1665 he was proclaimed as the true Messiah by a well-known mystic and faith-healer,

Shabbetai Zevi in prison in Adrianople. From Ketzer Geschichte, *1701.*

Nathan of Gaza. That launched the Shabbatean movement, with Nathan of Gaza acting as Shabbetai's prophet and ideologue.

Increasing persecution, and especially the Chmielnicki massacres in the Ukraine, had left a mood of gloom and despair in the Jewish communities of Europe. Many believed that the darkest hour had been reached, which would be followed by the redemption. The expectations were strengthened by the mystical doctrines, with messianic overtones, that had been enunciated in Safad by the Kabbalist Isaac Luria (*ha-Ari*) in the 16th century and had permeated Jewish scholarship everywhere. These factors accounted for the extraordinary spread and joyful acceptance of the news about Shabbetai's advent. It was confidently expected, even in some Christian circles, that he would soon be crowned in Jerusalem as king of the Jews. A circular was sent to all Jewish communities in the name of 'the first-begotten Son of God, Shabbetai Zevi, messenger and redeemer of the people of Israel'.

Alarmed by the ferment he had stirred up, the Turkish authorities arrested and imprisoned him. In 1666 he was brought before the Sultan in Adrianople and given the choice between conversion to Islam and death. He chose Islam and was converted together with a group of his disciples. Gratified at gaining so famous a convert, the Sultan granted Shabbetai an honorary title and a pension.

The apostacy stunned the Jewish communities everywhere. Some of his followers interpreted it as part of the divine plan, a mystical 'descent' to redeem lost souls among the infidels. Even after Shabbetai died in a small Albanian town, small groups of adherents continued to believe that he would return as a redeemer. That belief persisted for a century, after which it faded.

One Shabbetean legacy was a strong rabbinical distrust of any movement that appealed to the mystical and emotional elements in Judaism. That helps to explain the force of the opposition aroused in the Orthodox establishment by the revivalist movement of Chassidism in the 18th century.

(1391) and the Chmielnicki uprising in the Ukraine (1648), as also the Expulsions (especially that from Spain in 1492), were regarded as 'the birthpangs of the Messiah', the darkest hour before the dawn. False messiahs arose, then disappeared or were discredited, leaving their followers forlorn. But the recurrent experience with imposters and religious cranks did not extinguish the messianic yearning.

However, the modern Return came about in the form of a secular national movement, and not through the miraculous instrument of a Messiah. This fact caused deep perplexity to the Orthodox Jews. Most of them were opposed to Zionism, thinking it an impious and impatient attempt to pre-empt the advent of the Messiah. There were some 19th-century religious Jews who thought otherwise. Among them were Judah Alkalai, a rabbi from Sarajevo in Bosnia-Herzegovina; the German Talmudic scholar Zvi Hirsch Kalischer; and the Lithuanian rabbi Samuel Mohilever. These men contended that God expected human effort to pave the way for the Return, and they sought support for practical programmes. They were the forerunners of the Mizrachi (religious Zionist) movement.

Another road to Zionism in the 19th century was through the revolutionary socialist movement of the period. Moses Hess, a German socialist who worked for some years with Marx and Engels, became sceptical of the facile belief that socialism would eliminate anti-semitism. In 1862 he published a booklet, *Rome and Jerusalem*, advocating the revival of an independent Jewish State in Palestine on a basis of social justice.

In the mood of despair that followed the 1881 pogroms in the Pale of Settlement and the anti-Jewish May Laws, Leon Pinsker, a doctor in Odessa, published a pamphlet in 1882 called *Auto-Emancipation*. Attributing anti-semitism mainly to Jewish homelessness, he called on the Russian Jews to emigrate to a land where they could recreate their own independent nation. 'Help yourselves and God will help you!' Pinsker soon accepted that such a project was possible only in the ancestral homeland. He became a leader of the Lovers of Zion (Chovevei Zion) movement that sprang up in Russia and elsewhere. Its scattered societies joined into a single organization in 1884, at a conference at Kattowitz in Silesia. The same approach was developed by the Russian Hebrew writer, Moses Leib Lilienblum. His analysis of the Jewish problem in Europe concluded with the assertion that 'aliens we are and aliens we shall remain. . . . We need a corner of our own. We need Palestine.'

In the 1880s small groups of Jewish students started migrating to Palestine in order to live there on the land. They called themselves BILU, from the Hebrew initial letters of the phrase in *Isaiah*: 'O House of Jacob, come ye and let us go.' They were the vanguard of the first *Aliyah* (wave of immigration). The farm villages they set up could hardly have survived the grim local conditions without help from Baron Edmond de Rothschild.

The stirrings of Zionism among the Eastern European Jews was

Herzl

Dr Theodor Herzl (1860–1904) was the founder of the modern Zionist Movement. Born in Budapest, Hungary, of a well-to-do Jewish family, he became a doctor of law at the University of Vienna, and settled in Vienna as a journalist and playwright. Herzl was a striking-looking man, above average height, with a black beard and magnetic brown eyes. He was assimilated into the social and cultural life of the time, and uninvolved in Jewish affairs. But, while serving as the Paris correspondent of a leading Austrian newspaper, he became increasingly conscious of the anti-semitism that had persisted after the emancipation of the Jews in Western Europe.

The problem became an obsession with him as a result of the Dreyfus Affair, which he covered for his paper. In 1896 he published an epoch-making booklet, *The Jewish State*. Its sub-title read: *An Attempt at a Modern Solution of the Jewish Question*. In the preface he stated: 'We are a people – one people. We are strong enough to form a state...' The booklet set out a blueprint for such a State.

In 1897 Herzl convened the First Zionist Congress in Basle, Switzerland – the first international Jewish assembly for nearly 2,000 years. The Congress established the World Zionist Organization, with Herzl as its President. The programme adopted by Congress laid down that 'the aim of Zionism is to create for the Jewish people a home in Palestine secured by public law.' Herzl noted in his diary: 'In Basle I founded the Jewish State.'

Palestine at that time was under Ottoman rule. Herzl first sought German diplomatic support. In 1898 he was informed that the German Kaiser, Wilhelm II, was sympathetic to Zionist aims and would be willing to grant Herzl an audience in Jerusalem, which the Kaiser was about to visit. A preliminary meeting took place in Constantinople. Herzl requested the Kaiser's influence in favour of a colonization charter from

Theodor Herzl, who was the founder of modern Zionism.

the Sultan of Turkey. The response was non-committal. The following morning Herzl and his delegation sailed for Palestine. He found it a poor and largely barren country, after centuries of Turkish misrule. The meeting with the Kaiser was an anti-climax, as the erratic monarch had lost interest in the matter.

In 1901 and 1902 Herzl carried on negotiations directly with the Sultan Abdul Hamid II and his ministers in Constantinople. Herzl promised to raise a large loan for the bankrupt Ottoman regime, but his efforts to enlist the help of rich Jewish bankers was unsuccessful.

With the direct road to Palestine through Constantinople blocked, a promising detour seemed to open up through Britain, the mightiest imperial power of the time. Herzl was received in London by the powerful Colonial Secretary, Joseph Chamberlain. They discussed the possibility of a temporary Jewish settlement in the El Arish district of Sinai, but the project proved impossible because of the water problem.

On returning from a visit to East Africa in 1903, Chamberlain proposed that a commission be sent out to establish whether a suitable territory along the new Uganda Railway could be made available for an autonomous 'Jewish colony of settlement'. Herzl placed the proposal before the Zionist Congress, urging that it might provide a home at least for the time being, for the refugees from the bloody pogroms in Russia earlier that year. To his dismay, most of the Russian delegates were fiercely against the proposal, refusing to consider any diversion from settlement in Palestine. The Uganda Project, as it was called, split the Zionist Movement into two bitterly opposed camps before it was abandoned. Herzl, who had suffered from a heart ailment for some years, emerged from the controversy exhausted, ill and burdened by a sense of failure. But for millions of Jews, especially in the Russian Pale of Settlement, he had already become a Messianic figure, the personal embodiment of the age-old hope of a Return. His death in July 1904, at the

dramatically converted into an international movement by the Viennese journalist, Dr Theodor Herzl, who established the World Zionist Organization in 1897. Herzl died in 1904, worn out by his unsuccessful attempts to obtain a political charter for large-scale settlement in Palestine. For the next decade, practical colonization continued quietly in Palestine. A new type of *chalutz* (pioneer) appeared – the young, idealistic men and women of the Second Aliyah, bent on self-help and manual labour. David Ben-Gurion was one of that generation. The first kibbutzim (collective farm villages) were born, and Tel Aviv, an all-Jewish city, was founded. By the outbreak of the First World War the Yishuv (Jewish community of Palestine) numbered 80,000.

The war radically changed the prospects for Zionism. Partly through the efforts of Dr Chaim Weizmann, a Russian-born chemist teaching at Manchester University in England, the British Government on 2 November 1917 issued the historic Balfour Declaration, that pledged support for the establishment in Palestine of a National Home for the Jewish people. After the war, in which Turkey was defeated, the Declaration was written into the Mandate for Palestine accepted by Britain under the auspices of the League of Nations. The Mandate was the international framework for the return of the Jews to age of forty-four sent a wave of shock and bereavement through the Jewish world.

In 1949, when the State of Israel was a year old, Herzl's coffin was brought to Jerusalem and interred on a hilltop named Mount Herzl, looking out upon the Holy City from the west. Herzl's most fitting epitaph could be the words he wrote in his diary: '...it was, after all, no mean achievement for a Jewish journalist without resources...to turn a rag into a flag and a downtrodden rabble into a people rallying erect around that flag.'

The Pioneers

From the 1880s onward small groups of young Zionist pioneers (*chalutzim*) migrated from Eastern Europe to Palestine, filled with zeal to redeem the soil of the homeland. For centuries the Jews in the Diaspora had been cut off from agriculture. The chalutzim believed that the new society they wanted would develop on healthy lines only through a return to manual work, especially on the land.

Dedicated to this ideal, they went through great hardship and danger – draining malarial swamps, clearing stony hillsides, building roads, enduring heat, poor food and primitive living conditions, and protecting themselves against attack by armed Arab bands. Gradually the obstacles were overcome. They established farming communities centred on collective and co-operative villages (kibbutzim and moshavim); a progressive labour federation (the Histadrut); and a country-wide self-defence organization.

In the pre-State era of Zionist colonization, these chalutzim formed an elite serving in the forefront of the national effort, and viewed by the whole Zionist movement with admiration and pride. Their voluntary leadership role waned in the State of Israel, with its mass immigration, professional civil service and regular army.

Two of the tens of thousands of Jews from the European ghettoes who formed farming communities in Israel.

redeem their homeland – the equivalent of the Charter for which Herzl had so vainly struggled.

In the next two decades steady progress was made in developing the National Home. But the mass aliyah that Herzl had visualized did not take place at that time. The Russian Jews had been cut off by the Bolshevik Revolution of 1917. Economic conditions in Palestine were difficult. The Zionist concept was rejected by the Arabs, who plunged the country into disturbances in 1920–1, 1929, and 1936–8. In the Thirties, Britain started to retreat from the Mandatory obligation to promote the Jewish National Home. In May 1939, the British Government issued a White Paper (policy statement) that aimed at turning Palestine into an Arab State, with a Jewish minority that would not exceed one-third of the population. The Zionist leadership determined to fight the White Paper by every available means, as it spelt the doom of hopes for an independent Jewish homeland.

The crux of the conflict was aliyah, Jewish immigration. In the early years of the Mandate there had been a small-scale aliyah, with the number of immigrant certificates restricted to what the British authorities fixed as the 'economic absorptive capacity' of the country. The rate of aliyah increased somewhat in the Thirties, and included 70,000 refugees from Hitler Germany. Further immigration was drastically reduced when the Arab rebellion broke out in Palestine in 1936. When nothing came of the partition plan proposed by the Royal (Peel) Commission of 1936, an organized effort started to bring Jewish

refugees from Europe to Palestine without official immigration certificates. For the British Mandatory government this was an illegal and politically embarrassing movement that had to be blocked by any means. For the Jewish world it was a rescue operation of Nazi victims who had the right to come to their homeland; they called it Aliyah Bet (Immigration 'B'). Until the outbreak of the War, 41 'illegal' boats had sailed with a total of 15,500 refugees. Some of them succeeded in slipping through. Their passengers were disembarked at night and promptly mixed with the local Jewish population. Those who were intercepted were detained in the country.

During the early war years, a number of ships sailed from Rumania through the Black Sea and the Dardenelles. Several of them sank. Of the refugees who reached Palestine, 1,580 were rounded up and transported to detention camps on the island of Mauritius.

At the end of the war great numbers of the Jewish survivors gathered in the Displaced Persons (DP) camps, most of them in the American and British zones in Germany and Austria. The Jewish camps, with a population that rose to a quarter-million, were run as self-governing communities, with their own internal network of services. They taught Hebrew in improvised schools and adult classes, and a number of the young people went to agricultural training (*hachshara*) farms. The overwhelming urge of these DPs was to leave the bloodstained soil of Europe and start again in the National Home.

The renewed post-war Aliyah Bet was run by the Mossad, a clandestine body set up by the representative Jewish institutions in Palestine. It had its headquarters in Paris and a network of agents and

The 'Bericha'

A group of Holocaust survivors passing through Graz, Austria, in 1946, as part of the movement known in Hebrew as *Bericha* (flight). It was a large-scale underground migration of Jews at the end of the War, crossing borders at dead of night, moving westward to the DP camps in Germany and Austria and southward to the Mediterranean coast. Graz in southern Austria was one of the main assembly-points for crossing into Italy, where the refugees could be put onto the 'illegal' ships of the Aliyah Bet.

The Return from Arab Lands

Right *A mass meeting in front of the immigration offices, Tripoli, 1949.*

In the 20th century the situation of the Jews in the Arab countries became more difficult and insecure, owing to the growth of Arab nationalism and the conflict over Palestine. In 1947–8 the pressure on the Jews became intense in most of the Arab lands, and ugly anti-Jewish riots occurred in a number of places. After the birth of Israel two whole communities, in Yemen and Iraq, were evacuated by air to Israel. After the return of the Iraqi troops in 1949 from their inglorious Palestine campaign, resentment turned against the local Jews and repressive measures were imposed on them. The Iraqi government was willing to let them depart, while confiscating their homes, businesses and assets. In a matter of months in 1950–1, 120,000 Iraqi Jews were brought to Israel via Cyprus, by what was called 'Operation Ezra and Nehemiah'.

The immigration from other Arab countries was spread over a number of years, and was less dramatic. In Egypt and Libya the Jewish communities declined from 1948 but were finally evicted only in the aftermath of the Arab defeat by Israel in the Six-Day War of 1967. The Algerian Jews were French nationals and eighty per cent of them were absorbed in France when Algeria became independent in 1962.

In 1948, there were an estimated 870,000 Jews in the Arab world. Two-thirds of them were re-settled in Israel, and the rest absorbed elsewhere. The largest surviving number is in Morocco – 20,000 left of nearly 300,000 in 1948. In Syria 4,000 Jews are held virtually as political hostages.

In Israel the influx of Jews from the Arab lands accounts for about half of the Jewish population. When one adds the aliyah from the non-Arab Moslem countries, Iran and Turkey, it is evident that the Sephardi dispersion in the world of Islam has come round full circle to its beginnings in the Land of Israel.

contacts throughout Europe. The personnel and ships' officers were drawn from the Haganah, the self-defence organization of the Palestinian Jews. The 'Scarlet Pimpernels' of the Mossad operated with an incredible daring and resourcefulness. They smuggled refugee groups across frontiers, turned out thousands of forged travel documents, purchased and outfitted scores of old vessels, and carried on a battle of wits with British intelligence in Europe. Influenced by their recent experience of Nazi occupation, and by the ghastly facts of the Holocaust, many Europeans were sympathetic to Aliyah Bet. But their governments were under heavy diplomatic pressure from Britain to prevent Jews moving through their countries towards Palestine, or embarking from their ports.

Once the crowded boats had sailed, some of them evaded the Royal Navy blockade and succeeded in making secret landings along the coast of Palestine. The estimated numbers that had entered the country in this way were debited against the meagre quota of legal immigration certificates (1,500 per month). Most of the ships, however, were intercepted and boarded, sometimes after stiff resistance. They were escorted into Haifa harbour, often in a damaged state. The refugees were transferred to 'prison ships' with caged-in

Left *Jerusalem from a 15th-century French manuscript.*

Below *False Messiahs. The Messiah on a white ass at the gate of Jerusalem, from the Ashkenazi Haggadah, Germany, 15th century.*

The Gateway. Immigrants on board ship approaching New York.

Overleaf The Menorah. 'Wherever I go, I am going to Eretz Israel' Rabbi Nachman of Bratslav (1722–1811).

Lower East Side, New York. Tenement housing on Lower East Side, New York.

decks, and deported to detention camps in Cyprus. World attention became focussed on the plight of boatloads of Holocaust survivors trying to reach the forbidden shores of the Promised Land.

In the three years from the end of the war in 1945 to the birth of Israel in 1948, the Mossad was responsible for the despatch of 64 ships, carrying nearly 70,000 refugees. Of these, 56,000 were interned in Cyprus, and brought to Israel after it became independent. The total number of 'illegals' arriving by sea and land from 1934 to 1948 was 120,000.

When Israel became independent in May 1948, all immigration restrictions on Jews were scrapped and the gates flung open for the Return. In the first year of independence over 200,000 immigrants flooded in from forty-two countries. The Law of the Return passed by the Knesset (Israel Parliament) in 1950 formally reaffirmed that 'every Jew has the right to immigrate to Israel'. Furthermore, a Jewish immigrant automatically became a citizen of Israel on his arrival, unless he chose to opt out. In the first four years the number of Jewish inhabitants more than doubled. After thirty years the original 650,000 had become over 3,000,000.

The two main sources for the Ingathering were the Holocaust survivors in Europe and the Jewish communities in the Arab lands.

The first European Jews to arrive after independence were the detainees in the Cyprus camps; this time they sailed into Haifa harbour not as 'illegals' but as free citizens of the Jewish State. About 70,000 were brought in from the DP camps in Europe. 300,000 immigrants reached Israel from the Iron Curtain countries other than the Soviet Union – Poland, Hungary, Rumania, Czechoslovakia and Bulgaria. While emigration was barred from the Soviet Union itself at that time, Moscow did not intervene when other Soviet Bloc states let their own Jews leave, for their own policy reasons. Jewish emigration from the Soviet Union started in 1970, and in the next decade about 150,000 came to Israel. By 1980 nearly 800,000 Jews had been taken in from Europe. From 1948 onward nearly all the Jews left the Arab World, and nearly 600,000 were resettled in Israel.

There has been a steady but small-scale aliyah from Western Europe, the English-speaking world and Latin America. The importance of these immigrants does not lie in their numbers. They have brought with them energy and ideas; professional, industrial and technical skills; investment capital; and a political and social background that have strengthened democracy and the quality of life in Israel. Their presence in the country also provides an essential living link with the Jewish communities in the Western world.

Absorbing this mass of human beings and moulding them into a vigorous new nation has been the dominant purpose of the State since its inception. In the process of immigration and absorption, the age-old dream of the Return has become a reality, and the central place of the Land of Israel in Jewish life has been restored.

יציאת אירופה ת

HAGANAH Ship
EXODUS 1947

The Exodus 1947 arriving in Haifa
after being intercepted and boarded at
sea by the Royal Navy.

The 'Exodus 1947'

The Exodus 1947 provided the most
spectacular episode in the story of
Aliyah Bet, the 'illegal' immigration
from Europe to Palestine.

The ship was actually an old American river-boat of 1,800 tons that had
been called the President Warfield. It
was very high, with four decks and a
flat bottom, and had served as a
ferryboat across Chesapeake Bay
before being bought by the Mossad
and sailed across the Atlantic by a
Haganah crew of forty, under the
command of Captain 'Ike' Aranne,
early in 1947. At a port in Italy she was
fitted with stacks of bunks to take
4,500 people. That number of refugees were brought from DP camps
in Germany to Marseilles, all of them
equipped with travel papers for Col-
ombia in South America. The embar-

shadowed by British destroyers. Twenty miles from the Palestine coast, at three a.m., the naval vessels launched a surprise boarding operation. It was fiercely repelled, with a running radio commentary from the Exodus on the battle reaching Palestine and from there going out to the world's press. After two hours, the specially-trained boarding parties had still failed to gain control. At this point it was decided to hand over the ship. It had been battered by the destroyers and was holed on both sides. Of the crew and passengers, three were dead or dying and 200 more were injured.

The ship was escorted into Haifa and the stretcher cases taken to hospital. The rest of the refugees were moved onto three caged vessels, that headed out to sea under the control of British troops. On opening his sealed orders, the Commander discovered that he was not to head for Cyprus as usual but to bring the refugees back to Port-de-Bouc, their port of embarkation.

Furious at the escape of the *Exodus* from Sète, Bevin had obtained the reluctant consent of the French government to dump its passengers back on French soil. The British ambassador in Paris, Duff Cooper, warned against the 'unedifying spectacle' of dragging the refugees off British boats at a French port. The French, he noted, were not concerned with the complexities of the Palestine problem but saw only 'survivors of a persecuted race seeking refuge in their national home'. Bevin was adamant. He would make an example of the *Exodus* and thereby discourage further illegal attempts.

The magnitude of this political blunder became clear at Port-de-Bouc when the refugees refused to land and the French authorities refused to compel them to do so. A French official who came aboard read out a statement that 'those who wish to land of their own free will, will be given asylum on the national soil, where they will enjoy all the liberties which France traditionally bestows on those who fight for human freedom'. Only thirty sick people and pregnant women went ashore.

For the next three weeks of stalemate the refugees sweltered in the heat of the crowded holds, with their plight getting world coverage. Then orders were received from London that they were to be taken all the way back to Germany. After another month at sea the floating cages reached Hamburg, where their human contents were landed by force and taken to the camps in the British zone of Germany. Within the next few months, most of them had sailed again on other 'illegal' ships and had reached Palestine or the Cyprus detention camps.

The Exodus story dramatized the fact that Britain's Palestine policy was bankrupt. Earlier in 1947, the British government had referred the whole problem to the United Nations, that had appointed the eleven-nation UN Special Committee on Palestine (UNSCOP) to study it. UNSCOP was in Palestine during the *Exodus* affair, and members of the Committee were eye-witnesses to the boat's arrival. The United Nations endorsed UNSCOP's recommendation that the country should be partitioned into independent Jewish and Arab states. Britain terminated the Mandate and withdrew from Palestine by midnight on 14 May 1948. On the same day, the State of Israel was born, and threw open the gates to Jewish immigrants. Amongst the first to come in were those refugees from the *Exodus* who had ended up in Cyprus.

kation took place at nearby Port-de-Bouc. The vessel then moved to the small harbour of Sète, sixty-five miles to the west. Under pressure from the British Foreign Secretary, Ernest Bevin, the French authorities detained the ship at Sète, under armed guard; but it managed to slip away at dawn and manoeuvre itself through the narrow exit channel without a pilot.

At sea the *Exodus* was closely

A reunion in 1971 between an immigrant arriving from the Soviet Union and his sister living in Israel. In the decade from 1969, over 200,000 Jews succeeded in leaving the Soviet Union, and about 150,000 of them went to Israel.

The Renewed Russian Aliyah

While the Jews are officially recognized as a 'nationality' in the Soviet Union, the basic thrust of Soviet policy has been to bring about their assimilation and their ultimate disappearance as a separate community. Their religion, language and culture have been suppressed, and their ties with Jews elsewhere discouraged. Yet the reaction to the emergence of Israel, thirty years after the Russian Revolution, showed that Jewish sentiment remained strong. When Mrs Golda Meir arrived as Israel's first Minister to Moscow in 1948 and went on the Sabbath to the synagogue (usually attended only by a handful of old people), thousands of Jews gathered outside in an emotional mass demonstration of support for the Jewish State, to the dismay of the Russian authorities.

From the Sixties, Soviet Jews in increasing numbers took part in an open struggle for the right to leave. A few were let out to rejoin relatives in Israel. As a rule the applications for exit permits were rejected, and the applicants penalized by being deprived of their jobs, expelled from universities and other punitive measures. At the same time the Soviet state press, media and publishing-houses carried on a venomous propaganda campaign against Israel and Zionism, with strong anti-semitic overtones.

For the regime, these deterrent efforts proved counter-productive. They increased among many Soviet Jews their sense of alienation from Soviet society, and intensified their urge to identify with Israel and the Jewish people. These sentiments came more strongly to the surface at the time of the Six-Day War of 1967. The plight of Soviet Jewry was dramatized in 1970 by the trial in Leningrad of a group of Jews from Riga, Latvia, accused of planning to escape by hijacking a small plane. The harsh sentences imposed on them provoked an outcry in the world press. From that year larger numbers of Jews were allowed to emigrate to Israel, in the hope that this would dispose of internal and external pres-sures. That expectation has not been fulfilled. The number of 'refuseniks' (those whose applications were rejected) grew steadily, and included a list of 'prisoners of Zion' – Jews active in the emigration movement who were jailed, put in psychiatric wards or sent to labour camps in Siberia.

The solidarity in Israel and the Western communities with their Russian brethren became more active, vocal and organized. An international Jewish conference in Brussels at the end of 1970 adopted a programme of co-ordinated efforts on behalf of Soviet Jewry. Generally speaking, these efforts have met with the sympathy of Western governments and public opinion, and has thereby had some impact on Soviet policy. Next to support for Israel, no cause has aroused and united the Jewish people to such an extent in recent decades. But the primary factor has been the tenacity and courage of the Russian Jews themselves. The Soviet Union has tried in vain to stifle the revived cry of the biblical Exodus: 'Let my people go!'

Important Events

The Messianic Hope

*c.*132	Bar-Kochba Revolt with messianic overtones.
*c.*1124	David Alroy appears in Kurdistan.
1522	David Reuveni reaches Western Europe.
1525	Shlomo Molcho declares himself a Jew.
1532	Arrest of Reuveni and Molcho.
1648	Shabbetai Zevi proclaims himself the Messiah.
1666	Shabbetai Zevi converts to Islam.

The Zionist Movement

1882	Pinsker's 'Auto-Emancipation'.
	Beginning of BILU settlement in Palestine.
1884	Kattowitz Conference of Chovevei Zion.
1897	First Zionist Congress convened by Herzl.
1917	Balfour Declaration pledges support for Jewish National Home in Palestine.

The Palestine Mandate

1920	British Mandate over Palestine.
1936	Start of Arab Rebellion in Palestine.
	Palestine Commission proposes partition.
1937	Start of 'illegal' Jewish immigration.
1939	Palestine White Paper restricts immigration.
	Start of the Second World War.
1946	Renewal of 'illegal' immigration.
1947	Palestine Question referred to United Nations.
	The 'Exodus 1947'.
	UN partition plan adopted (29 November).

The Ingathering

1948	State of Israel proclaimed.
	Start of mass immigration into Israel.
1970	Immigration started from Soviet Union.

Chapter Eighteen

The Making of the Museum

Is it possible to portray in a single three-storey building, twenty-five centuries of Jewish wanderings in a hundred lands? That is the challenge successfully met by the Nahum Goldmann Museum of the Jewish Diaspora (in Hebrew Beth Hatefutsoth) opened in May 1978 on the campus of the Tel Aviv University. Using colour, light, sound, movement and bold innovations in museum technology, it presents a rich and profoundly moving panorama of Jewish life in the Dispersion.

The Museum emerged from years of discussion and discarded plans. Two decades ago Dr Nahum Goldmann, then President of both the World Jewish Congress and the World Zionist Organization, proposed the setting-up in Israel of a museum to commemorate the ancient Jewish communities that were destroyed on the European continent in the Nazi Holocaust. It was originally intended to do this on a geographical basis. Each major community wiped out in the Holocaust, such as Poland, Lithuania, Hungary or Germany, would have its own exhibition, recalling its distinctive life and culture. Approaches were made to the *Landsmannschaften* in the United States – associations of Jews based on a common origin in Eastern Europe, from the same city, province or country. They agreed to collect from their members and to participate fully in the enterprise.

It was then pointed out that many other historic Jewish communities had ceased to exist in recent years as a result of the mass exodus from the Arab lands to Israel. For instance, the world's oldest Diaspora in Iraq, going back to biblical Babylonia, was no more; it too had to be commemorated, as did communities like those of Egypt, Libya and Yemen. The scope was widened to cover the entire Jewish Diaspora. Later, however, the regional framework was dropped, as being too restrictive and uneven.

It was next proposed to create an academic research centre that would contain all available documents – written or pictorial, originals or copies – with a bearing on Diaspora life and history. But this concept was also rejected. It would serve the needs of researchers and students but would lack wide popular appeal, and would cut across existing libraries.

Another plan put forward and discarded involved a series of life-

The photographing of the wall frieze in the 14th-century synagogue in Toledo, Spain. The synagogue was turned into a church and is now used as a Jewish historical museum.

size 'environments', each representing a home, a synagogue, the court of a Chassidic rabbi or some other focus of Jewish life.

The protracted debate among the Museum's planners did serve to clarify certain broad principles:

a The Museum should project the Diaspora story in a dramatic and popular form, and thereby serve an educational purpose.

b While martyrdom and persecution were a central theme of Jewish history, the Museum should also bring out the positive and creative aspects of Diaspora experience.

c The Museum should stress the pluralism of Jewish culture, and give due weight to the cultural background of Jews from Moslem lands.

d The presentation should be thematic rather than chronological. The wide dispersion of the Jews made it impossible to tell their story in a strictly 'linear' order.

On the basis of these principles, the Museum's permanent exhibition was divided into six sections:

The Family, based on the life-cycle from birth to death and the annual succession of festive occasions;

The Community showing the infra-structure of Jewish communal life and the extensive self-rule enjoyed by Jews.

Faith, paying particular attention to the synagogue and to religious learning;

Culture, covering a whole variety of sub-themes – the Hebrew and Yiddish languages, education, literature and the arts, the press, and the role of Jews in world civilization;

Among the Nations, reflecting the interaction between Jews and their non-Jewish environment in certain outstanding communities from different periods;

The Return to Zion.

These sections would hold a balance between elements special to individual communities and the basic features common to them all.

The general themes had to be translated into tangible exhibits, and that created a dilemma. An historical museum is normally based on collections of authentic artifacts surviving from the past. For a number of reasons, that basis was not feasible for the Diaspora Museum. Existing buildings and architectural remains could hardly be acquired or transported. Objects of ritual art and of Jewish ethnological interest were scarce and costly, and anyway were represented in the Israel Museum in Jerusalem and Jewish museums elsewhere. Moreover, such objects reflected Jewish life not in its totality but in a fragmentary way; indeed, there were entire regions and periods which could not be represented at all by material remains. The idea of gathering authentic objects was abandoned altogether. Instead, the exhibits would be specially designed and constructed, since the aim was to communicate, not to collect.

The reconstruction approach had its own problems, owing to the paucity of visual clues. For instance, the daily occupations of Jews in 1st-century AD Egypt are depicted in the form of a mural in the contemporary art-style of the period. To paint the mural, the general Egyptian civilization of the period had to be studied to learn how people dressed, what sort of houses they inhabited and what tools they used. Similarly, in making the striking bas-relief of a 5th-century AD Babylonian Talmudic academy, the artist relied on the Persian culture of the time. In reproducing the relief on the Arch of Titus, missing heads and limbs were added without any certainty that they resembled the original ones.

The Museum's concern for accuracy of detail is admirably illustrated in its exhibition of synagogue models. Thousands of photographs and measurements were taken of the synagogues concerned that were still extant in various countries, while documentary research and personal interviews with local Jewish families helped to reconstruct models of some that had been destroyed. Roof-top photographs were obtained in Amsterdam from a chartered helicop-

An early stage in the construction of the model of the Great Synagogue in Amsterdam. The model was based on photographs, drawings and measurements.

ter, and in Florence from a fully extended, swaying fire-brigade ladder. In Toledo, Spain, the interior frieze high up around the four walls of a former synagogue was photographed from scaffolding set up each night and removed each morning, as the building is now a museum open to the public. The massive key of the Danan synagogue in Morocco was found under the bed of a ninety-year-old Jewish lady, to whose family the building belonged. The vanished synagogue of Kai Feng-Fu in China had to be reconstructed on the basis of drawings made by an Italian Jesuit missionary in the 18th century.

The materials used in the synagogue models include gold, silver and zinc, plexiglass, chemical fibres, resins, dental cement and special alloys developed for the US space programme.

The Museum's academic research team collected reference materials from all over the world and prepared briefs for the workshops in Israel, Britain and the United States, where the paintings, models, dioramas and sculptured figures were produced. The making of the permanent exhibition took eight years and engaged the talents of hundreds of specialists: Jewish, general and art historians, architects and designers, painters, sculptors and model-makers, audio-visual, electronics, lighting and sound experts, photographers and documentary film producers. The craftsmen included a woman who designed figures for Madame Tussaud's wax museum in London, and technicians from the US space programme.

The complexity of translating abstract concepts into tangible form is shown by the Museum's largest exhibit, the Memorial Column. It symbolizes the theme of Jewish survival and continuing life in the midst of persecution and death. After many experiments, the design accepted was a thirty-foot structure suspended from the ceiling and stretching down for three floors in the interior well of the building. It consists of concentric black cages constructed of aluminium, enclosing a central core made up of 2,400 small light-bulbs, so arranged that the light gleams through the spaces in the grid from all angles. At first the cages were covered with light-refracting paint, but the effect was too bright, and the aspect of darkness too diminished. The dramatic balance between light and dark was achieved when the cages were covered with light-absorbent paint.

A number of sophisticated audio-visual techniques and special features enable the Museum to treat its subject-matter in far greater depth than would otherwise be possible in the limited floor space. Thus:

> The Museum collects short documentary films from many countries and has others specially made from its own stills. Each of the three floors has one or two study areas equipped with mini-screens for the projection of selected documentary films on request.

> There are 11,500 slides in daily use in the Museum's 'carousels'.

> Recorded music, conversation and sound effects accompany a number of the visual exhibits.

> An electronic computer is programmed to furnish 'print-outs' on over 3,000 Jewish communities. Eventually a comprehensive Jewish data bank will be computerized.

> The Chronosphere is an imaginative feature of the Museum. It is a small circular hall resembling a planetarium, with a seating capacity of fifty. In a half-hour programme the ebb and flow of Jewish migration down the ages is presented in maps and pictures screened onto the curved walls and domed ceiling by thirty-five projectors, with a sound-track commentary.

The Permanent Exhibition is supplemented by temporary exhibitions on specific communities or topics. Among those already held have been:

'Beyond the Golden Door' – a picture history of New York Jewry;
'Image before my Eyes' – Jewish life in Poland, 1864–1939;
'The Ghettoes of Venice and Rome';
'Judaism in Mediaeval Art';
'Kafka and his Prague';

'Moses Mendelssohn and his times';
'The Jews of Manchester, 1780–1945.'

The Museum's photo archive will in due course cover Jewish life everywhere in modern times.

The Museum is wholly bilingual, operating in English and Hebrew. Such texts as exhibit captions, Chronosphere and film commentaries and computer data are in both languages.

The special character of this 'museum that is not a museum' is reflected in the make-up of its staff. A traditional museum relies on curators who are experts in their artistic or scientific fields, and are responsible for acquiring objects and selecting exhibits from those in storage. The Diaspora Museum does not acquire or store objects – hence, it has no curators. Its departments are functional and technical, and their main concern is the maintenance of the Museum's exhibits and equipment. Slides, for instance, become worn and need to be replaced four to five times a year, making a total of some 50,000 slides produced annually.

The Museum's network of educational activities extends through the school system (with the Youth Wing as its focus), the universities, the armed forces, adult education courses, and groups from abroad attending seminars conducted in English, French, Spanish and other languages.

Through the Museum, a new generation of Israelis is absorbing a more positive and knowledgable attitude to Diaspora life, past and present. Tens of thousands of Jews from abroad are gaining a renewed sense of identity with their Jewish roots. Jewish and non-Jewish visitors alike begin to understand how this small, gifted, embattled people was able to outlive its persecutors and retain the creative energies that have enriched the civilization of the world.

Acknowledgments

The author and publisher would like to thank the following museums, collections and private individuals by whose kind permission the illustrations are reproduced. The page numbers of those pictures reproduced in colour are italicized.

The Art Gallery, York 140
Avila Municipal Archives 135
Micha Bar-Am, Tel Aviv 61
Clive Barda, London 222 below right
Bayerische Staatsbibliothek, Munich 72–3
Beth Hatefutsoth 12, *17*, *18*, *19*, 22–3, 26, 31, *40 below* (David Harris), 62–3, 63, 103, *105 above*, *108–9*, 113, 143, 146, *178–9*, *183 above*, 194–5, 204, 206–7, *223 above, left and middle*, 229, 241, *249–51*, 252, 253, 258 above, 267, *270–1*
Beth Hatefutsoth (Edgar Asher) 8, 15, 16, 28, 28–9, 30, 44–5, 48, 49, 50–1, 51, 53 above and below, 54, 56, 57, 59, 60 left, 66–7, 70, 79, 80, 84, 86, 104, 120–1, 124 above, 124 below, 127, 129, 138–9, 139, 186, 175, 206 right, 231, 235
Beth Hatefutsoth (David Harris) 27, 33, 35, 41, 74–5, 106, 117, 118–19, 131, 132–3, 134, 136–7, 160–1, 177 above, 190–1, 198, 205, 220–1
Bibliothèque Nationale, Paris 132, 151
Bibliothèque Royale, Brussels 142–3, 150
Bildarchiv d'Osterrische Nationalbibliothek, Vienna 222 middle
British Library, London 163
British Museum, London 225 top right
Brooklyn Museum, New York 115
Central Zionist Archives, Jerusalem 268, 274–5

Church of San Ambrogio, Florence 153, 158–9
Collection Viollet, Paris 222 above right
Einhorn Collection, Tel Aviv 206 left
M. H. Gano Collection, Amsterdam 162–3
Government Press Office, Tel Aviv 90, 200–1
Philip Halsman, New York 223 below right
Hermitage Museum, Leningrad 122
Israel Museum, Jerusalem *40 above*, 98 top left, 169, 261 (Teddy Kollek Collection), *263*
Israel State Archives, Jerusalem 95
Jack Resnick Collection, New York 83
Jacob Shulman Collection, New York 242 bottom right
Jewish Agency Photo Service, Jerusalem 96, 228
Jewish Chronicle, London 89
Jewish National and University Library, Jerusalem *20 above*, 64, 91, 94, 98 below, 145, 158, 192, 193 left and right, 196–7, 218, 222 top left, middle left and bottom left, 225 top left, 225 below, 226, 240 left, 258 below
John Rylands Library, Manchester *269 below*
Dmitri Kessel *20 below*, *39 above and below*, 100, *105 below*, *110–11*, *112*, *177 below*, *180–1*, *182 above and below*, *183 below*, *184*, 208, *272*
Kupferstich Kabinet, Munich 148
Leo Baeck Institute, New York 168
Paolo Lombrozo, Venice 156–7
London Library 223 above right
Municipal Archives, Koblenz 154
Municipal Archives, Rome 157
Municipal Museum, Rseszow 209
National Film Board of Canada 248
National Historical Museum, New York 245

National Theatre Habimah Archive 92 below
New York Historical Society 92 above, 234–5, 237, 238–9, 239
Photo Mas, Barcelona 129
Popperfoto, London 240 right, 242 bottom left, 243, 256–7, 265
Public Records Office, London 98 top right
Repartagebild, Stockholm 96–7, 242 above right
Rijksmuseum, Amsterdam 164, 166, 166–7
Royal College of Art, London 223 below left
Sachsische Landesbibliothek, Dresden 141
The Salk Institute (D. K. Miller) 242 top left
Sarajevo National Museum 60 right
Stadtarchiv, Worms 34
Sherry Suris, New York 276
Tel Aviv University Theatre Archives 93
University Library, Bologna *38*
University Library, Wroclaw 152
The Vatican, Bibliotheca Apostolica, Rome *37 above and below*
Weidenfeld and Nicolson Archives 254–5
Winchester Cathedral 149
Yad Vashem Archives, Jerusalem 82–3
Yivo, Institute for Jewish Diaspora, New York 88–9, 212–13, 266

The author and publisher have taken all possible care to trace and acknowledge the source of illustrations. If any errors have accidentally occurred, the publishers will be happy to correct them in future editions, provided that they receive notification.

Index